AF449428

HOW TO PROFIT
FROM
THE COMING
HYPERINFLATION

HOW TO PROFIT FROM THE COMING HYPERINFLATION

HENRY B. ZIMMER

and

DAVE GREBER

BEAUFORT BOOKS, INC.
New York

Library of Congress Cataloging in Publication Data

Zimmer, Henry B.
How to profit from the coming hyperinflation.

1. Investments—United States—Effect of inflation on.   I. Greber, David.   II. Title.

HG4910.Z55   1984   332.6'78'0973   84-11107
ISBN 0-8253-0253-6

Published in the United States by Beaufort Books, Inc.,
9 East 40th Street, New York, N.Y. 10016.

Published in Canada by Methuen Publications,
2330 Midland Avenue, Agincourt, Ontario M1S 1P7.

First American Edition

Printed and bound in the United States

10 9 8 7 6 5 4 3 2 1

ACKNOWLEDGMENTS

We wish to dedicate this book to the black market currency traders in Israel and Argentina, who taught us the true meaning of a dollar.

We would like to thank Harvie Andre, member of Parliament, Calgary Centre, for his courtesy in providing formal introductions to Canadian embassy staffs. It helped smooth out an otherwise rough road.

Thanks also go to the commercial secretaries at the embassies in Israel, Argentina, and Mexico, and the cultural secretaries in Italy and Spain. Their invaluable aid reduced a Herculean task to human proportions.

Our appreciation is extended to Greg Cable of Methuen Publications for his faith in our idea, to Shana Zimmer for her valuable editorial assistance, and to Somigo MacLean for emotional support.

Special thanks go to our editor, Natalie MacLean, whose patient and demanding supervision ensured completion of this project.

CONTENTS

PREFACE

EVER SINCE the federal budget of November 1981, I have been convinced that hyperinflation—high double- and, eventually, triple-digit inflation—is inevitable in Canada.

I have lectured on this subject and discussed it at hundreds of seminars over the past few years. Until now, however, I was incapable of assisting anyone in proper financial planning, because I have not operated in an economic system that has been inflationary for thirty or forty years, nor in one that has exploded into hyperinflation. I had no way of knowing, for example, whether gold values would continually increase under these circumstances, or if they would reach a leveling point. I could not advise anyone as to when real estate should be bought, either as a home or investment property. Nor could I tell whether anything—gold, property, whatever is thought to be of value—would be a good investment despite continual appreciation.

My gut feeling was, and still is, that real estate values always will appreciate tremendously in inflationary times. The big questions are: When do you pay for your property and when do you sell if, in fact, you should? All markets tend to be cyclical, and it doesn't appear that any investment can be held "from cradle to grave," so there must be a point of optimum divestiture. And what about the stock market? How will it perform in a hyperinflationary environment?

Answering these questions seemed impossible until one day Dave Greber suggested the best way to find out was to ask the people who know, the ones who live in countries with long-term inflationary and hyperinflationary economies.

In general, the degree of prosperity in North America is far greater than anywhere else in the world. While we have our problems, they have been perceived as relatively insignificant in comparison to other countries. Daily we read and hear of countries with inflation rates of 15, 50, 200, and even 500 percent. But those are only numbers. What is it like to live in a country where the inflation rate has been double-digit for decades or runs in three-digit numbers? How do people organize their finances? How do they cope? And how, if possible, do they prosper?

Dave traveled to Italy, Israel, Spain, Argentina, and Mexico to find out. From his research we determined that varied circumstances cause inflation to become hyperinflation, but there was a common denominator: governments spending more than they earn and playing with fiscal and monetary policies to cover their deficits. Whether it's defense spending in Israel, spending based on an assumption of ever-rising oil prices in Mexico or, as I believe, excessive social spending in Canada, the result of overspending is always the same.

We also found it will be possible for you to cope with hyperinflation if you order your financial and economic life starting *now*.

We all have much to learn from those who were not able to protect themselves. It is up to each of us to face our problems squarely and prepare for the future. The alternative to action is to sit back complacently and hope someone, perhaps the government, will do something about the situation. The problem is that an attitude of dependency on government is what allowed government to go its free-spending ways. Despite the fortunes made during the inflationary 1970s, we all paid a price, and we paid a heavier one during the recessionary early-1980s. If we

continue to think government will take care of us, each of us will
pay an even higher price during the hyperinflationary future.

A few words now on the organization of this book. In the
introduction which follows, the historical background of inflation is examined. In Chapters One and Two I explain how
inflation works in our economy, and why I believe hyperinflation is inevitable in North America.

Part Two is an account of Dave's investigations. He interviewed manufacturers, bankers, brokers, financiers, government officials, and small business people. He also spoke with
wage earners, housewives—just about anyone who would consent to being questioned, so he could take us into the homes,
businesses, and lives of people in the countries he visited.

In the final segment of this book, we construct a blueprint of
how to prepare for, and even profit from, the coming hyperinflation, again, based on the experiences of people in other lands.
Unfortunately, there is no single answer: Survival depends on
your economic circumstances, how you earn your living, your
financial status, and how you learn to manage them under
existing, and projected, circumstances.

In the last chapter, we show you how we believe hyperinflation can be avoided in North America. Our suggestions are
undoubtedly controversial and in conflict with many programs
introduced by our governments over the last two decades.

We believe a majority of North Americans will never be
persuaded to vote for some of the measures we suggest. So we
have no illusions. The die is cast and, it appears, the flow is
irreversible.

HENRY ZIMMER
Calgary, Alberta
August 1984

Part 1

THE PROBLEM

INFLATION TO HYPERINFLATION

T HE ROUND OF INFLATION which became a major part of the economics of the 1970s was a worldwide phenomenon rooted in a 1964 tax cut in the United States when Lyndon B. Johnson was president.

The twenty years after World War II were an economic Golden Age for the United States, a period of continual growth and economic expansion with a minimal inflation rate of approximately 1 percent. Shortly after the tax cut, however, the American economy experienced a series of shocks.

To begin with, from 1964 until 1968, Johnson fought the Vietnam War while maintaining a "Guns and Butter" policy at home. He spent as though the economy were on a war footing, diverting large amounts of money into armaments and the military. At the same time domestic policy directed massive amounts of money into "Great Society" social programs. Taxes, however, were still low, and government spending outstripped revenues.

Inflation is basically a steady rise in prices that results in the erosion of the purchasing power of money. Aside from a few notable exceptions among the defeated combatants of the First World War, inflation has most notably been a factor affecting economies and peoples' lives since the Second World War.

One theory explaining the origins of inflation is the demand–pull theory, which says that inflation results when demand for goods and services by government, business, and consumers outstrips the supply of those goods and services. This excess of demand over supply drives up prices and keeps them rising.

The U.S. economy during the Johnson administration operated as a war economy, a consumer economy, and a business- and investment-spurred growth economy, all at the same time. The forces of the demand–pull theory were in effect. Johnson was faced with the difficult choice of having to cut expenditures or increase revenues. The combination of government, business, and consumer spending, all competing for the same goods and services, was driving up prices.

Johnson's options were to adopt the traditional approach to fiscal policy, which manipulates taxes and spending, or to manipulate the money supply. Specifically, he could cut government spending to reduce government's competition in the marketplace for goods and services, thus relieving pressure on prices. At the same time, he could raise government revenues by taxing money away from business and the consumer. This would take money out of the hands of the other two elements in the economy competing for goods and services, relieve pressure on prices and give government the money to pay all its bills.

Alternatively, his option was to expand the money supply, and allow everyone to keep on spending, which only enhances the power of the demand–pull forces.

Johnson made no decision, and the result was an inflation rate that by 1969 was running at 5.4 percent a year, compared to the 1 percent per year at the beginning of the decade.

There are three reasons why American inflation affected the economies of the rest of the world. *First*, the American economy is the dominant free-market economy in the Western world: When it suffers, the rest suffer; when it's buoyant, the rest keep their heads above water.

Second, at the time the American dollar was inflating, it was still the benchmark against which other currencies throughout the world were valued.

At the Bretton Woods conference in 1944, the Allies gathered at the invitation of the U.S., Canada, and Britain to discuss the structure of the post-war world economy. They established a currency exchange system based on the U.S. dollar, which was then backed by gold.

The dollar's value wasn't set as the highest. If anything, the U.S. dollar was only a benchmark against which other currencies were measured. The Bretton Woods arrangement was a financial set-up to ensure that countries in debt to the U.S. after the war could repay those debts easily.

For example, the Canadian dollar was pegged at a value higher than the U.S. dollar, and the British pound was made almost three times as valuable as the U.S. dollar. Repaying war debts in the billions would be easier if Britain were paying with a three-to-one pound rather than today's 1.5-to-one pound.

By the same token, even though a Canadian dollar valued at $1.05 American would make paying off debts easier, Canadian exports would be costly for American buyers. In 1944 and the immediate post-war years, however, Canadian production costs and wages were much lower than American production costs and wages so, despite the high-valued Canadian dollar, Canada's exports were cheap.

Third, other world economies were affected by the inflated U.S. dollar because it is, very simply, the currency of international trade. When the dollar inflates and loses purchasing power, anything priced in dollars gets more expensive.

By 1970 the American economy and, consequently, the world economy were experiencing inflation in the 6 percent range. To combat the problem, President Richard M. Nixon surprised the world by imposing wage and price controls in August 1971 and ended convertability of the American dollar into gold, essentially taking the dollar off the gold standard. He then set out on a program of economic stimulation by expanding the money supply.

Money is like any commodity. When it's in short supply and high demand, it holds, and trades for, high value. When it's in high supply and low demand, its value decreases.

When government prints money to pay the bills, without there being an increase in the gross national product, the new currency dilutes the overall value of all money in circulation and decreases its purchasing power.

The aim of Nixon's stimulative monetary expansion was that the ensuing spurt of economic growth would outstrip inflation. The actual result was international economic chaos as, over the next two years, the American money supply grew rapidly and inflated. The Bretton Woods agreement fell apart, fixed exchange rates broke down, and currencies floated in value relative to the now-floating American dollar.

There's a second theory about the sources of inflation: the cost–push theory, which says that inflation results from increases in production costs unrelated to the demand for goods or services.

In late 1973, following the Yom Kippur War, the Organization of Petroleum Exporting Countries (OPEC) raised oil prices fourfold.

Inflation hit the world with a vengeance. Oil importing nations were caught in a vise as production costs increased dramatically following the explosive energy-price hikes. Inflation soared, and the industrial output of the oil importers was no longer price competitive. To regain a competitive position, they could: cut oil imports, choke off their industrial development programs, and face massive unemployment; maintain oil imports and subsidize energy costs through deficit-producing transfer payments to industry so their output would remain price competitive; or maintain oil imports and subsidize energy costs by borrowing overseas.

Most governments initially chose the second option, rather than face the domestic political implications of allowing massive unemployment. The third option was not heavily employed until 1974 and 1975, when international banks found themselves awash with dollars—the "petro-dollars" that had flooded into OPEC coffers since the price hikes.

As one South American representative of a multi-national bank puts it, "It isn't common knowledge, but the International Monetary Fund and the World Bank came to us and asked us to lend out that money. We only got greedy when we saw how much money we could make in commissions and interest."

The banks were asked to lend out the money because the money was sitting in bank accounts gathering interest, while OPEC countries decided what they would do with it. The money, however, was not creating more wealth nor contributing to the gross international product; but it *was* causing worldwide inflation to pick up speed.

The banks went on an international lending binge and developing nations went on a borrowing binge, assuming they would pay back the debts with further-inflated dollars in the future. The expectation of rising inflation was met as the money flowed freely and easily around the world. The OPEC nations also went on multi-billion-dollar spending sprees. For example, Iran under the Shah built a massive military establishment on oil revenues; Saudi Arabia bought an industrial infrastructure as a hedge against the day the oil ran out. And they paid whatever was asked. Prices continued to soar.

Suddenly, a whole new economic regime took shape in the world. Not only were government, consumers, and businesses within countries competing for goods and services, but governments were competing with each other for goods and services from the industrialized nations.

As these new pressures forced up prices and spurred international inflation, OPEC nations found their petro-dollars bought less, but they were still spending freely. So in 1979 the second oil shock hit the world as OPEC doubled the already-inflated oil prices.

At the same time, to control inflation, the chairman of the U.S. Federal Reserve Bank, Paul Volcker, changed American policy from one of monetary expansion to monetary control and stopped trying to hold down interest rates. As a result, interest rates soared during 1980, the last year of Jimmy Carter's presidency. The Carter recession was on.

The runaway inflation of the 1970s was brought under control because, for a short time, President Ronald Reagan, using the monetary brake of intolerably high interest rates, brought the American economy to a standstill. Despite a tax cut, business and consumers were forced to stop spending because of expensive credit. Inflation was subdued at the cost of a deep recession. As the recession spread to the trading partners of the U.S., they too experienced drops in their inflation rates.

The United States is Canada's chief trading partner. When demand from the American market for Canadian goods stopped, the Canadian economy suffered a slowdown. At the same time, to prevent the flight of Canadian dollars to the United States, Canadian monetary authorities had to keep interest rates at an attractive premium above those in the U.S.

These painful interest rates kept money in Canada but, as a result of this policy and economic uncertainty, Canadians also stopped spending and the Canadian economy simply shut down. The result has been the worst recession in more than fifty years coupled with severe unemployment.

A year later, in August 1982, the U.S. dollar began to strengthen, and the American economy commenced a strong recovery, which spurred weaker recoveries among her trading partners. It appeared for a short while that U.S. policies had been successful. But, at the same time, a world debt crisis erupted as countries with huge debts found they no longer had inflated dollars with which to pay their debts, and that their debts were compounding at an alarming rate because they had been negotiated with floating interest rates.

Stable inflation of about 1 to 3 percent, in modest figures, depending on a country's average efficiency and productivity, tends to be part of a growing economy. Factories are built to produce the goods that people buy, mines are developed, forests are opened up to loggers, oil wells are drilled, houses are built. Investment in these ventures is money spent against a long-term payoff. Until an investment contributes to expansion of the gross national product—the total value of goods and services produced by a country—it is non-productive and, therefore, inflationary.

In this kind of environment the consumer finds over the

course of a year that prices for perishables and durables rise a few pennies. These increases are far outstripped by annual wage and salary increases that result from increased productivity.

The real problem with modest inflation (as happened throughout the 1970s) is that it can accelerate and become runaway inflation. If employers' costs rise faster than productivity increases, consumers find prices climbing every few months. Those pennies add up, and productivity-linked salary and wage increases don't cover the increases in the prices of goods and services. So wage and salary earners demand inflation-linked "cost of living" increases, rather than live with the continual erosion of the purchasing power of money they earn.

Employers build these cost of living increases into their selling costs to maintain profits and, suddenly, consumers at every level of society notice that "a dollar won't buy what it used to." A runaway inflationary spiral has begun.

Government intervention to arrest the spiral through, for example, wage and price controls creates its own problems, especially administrative ones, which result in unwieldy civil service structures to manage the controls. The real problem in combating inflation is finding a balance between the costs of inflation and the price society pays for avoiding it. The price, unfortunately, is usually recession, with high unemployment and cuts in production of goods and services.

To date in Canada more than 1.5 million citizens and their families have suffered in the fight against inflation. The cost of controlling Britain's inflation was 3 million unemployed and, by the time the 1982 recovery began in the United States, the unemployment rate was 10.7 percent of the work force.

The problem in all countries has been that, while recession may have caused the consumer to stop spending for a while, governments did not, have not, and do not appear about to stop spending under any circumstances.

In response to inflation and to protect jobs, governments generally try to spend their way out of the problem, either directly by subsidizing the rising production costs of industry, or indirectly by providing programs that subsidize the cost of living.

When this increased spending outstrips income, and government budgets go into deficit, government finances the deficits by squeezing taxpayers, borrowing, and speeding up the press that prints the money. Purely short-term measures, these techniques further devalue currency and encourage inflation.

Money that is not backed by a tangible commodity, such as gold, is "fiat" currency; it holds value by government decree alone. Fiat money is a representation of value that government says can be traded for goods and services equal in value to the denomination of the currency. The ability of a country to produce and distribute those goods and services backs up its currency. There is not, however, and cannot be, one dollar for each dollar's worth of goods and services out on the street. If there were, we would be swamped by pretty, multi-colored bits of paper with lots of zeros and very little purchasing power.

So, when government presses churn out more currency, it devalues the existing currency. When the currency is backed by borrowed money that eventually has to be paid back with interest, it is further debased. Prices, in response, continue to climb.

Workers demand more money and prices shoot up, but wages always lag behind price hikes. People never keep up with inflation; they're always trying to catch up. So they look to ways of protecting the value of money they earn. Wage demands get tougher and prices shoot ever higher. Houses that ten years ago would have been overpriced at $25,000 sell for $90,000.

Meanwhile, government presses keep churning out more money, and inflation is out of control.

The final stage of inflation is hyperinflation. The historic example of hyperinflation is that of Germany in 1923 under the Weimar Republic. Under the crushing demand for billions of marks in post-First World War reparations imposed by the Treaty of Versailles, the government printed massive quantities of currency during 1922. By 1923 inflation was raging at 1,000 percent per year, but interest rates hovered in the 3 percent range, so the German middle class—the savers—saw their savings, pensions, insurance plans and, ultimately, themselves wiped out.

Germans with jobs were paid daily. Currency was printed blind—without denominations—and each day values were printed on that day's supply of money and issued to meet the demand for notes of exchange. This was the economic backdrop for the famous story of people trundling wheelbarrows full of money to the baker to pay for a loaf of bread.

Meanwhile, people who had borrowed money before, or in the early days of the hyperinflationary cycle at 3 percent, were paying off their loans with inflated marks. Many laid the foundations of immense fortunes during this period that grew during the following decade and the ensuing Nazi regime.

The German hyperinflation also brought with it the social violence that accompanies massive economic confusion and widespread discontent. The authority of the Weimar Republic was undermined, and the stage was set for anyone who could offer a solution to the problems that accompany free-enterprise democracy.

Hyperinflation on the scale of the German experience isn't possible any more. Should an economically explosive situation like this occur, the one critical factor that existed in Germany—fixed, stable interest rates—wouldn't occur. Even with moderate inflation, interest rates these days are adjusted periodically.

Modern hyperinflation is, essentially, the inflationary spiral gone mad, with everything rising—prices, wages, interest rates, exchange rates, unemployment. Its main characteristic is fear, not only for the future but that the government has lost control of the economy.

Modern hyperinflation usually occurs when government allows a rapid expansion in the money supply. The expansion is to meet the demand of all sectors of the economy for currency with which to pay their bills; it usually happens when prices increase, not annually nor semi-annually, not even quarterly or monthly, but weekly or daily. Under these conditions everyone suffers, except those who have built tangible financial buffers around them.

———— ∿∿∿ ————

Chapter 1

WHY MODEST INFLATION IS NOT AS BAD AS WE THINK

FOR THE PAST THREE YEARS the Canadian government has been trying to convince us that inflation is the dirtiest word in the English language. Since then, government policies have been directed towards defeating inflation at all costs. In the process interest rates were forced up and remained relatively high even during the recession. As this is being written, the fear of high interest rates threatens any sustained recovery. Meanwhile, high unemployment has become something we are expected to live with as the cost of the victory over inflation.

A propaganda campaign was mounted by government to convince us that curbing inflation requires consumers to curtail personal spending. We have been conditioned to cheer each time Statistics Canada announced a drop in the cost of living index and to become despondent any time the figures show inflation on the rise.

No doubt, inflation strikes fear in the hearts of pensioners living on fixed incomes and people earning minimum wages. Certainly, if prices go up while income remains static or rises slowly, anyone's standard of living suffers, no matter what income bracket.

For part of our society, however, modest inflation is productive. Specifically, modest inflation contributes to the prosperity of business. This may sound like a strange statement, especially since government has succeeded in labeling inflation as Public Enemy Number One, and very few people today would live with even modest inflation if they could avoid it.

Remember how a salesperson would clinch a sale in the 1970s? Perhaps you were looking at some furniture for your home or apartment and were undecided whether or not to buy. The salesperson would tell you how lucky you were that you hadn't waited until the beginning of the following month, when a 10 percent price increase was anticipated. The consumer psychology of the late 1970s was to buy now, even if it meant paying later, so the purchase would be paid for with inflated dollars and the next price increase would be avoided.

Today the psychology has turned around, and the consumer attitude appears to be: Why buy today if the price is going to be the same or perhaps even lower tomorrow? In fact, rather than seek "the best deal this very minute with easy credit terms and no downpayment," as in the 1970s, astute buyers now sniff out financially troubled businesses, wait until one goes bankrupt, then purchase the goods from the receiver, often for as little as 50 cents on the dollar.

Today's consumer psychology can be illustrated with a simple example involving middle- and upper-income Canadians. As you read this example, apply it to your circumstances.

Assume that you're suddenly handed $10,000 to spend. You may not invest the money; rather, you must buy some consumer product.

What would you buy?

If you're like many people these days, you want a personal computer for your home. You're also likely in the market for a video-cassette recorder to go along with your color television. Pick up virtually any publication today, and you'll be assaulted by a tremendous amount of advertising for these two products.

In early 1984 figures in the financial press showed that approximately one out of every ten Canadian households owns video-cassette equipment. By the end of 1984 projections are that almost one out of every four households will have a VCR. It's safe to say that today's video revolution is akin to trends of twenty years ago, when color television first became popular, and thirty years ago, when black-and-white televisions were introduced into most households.

If you're like many people, you haven't yet committed yourself to the purchase of either a home computer or video equipment. Normally, according to marketing trends, now is the point in the computer and VCR product cycle where the cautious consumer enters the market to buy. You, however, have watched computer and VCR prices drop drastically in the last three years and you expect prices to drop even further. You don't want to buy now and, three months later, see your equipment advertised at half the price you paid.

Perhaps you're also a little hesitant about making a big expenditure when you're not sure how strong, or how real, the economic recovery is. So your overall judgment is to leave your money in a savings account or term deposit, sit back, and wait to see what happens.

Everyone, however, is sitting back doing the same thing. When consumer psychology is recessionary, consumers don't buy, merchants don't sell, and manufacturers don't manufacture. When manufacturers don't manufacture, they don't need workers, so people with jobs lose them, and those without jobs don't get any. In turn, people without jobs also don't buy.

By all accounts it appears that the Canadian economic recovery, which seems to be operating in fits and starts, has been real and consistent in only one sector—the automotive industry. Economic reports indicate that the statistics supporting the existence of an economic recovery are heavily skewed by the large consumer spending on automobiles.

There are several factors that perhaps should be considered in accounting for this phenomenon. Consumers who held on to cars longer than the traditional two-to-four-year ownership cycles when prices and interest rates skyrocketed in the 1970s have reached the point where they have to either invest large amounts of money to extend the lifespans of their cars, or buy new ones. Many are buying new ones.

The rising prices of the late 1970s followed by the uncertainty of the early 1980s—our recession years—led to poor sales in 1981, 1982, and 1983. Those consumers who didn't buy during those years and whose personal economic situations appear to be improving are feeding their pent-up demand.

Cars, like homes, are generally financed when purchased, and interest rates during the recovery have been lower than in 1981 and 1982. Moreover, by buying a car on time, you can get a guaranteed interest rate over the length of the loan, without any risk of higher interest making your purchase more expensive.

Most important of all, car prices continue to increase, albeit very slowly. On average, a 1984 model car costs about 3 percent more than last year's model. The consumer is electing to buy now to avoid anticipated price increases.

An inflationary consumer psychology which results from modest price increases and the expectation of further modest increases would not be unhealthy for the North American economy. These factors are components of an expanding economy. The prospect of price increases gets people spending money, which circulates through the economy, and wealth and value are created and distributed. As long as no sudden increases occur in the costs of any sector, productivity and profitability will outstrip inflation.

If a business can increase its income, it can also increase wages and salaries to its employees. It is best if the increased income results from increased productivity and efficiency that produce economies of scale. As far as business is concerned, however, no matter how they develop, increased profits are pleasant entries on a balance sheet.

On the consumer's end, price increases are not necessarily frightening to those with jobs and secure income that can be expected to increase proportionately. When the consumer is on a fixed or slowly increasing income, and inflation is rapid, then it is a frightening phenomenon.

Is an Economic Recovery Really Taking Place?

Whether or not a real economic recovery is occurring is a continuing and inconclusive debate: Some economists feel the worst is over and things will continue to improve gradually; others predict that this is just the lull before the storm, and 1985 could be worse than 1981 or 1982.

No one knows for certain what is happening. The government tries to encourage the country to believe, but only with moderate success, that all is improving.

In addition to minor private-sector inspired inflationary pressure motivating consumers to buy, and increased profits through greater efficiency and productivity, a stable interest rate is critical to an economic recovery. Without a stable interest rate, or an interest rate which fluctuates in direct proportion to inflation, business can't possibly prosper.

A few years ago, when interest rates took a dramatic upward leap, the monetary authorities decided that, rather than having a fixed interest rate, it would be better to allow the interest rate to float. The theory behind the floating rate is that, if the cost of money goes up one-tenth of 1 percent each week for five weeks in a row, no drastic economic consequences will arise, and the economy will adjust gradually.

For example, should an upward trend develop, so the theory goes, borrowers can stop borrowing, repay their debts and wait until money becomes cheaper. On the other hand, if the rate declines for four or five successive weeks, the appropriate adjustments will be made all around. So, every Thursday at noon, Ottawa time, the Bank of Canada announces the interest rate for the following seven days according to the bids on treasury bills.

On the surface floating interest rates make sense, but in practice a floating interest rate policy is economic folly. A business cannot survive if it must adjust its borrowing each week.

The business owner has to count on a stable interest rate not for this week, next week, or the week after, but for two, three, or even five years at a time. Otherwise, it becomes impossible for business to plan or borrow for capital expansion, to purchase inventory, or to finance accounts receivable.

The one sector of the economy in which buyers can now make long-term decisions is real estate, for which it is possible to get mortgage financing of up to five years at a predetermined, fixed interest rate. At least a buyer of real property knows what the financial commitment will be over a relatively long term and can decide whether or not to buy.

Now look again at the position of the merchant or entrepreneur. Most business financing is arranged on a demand loan basis, which places the business at the mercy of changes in interest rates when and if they occur.

For sustained economic recovery to occur business needs:
* the opportunity to raise prices periodically;
* increased productivity and efficiency; and
* a fixed, long-term interest rate or a rate linked to the inflation factor.

These points can be illustrated with two examples: one a resource mega-project involving millions of dollars of expenditure, creating hundreds of jobs, and the other from the small business sector. After reading the next few pages, you should appreciate the problems of today's economy.

As a resident of Calgary, Alberta, I witnessed the economic collapse of the early 1980s far more vividly than people in most other parts of the country. The old saying, "the higher the climb, the longer the fall," certainly held true in this case. Alberta's prosperity is linked inexorably to international oil prices, which ultimately collapsed.

Alberta's government has been criticized for not having pushed the province aggressively enough to diversify during the prosperous good years. Unfortunately, diversification is not as easy as it sounds. The markets, in terms of population, simply do not exist in Alberta.

If you stand in downtown Toronto, and count the population within a radius of two hundred miles, you will find more people than the entire population of Manitoba, Saskatchewan, Alberta, and British Columbia combined. It is impossible to sustain manufacturing, or other industry, in places where the markets and the population are sparse. So, it appears that Alberta's fortunes will always be tied to oil and gas in the same way British Columbia's depend on lumber and Saskatchewan's are linked to agriculture.

Go back to the late 1970s. Assume that you are a senior executive with a multi-national oil company. It is your decision, and yours alone, whether or not to proceed with a mega-project. If you give the go-ahead, the plant will be under construction for some time, providing hundreds of jobs at a cost of millions, perhaps billions, of dollars.

Keeping in mind that inflation was on a sharp rise in the late 1970s, your projections assume that you'll be paying off your debts with dollars that are worth less and less over time. Assume, also, that it will take two years for this mega-project to be completed, at which point, the plant will start producing revenue.

In an inflationary environment, you could expect your revenue to increase periodically. Figure 1–1 illustrates your projections in graph form. You can see that, as time passes, your decision to build looks better and better as you pay off your debts with less valuable dollars generated from increasing revenues.

Figure 1–1: How Inflation Helps Business Grow

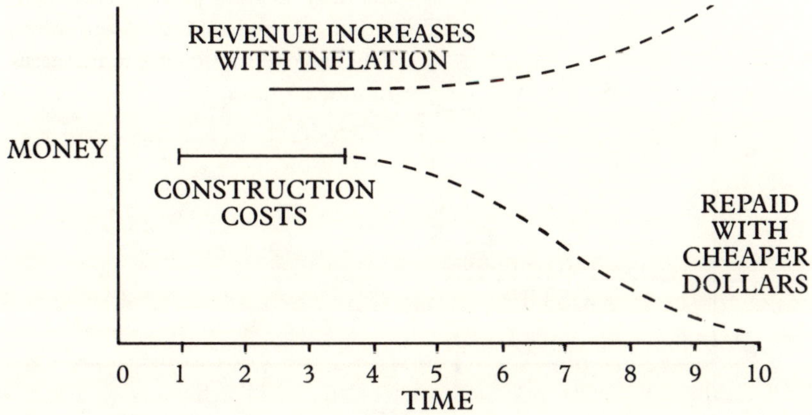

Let's now re-examine your mega-project in today's environment. First of all, as will be explained in the next chapter, there is no appreciable price inflation within the private sector. So, if you commit your business to a multi-billion dollar expenditure, there is no guarantee that you will be able to repay your debts out of increasing revenues, or with dollars that become worth less and less over time.

On the other hand, you recognize that interest rates remain unstable, and you're forced to finance your project through a lending institution under terms where the interest rate fluctuates according to variations in the prime rate. Assume interest rates then shoot up to 18, 19, or 20 percent because of an economic crisis, for example, a repayment default by a Third World country on its foreign debt. You would then find yourself paying your costs with very expensive dollars!

If there is no price inflation when the project is finished, you have no guarantee revenues will increase. In fact, if you work in a price-regulated industry, such as oil and gas, your revenue might even *decrease* if the government increases its tax bite. Over time your income could actually drop!

This unpleasant situation is illustrated graphically in Figure 1–2. By the time the two lines intersect in this second example,

Figure 1–2: How Unstable Interest Rates, Government Taxes, and a Lack of Inflation Can Cause a Business to Collapse

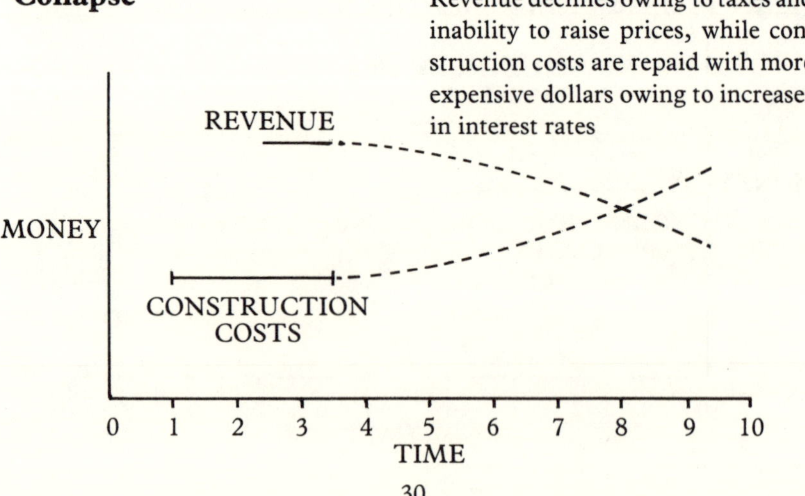

Revenue declines owing to taxes and inability to raise prices, while construction costs are repaid with more expensive dollars owing to increases in interest rates

your business is bankrupt. Of course, you don't take on the project. It doesn't make economic sense. This is one of the major reasons hundreds of thousands of people are now without work.

Now, for a second example. Let's pretend that I'm an accountant and you're a business owner. Your business has $1 million in inventory, financed through an $800,000 bank loan and $200,000 of your own equity.

You call me and ask for help preparing a budget projecting your operating expenses for the next twelve months. It's good business to prepare these periodic budgets, so business costs can be determined and profitable selling prices can be set.

We sit down and work through the figures. For the most part, it isn't too difficult to prepare an accurate budget for a small or medium-sized business. Salaries, for example, are known and, if you want to give your employees a 5 percent increase in three months, we can account for that contingency. You know your rent; utilities, phone, and fringe benefit costs, such as Canada Pension, unemployment insurance, and group insurance, can all be built into the budget. As for advertising, the word budgeting may be used in a slightly different sense: An advertising budget is a ceiling figure of how much the business is willing to spend to advertise its products, goods, or services.

Almost every cost can be budgeted fairly accurately with one exception: interest on the bank loan. Over the next twelve months, it's certainly conceivable that the retail interest rate, which I define as prime plus 1 or 2 percent, can be as low as 10 percent, because of low demand for borrowed money within the private sector. On the other hand, it's just as conceivable that the retail interest rate will be as high as 16 percent. This could happen as early as tomorrow if some simmering world troubles were to explode into a full-scale crisis.

The way things are now, with a floating interest rate, I don't care who you are—prime minister or finance minister of Canada, or president of the United States: *No one can predict with any degree of certainty what the interest rate will be in twelve months' time within an accuracy factor of plus or minus six percentage points.*

In the national budget of 15 February 1984, the Canadian finance minister introduced a mortgage rate protection plan as a discussion paper. The gist of this program is that the government is willing to enter into an insurance arrangement which would protect Canadian individuals against significant rises in interest rates on home mortgages. While the plan is to be commended, take a moment and read between the lines. If the government had any guarantee that the interest rate would be stable, or had any ability to control the rate, such a protection plan would not be necessary in the first place! So, if the politicians can't control or predict interest rates, can we as individuals or as business owners?

Let's turn our thinking back to what to do with your small business budget. The onus is on me, the accountant, to help you, the business owner, make a decision. If I'm optimistic, budget interest at 10 percent, and I'm wrong, your business could lose approximately $50,000. This is assuming that the interest rate really does average 16 percent instead. The 6 percent differential on $800,000 is the difference between a profit and a loss for most small businesses. On the other hand, what I would likely do is make the "conservative" accountant's decision and tell you to budget at 16 percent.

If I'm wrong on the high side, I could cost your business more than $50,000, because you would price your products so high they wouldn't be competitive. There really is only one alternative: You budget somewhere in the middle, at 12 or 13 percent, which, coincidentally, is where the rate is at the time this is being written.

I would also advise you against any expansion. Because of the specter of higher interest rates, I would advise you to reduce your inventory, if at all possible, and warn you away from any major investment in plant and equipment. I would suggest that two or three more employees should be dismissed if possible. The next step would be to use every penny of cash flow not needed to finance business operations to pay down your business loan. In short, I would force your business into a debt-reduction program.

While this strategy makes sense for your individual business, a policy of debt reduction and business contraction is certainly not good for the economy as a whole. If you lay off two or three employees, that will create two or three fewer consumers throughout the system, which will only aggravate the unemployment and recession problems. When many people suddenly have less money to spend, there's a ripple effect which contributes to recession.

What About Government?

Ironically, however, by paying off debt, we fall right into the government's trap. The government first tells us not to raise *our* prices so government can raise *its* prices. The government tells us not to borrow money; then it borrows every available penny. For example, in 1983, *government borrowed 76 cents out of every dollar borrowed by the private and public sector in Canada.*

Our major objective in writing this book is to get you to think independently, and understand what's happening around you. Don't take anything that is said to you at face value when it comes to government action. For example, many people believe that interest rates have come down from their peak in 1981 and 1982. In reality, interest rates have gone up in the last two years.

The interest rate in 1981 and 1982 averaged around 18 percent. If you borrow money for business or investment, your interest is tax deductible. So, if you are an investor in a high tax bracket, the cost of borrowing at 18 percent reduces to only 9 percent. At the same time, the inflation rate was almost 12 percent. Would you borrow at 9 percent (after tax) to buy property which is appreciating at 12 percent a year?

While the return is not exciting, it certainly doesn't appear to be a bad deal. Today, if you were to borrow money from a lending institution, you would probably pay around 13 percent. If the money is borrowed for business or investment, your after-tax cost could be as low as 6.5 percent. The present published inflation rate, however, is only around 5 percent. Would anyone in their right mind borrow at 6.5 percent to earn 5 percent?

You cannot look at either the inflation rate or the interest rate in a vacuum. They must be examined one against the other. The big dilemma facing business today is that the risk–reward ratio just doesn't work out. One way to explain this is to say that today's interest rate is too high. On the other hand, it can just as easily be said that the inflation rate is too low!

Figure 1–3: Comparing the Cost of Borrowing Money to the Inflation Rate

	1981	1984
Inflation	12%	5%
Interest rate	18%	13%
Less tax saving to borrower in 50% tax bracket*	9%	6.5%
Net cost to borrower	9%	6.5%

* This assumes that the interest is tax deductible.

As mentioned earlier, I have conducted perhaps one hundred seminars over the last twelve months in which I have dealt with the question of inflation and whether it really is as evil as the government insists. In all these seminars I have asked participants to indicate whether or not they have reduced their personal debts in the past couple of years. My informal findings are that approximately 70 percent of middle- and upper-income Canadian families have reduced their debt loads over the last two years. If this is the case, it is my guess that approximately 90 percent of Canadian businesses have done the same. This is the only reason that the government of Canada is "solvent" today. It can borrow $30 billion a year because it has no competition for lending capital. The government cannot afford to encourage business to expand, because a competition for money would only increase the government's deficit in the short run by pushing up interest rates. Government is too blind to see that, in the medium term, by encouraging business instead of stifling it, tax revenues would increase and deficits would eventually drop.

You've likely heard the term "the domino effect." It refers to a game where children line up a series of dominoes close to each other, gently tap the first one, and cause all the dominoes to fall in succession. Look back again to the late 1970s. But first, when I suggest to you that modest inflation is healthy for the overall economy, I emphasize the word "modest."

By the end of the 1970s inflation was getting out of hand. At that time a portion of the domestic inflation could not be blamed on government's spending and was, in fact, attributable to the private sector. Inflation was tied in to real estate speculation. Those were the years when traders were flipping properties at a tremendous pace. The idea was to buy property and sell it a month or two later to someone else at a higher price who, in turn, would sell to someone else, and so on. In the final analysis, though, the tenant of the property paid for the owner's greed and profit taking through higher rent.

Of course, hindsight is 20–20 vision, and to keep private-sector inflation down to modest levels, speculation of that sort should be penalized through, perhaps, severe taxation. After all, there is quite a difference between speculation and legitimate investment. Politicians, however, panicked when they saw the pendulum swinging too quickly in the direction of inflation, and government brought its economic weight to bear against inflation and pushed back with tremendous force.

The lesson Canadians have learned since is that the opposite of rampant inflation is severe and prolonged recession. Recession continues, despite government attempts to encourage the market and public by telling us the worst is over.

Return to the domino effect. In 1981, when interest rates jumped dramatically, and the Canadian government introduced the harsh tax measures of the November budget, business was the first to falter. Suddenly business accumulated less profit and paid significantly less tax. The people who were laid off and found themselves without jobs also ceased to be taxpayers.

Provincial and municipal governments were next to suffer. With reduced tax revenues, those governments were forced to introduce their own restraint programs. They began to freeze civil service salaries and, in some cases, threatened huge layoffs. In other cases governments actually followed through with major reductions in the civil service.

Recall the Solidarity Movement in the summer of 1983 in British Columbia. Premier Bennett made the honest statement that his province could no longer afford its large civil service because of declining revenues from the lumber and construction industries. He became perhaps the most unpopular person in western Canada, though it appears that he did not follow through with many of his threats.

Bennett's proposals may not have solved his province's problems. Realize that a civil servant is as much of a consumer as any individual working in the private sector. Any time there's a massive reduction in the civil service, the accompanying reduction in consumption puts further pressure on business. Business revenues drop accordingly, along with the ability to pay taxes. This, in turn, reduces government revenues and forces more and more layoffs. The cycle simply continues in this direction.

In Alberta Premier Lougheed, who in 1982 was sitting on top of the world with a growing multi-billion dollar Heritage Fund and seemingly endless revenues, suddenly found the tables turned. In the early spring of 1984 nine hundred liquor board employees were laid off, an incredible statistic when you consider the families of these people and the ripple effect through the economy. The reduction in consumption only puts further pressure on business and reduces government income. In April 1984 it was announced that another 1,100 civil servants would also face layoffs in the near future.

Of course, there is one major difference between government at the provincial and municipal levels and the federal government. Times are tough for the federal government the same as they are for everyone else, but the federal government has an ace in the hole: *When the federal government can no longer borrow money, it will start to print money. And when it starts to print money, we will see hyperinflation.*

Figure 1–4 provides a synopsis of the government of Canada's budget for 1984–85. The bottom line is a projected deficit of close to $30 billion, an incomprehensible figure.

In November 1981 the government projected a deficit of $10 billion. Seven months later, in June 1982, it was disclosed that the actual deficit would be double the projected amount. No one reacted then, and few people react today when the 1984–85 deficit projection is $30 billion. By way of dramatizing what this means, consider that $30 billion in $100 bills would comprise a pile over five times the height of Mount Everest—8848 meters/ 29,028 feet.

Figure 1–4: Government of Canada Budget, 1984–85

	(Millions of dollars)	
Projected revenues		$ 67,326
Projected expenditures		
Social affairs (UIC, old age security, family allowances, Indian affairs, CBC, CMHC)	$39,707	
Public debt charges	20,350	
Economic development	11,251	
Defense	8,782	
Government services, justice and legal, Parliament	6,503	
Fiscal arrangements (transfers to provinces)	5,898	
Energy	4,016	
External affairs and aid	2,721	
Other	(2,302)	96,926
Projected deficit		$(29,600)

Expenditures:Revenue ratio
$1.44 $1.00

Social affairs:Revenue ratio
$0.59 $1.00

Public debt charges:Revenue ratio
$0.30 $1.00

Overall, Canada's *cumulative deficit*—the total of accumulated budget deficits since the government ran the spending into the red—is about $180 billion. Canada's deficit for one year is larger than the total debt Poland owes the Western world! For all intents and purposes, the country is bankrupt. So why do we still have an aura of complacency? Things don't look that bad, there are no riots in the streets, and the situation appears to be relatively healthy.

The difference between Canada and Third World countries is that Canada has no problem meeting its international debt payments, which are all financed internally. As long as you and I continue to buy Canada Savings Bonds and treasury bills, the government can keep borrowing to meet its cash requirements.

Perhaps you don't own any Canada Savings Bonds and you've never seen a treasury bill. But, if you're like most Canadians, you have reduced your debts over the last two or three years, and the lending institutions which have taken your money have lent it back to the only major borrower, the federal government.

Now, the day is rapidly approaching when the Canadian government will find that it has to borrow more than you and I can possibly save. Remember, government interest charges escalate as the debt increases. Already, public debt charges amount to 30 cents out of every dollar collected. If the interest rate should go up from, say, 10 to 15 percent, this would mean a 50 percent increase in the public debt cost and an additional $10 billion deficit. As you will see as you read on, it is government spending that leads to hyperinflation.

During the worldwide depression fifty years ago, a noted economist by the name of John Maynard Keynes contributed a resolution of this problem. Lord Keynes suggested that all a government need do is give people money to spend. If people have money to spend, he said, they circulate it through the economy and a depression ends. To some extent Keynes' concept worked. Of course, what really helped end the last depression was World War II. A war encourages the production and consumption of goods and services (as well as people).

Government also discovered another important fact: Taxpayers vote for the political party with the greatest giveaway programs. In Canada governments led by Pierre Trudeau ruled for approximately fifteen of the sixteen years from 1968 to 1984. Trudeau has been described as a socialist. There are several definitions of the word "socialist," one being a person who furnishes social goods and services to the public; in this area, Trudeau excelled.

Canada has a generous unemployment insurance plan, an old age pension with a guaranteed income supplement, family allowances, welfare, and medical care. Turn back to Figure 1–3, and you'll see that social service spending accounts for 59 cents out of every dollar collected by the Canadian government. Add the social services portfolio to public debt charges, and it turns out that almost 90 cents out of every dollar collected by the government is expended in these two areas. This means that there is virtually nothing left for anything productive. Aside from $8 billion earmarked for defense, there is virtually nothing left to allocate to economic development, energy or, for that matter, anything else.

These social giveaway programs exist for a very simple reason: It doesn't pay to be a politician unless you can get elected and are a member of the party in power. The Liberals have been electorally successful for so many years because the party has been ruled by pragmatic decisions to do whatever was necessary to get re-elected. Prime Minister Trudeau was able to retain power through most of the last sixteen years by gearing his giveaway programs to a majority of Canadian voters, including pensioners and low-salary workers.

What went wrong? The pensioner and the person on a fixed income are those people who are chronically opposed to any inflation—it means their dollars don't go as far. But what Trudeau failed to realize in waging war against inflation is that the first person to lose a job is the individual working at a low salary, for example, the unskilled worker.

All of a sudden Liberal party popularity dropped substantially in the polls, because anyone who is unemployed or threatened by unemployment will not support the party in power. Any alternative has to be better. No doubt pensioners still support the government's anti-inflation program. But, if unemployed workers stopped to think for a moment, they might begin to realize that, with modest inflation in a vibrant economy, there is the opportunity to hold down two jobs, if necessary, to make ends meet, and perhaps buy the occasional luxury. And holding two jobs is a great improvement over having no job at all.

Unfortunately, even if the government were to reverse its position and encourage business to raise prices 5 percent every six months, there would still be massive dissatisfaction. The fact is that unemployed workers can't see beyond today or tomorrow. They would only perceive costs going up without realizing that in two or three weeks or, at worst, a month or two, they would find the job market opening up and would become re-employed. In the short run the unemployed might suffer, but in the long run they would have to prosper.

What about the pensioner? Unfortunately, with the system now in place, people living below the poverty line or on fixed incomes, or both, are going to suffer no matter what happens. The problem is that government can no longer continue to provide the level of social services support now being given across the board. The cost is too great. Already more than 1.5 million productive Canadians have been sacrificed for the sake of 600,000 pensioners on fixed incomes.

Whether economic conditions are inflationary or recessionary, low-income earners, pensioners, and the poor are going to suffer. If government stops spending and cuts back on social programs, these individuals will get less; if inflation returns, their purchasing power will be reduced; if hyperinflation results, their money will be worthless in the ensuing economic collapse. Again, look at the numbers in Figure 1–4.

In October 1983, during Small Business Week, I was guest speaker at a luncheon sponsored by the Calgary Chamber of Commerce. I put forth my suggestions that modest inflation is not unhealthy, and that government policies are leading us down the path towards destruction. After I had finished speaking, a radio commentator asked if anyone takes what I am saying seriously. At first I was a bit taken aback, then I stopped to reflect on why other people aren't saying the same thing I am.

Now I must be completely honest. Certain people profit more easily than others from inflation, and I admit that I am one of them. During inflationary times businesses earn lots of dollars and pay lots of taxes, but no one wants to pay any more taxes than absolutely necessary. Consequently, accountants, business owners, and executives buy my books, attend my seminars, and listen to my audio tapes. I make a lot more money when times are good than when times are bad. So, of course, modest inflation would benefit my position greatly.

Alternatively, consider who is against inflation and their positions in the economy. Economists don't appear to advocate even modest inflation, nor do the media. Let's take a moment or two to examine these groups objectively.

An economist is usually a highly paid, well-educated individual employed by government, an educational institution, or some kind of company, foundation, or non-profit organization. In times of little or no inflation, the economist's income stretches further, and he or she benefits from the opportunity to buy consumer goods and services at lower or relatively fixed prices. So, naturally, the economist sees a benefit to a non-inflationary environment and speaks against inflation. But remember the domino effect. When the economy is bad, the 12 percent annual raise disappears as the institutions are forced to cut back.

The raise first drops to 6 or 5 percent, then in the next year there are further budget cuts and the salary is frozen. After that, the economist is asked to take a cut in pay. If the individual is associated with a university and doesn't have tenure, dismissal may result if salaries are rolled back. At that point—which under present conditions could be a year or two from now—the economist could very well start singing a different tune when he or she remembers that "inflation," "boom," and "appreciation" mean more or less the same thing. But all this takes time.

Similarly, let's look at media people. Those who didn't lose their jobs during the recession hold relatively secure positions and receive the majority of their incomes by way of salary. Initially, their dollars stretch further when there is no inflation. But advertising revenues earned by newspapers, radio, and television might suddenly begin to drop if the recovery proves to be an illusion and falters. Salary hikes become smaller, or salaries are frozen, and junior people in all departments are laid off. Eventually the thinking of the media also changes.

To some extent part of what I'm telling you here is admittedly academic. I don't believe that any government in North America can campaign on the basis of admitting that it was mistaken and modest inflation is, in fact, tolerable. Politically, such an admission would be suicide. Also, critics would say that conceding the benefits of modest inflation would ultimately lead to hyperinflation. This may very well be true. But hyperinflation is inevitable either way.

If government encourages business to raise prices and doesn't monitor them properly, we could conceivably have hyperinflation. On the other hand, if business continues to falter, and government deficits escalate, we'll have hyperinflation when the government starts to print money. All roads lead to the same thing. It's just a question of one, two, or maybe three years' difference in the critical path from inflation to hyperinflation.

What I suggest you consider at this time, however, is: Which is more appealing, either slowly starving to death, or eating yourself into oblivion for two or three years?

In the long run, there may not be a total disaster. If the dollar is debased far enough, government can simply recall the old currency and issue new bills. Modern society is dependent on paper money as a means of everyday exchange. Despite advances in banking and commercial technology, I don't believe that we will see a completely cashless society in the near future; such a society would be dependent on the universal granting of credit, which is unrealistic to expect. So, we'll simply start over with a new currency. If we can spare the pain of a prolonged recession, however, I think, overall, many of us will be better off.

Let's return to the statement that we all tend to vote for politicians who offer, and deliver, the biggest giveaway programs. Think back to 1979 and the short period of time when Joe Clark was prime minister of Canada. In campaigning against the Liberal party, Clark promised that if he became prime minister, he would make mortgage interest on a principal residence tax deductible, as it is in the United States.

Once Clark became prime minister, however, he discovered the government couldn't afford such a generous program. When he failed to follow through, and his finance minister had the audacity to propose raising gasoline prices 18 cents per gallon to rationalize the government debt situation, Clark's days were numbered.

On 30 April 1982 the economy of Alberta fell apart when it was announced the Tarsands project was going to be shelved. A month or two later, Peter Lougheed's Progressive Conservatives were returned to power in an election which resulted in a mandate stronger than any Lougheed government had previously enjoyed.

During his campaign Lougheed promised to subsidize home mortgage interest. This was at a time when interest rates were hovering between 18 and 20 percent. Lougheed declared that Alberta Heritage Trust Fund income would be passed back to Albertans in the form of mortgage subsidies. For a two-year period after that, I received $129.61 on the first of every month. For that money, I would have voted for Jack the Ripper.

Take a look at your newspapers today. Politicians at the provincial and municipal levels are not the most popular people around these days. They preach restraint, threaten to cut back services, lay off civil servants, and raise taxes. From a politician's standpoint, it's a no-win situation. In times of modest inflation, the politicians can afford their giveaways. At present there is no hope and, when the hyperinflation sets in, things may be even worse.

This is not necessarily a picture of doom and gloom. We'll show you later in this book how you can prepare yourself for what is just around the corner. But what we hope you've seen so far is that you can't rely on government to bail you out. Your financial survival is largely in your own hands.

The following chapter explains what inflation really means and how the consumer price index works. It shows you how government misleads us and blames us for things which are the fault of government itself. You'll see that you must understand clearly how you spend whatever money you have coming in. Otherwise it is difficult, if not impossible, to plan properly.

⁓⁓⁓

Chapter 2

UNDERSTANDING THE CONSUMER PRICE INDEX

I FIRST BECAME INTERESTED in the subject of inflation in May 1982, when the economy of Alberta collapsed after the announcement that the Tarsands projects were being shelved. All around me prices in Calgary dropped dramatically; yet in the same month, when Statistics Canada announced the inflation figures to the end of April, the percentages were still in double digits. This didn't make sense, so I asked Statistics Canada how the consumer price index is calculated. The information I received is summarized in Figure 2–1.

The consumer price index works in the following manner: Seven categories of costs—food; housing; clothing; transportation; health and personal care; recreation, reading, and education; and tobacco and alcohol—are taken into account in the calculations. Price changes in a basket of goods in each of these seven categories are measured over a twelve-month period. Each month, month-end costs are then compared to equivalent costs for the same goods and services the year before. Percentage increases are then calculated.

The numbers in Figure 2–1 reflect the percentage changes from April 1981 to April 1982. Perhaps the easiest explanation would be to examine the price of a loaf of bread. Statistics Canada asks what the price was a year ago, what it is today, and

Figure 2–1: Major Components of the Consumer Price Index

All items	% Change April 1982 from April 1981 11.3%		Statistics Canada weighting % 100.0%		Weighted changes (column 1 × column 2) 11.3%
Food	6.1	×	21.1	=	1.3
Housing	13.8	×	35.4	=	4.9
Clothing	6.0	×	9.6	=	0.6
Transportation	16.3	×	16.2	=	2.6
Health and personal care	10.3	×	3.7	=	0.4
Recreation, reading, and education	8.7	×	8.6	=	0.7
Tobacco and alcohol	15.7	×	5.4	=	0.8
			100.0		11.3

calculates the percentage difference.

You can see from the numbers that, during the period April 1981 to April 1982, prices went up in all categories, from a low of 6 percent for clothing to a high of 16.3 percent for transportation.

The next step is that Statistics Canada takes a weighted average. The weighting recognizes that all of us tend to spend more on certain components of our cost of living than on others. For example, our single most significant cost is housing.

The average family spends 35.4 cents of each dollar of disposable income on housing costs. Then comes food, followed by transportation, clothing, recreation, reading and education, tobacco and alcohol, which is almost double what we spend on health and personal care! The raw data are then multiplied by the weighted averages. The results are added together, and the sum is the annualized increase in the consumer price index.

Here's the problem, though: We all look at the so-called bottom line, which as of April 1982 was 11.3 percent. Few people, if any, bother to look at what happens to the individual components that make up the total.

When the inflation factor was in double digits, two items alone made up 7.5 of that 11.3 percent—housing and transportation. From this you can learn one of the most valuable lessons in this book. No matter who you are, no matter how aggressive or passive you are when it comes to your investments, there are two goals that you must achieve as soon as possible. Your ultimate aim is not to go into retirement without having achieved these goals in light of the heavy inflation expected.

Specifically: *you must go into retirement with a house that is fully paid up; and with one or two late-model cars, also fully paid.*

As far as your house is concerned, the reason why it should be completely paid off is clear once you see what percentage of your present take-home pay is devoted to mortgage payments, which are subject to periodic renewals and interest-rate fluctuations.

If you decide you want a car after retirement, it should be a late-model, fully paid vehicle that you could drive for up to ten years, from age sixty-five to seventy-five. If your house and car are paid for, you are generally immune from changes in interest rates. Without question, when hyperinflation hits Canada, interest rates will start to skyrocket.

Alternatively, if you can structure your lifestyle so you can get by comfortably without a vehicle after retirement, this is just as good.

Take another look at Figure 2–1. Note that inflation affects different people in different ways. For example, in 1982 the inflation factor for tobacco and alcohol was almost 1 percent of the total. If you and your spouse neither smoke nor drink, this means your inflation rate is lower than that of people who do.

One mistake people make in dealing with inflation is assuming that a cost of living always goes up. Everyone should examine their position at age sixty-five. Assuming that at that age you no longer have dependent children, your cost of living should drop substantially. This is especially true if you aren't making house or car payments. Your food and clothing costs drop when you no longer have dependent children. After retirement much of your health and personal care is covered by government programs. You no longer have to worry about education costs, and you can tailor recreation expenditures according to your ability to pay. The graph in Figure 2-2 points this out.

Figure 2-2: Comparative Increases in Cost of Living

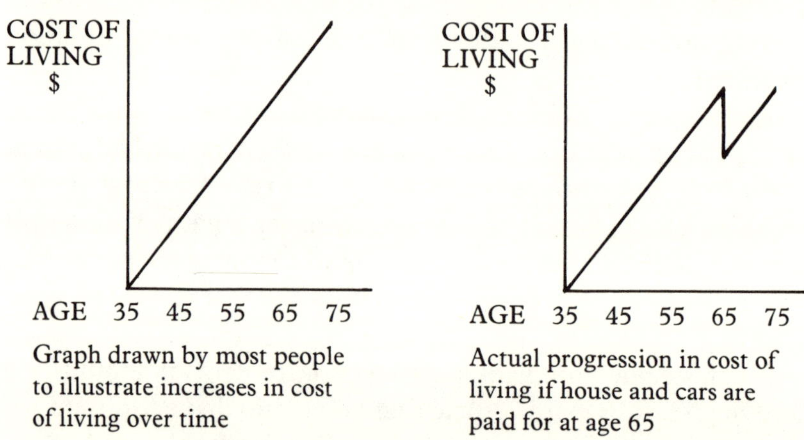

Graph drawn by most people to illustrate increases in cost of living over time

Actual progression in cost of living if house and cars are paid for at age 65

Of course, no one can avoid inflation completely. While I strongly recommend paying for your house as quickly as possible, not only to improve your after-tax cash flow but also to avoid exposure to high interest rates, I recognize that you are still subject to changes in utility costs, municipal taxes, repairs, and so on. Similarly, while it makes sense to own fully-paid, late-model cars, you still have to worry about gasoline prices. So, even if you're relatively insulated, you should still be concerned about inflation and hyperinflation. Moreover, for some people living comfortably is just not enough. You may want to become wealthy and profit from hyperinflation. So keep reading.

What our government has done in dealing with the subject of inflation is nothing less than fraud. Especially during 1981 and 1982 we, the Canadian public, were blamed for inflation while, in reality, inflationary factors are beyond private-sector control.

Let's take a look at housing, again with reference to Figure 2–1. From April 1981 to April 1982 house prices in most parts of the country dropped, but the entire index rose. This can only mean the cost to *keep* the house you *already owned* rose during that period.

Your single largest cost when it comes to housing is mortgage interest. And here is the fraud. From April 1981 to April 1982 interest rates rose dramatically. Anyone who previously had a mortgage at, say, 10 percent and was facing renewal was now required to renew at rates from 18 to 20 percent. The consumer's cost of home ownership actually went up—not based on the price of buying a house but on the price of the money needed to keep the house.

We're told constantly that low interest fuels inflation, because money is easily available for spending. We're also told high interest stops inflation by choking off spending. To a large extent, in the medium and long term, this is true. If, for example, the government suddenly declares that for the next two years it will be illegal to charge interest on borrowed money, we would all rush out to borrow, we would buy things, and prices would climb. The basic laws of supply and demand would come into play. On the other hand, when interest increases, we are reluctant to buy and prices fall.

In the short run, however, the result of changes in interest rates is exactly the opposite. If you're locked into borrowed money—a business loan with floating rates or a mortgage facing renewal—and interest rates jump, your consumer cost jumps. Yet, in 1981 and 1982 the Canadian finance minister laid the blame for inflation on the Canadian consumer, who had absolutely no control over interest rates.

It is certainly easy to condemn the Canadian government for many of its policies. To be fair, however, part of the blame rests elsewhere, outside the country. Canada willingly operates within a global economy. Under existing policies Canada cannot independently control domestic interest rates without paying a heavy price in lost investment capital—domestic and foreign— trade, unemployment, short-term inflation. Our interest rate is strongly linked to the American rate. In fact, the rates of all Western industrialized nations are linked to the U.S. interest rate.

The high interest rate policies of 1981 and 1982 were not the brainchild of the Canadian government. The concept was developed by Washington in an attempt to curtail inflation. But the anti-inflation movement in North America has done too good a job, which top politicians undoubtedly realize but are not ready to admit.

In June 1982, at the economic summit conference in Versailles, France, virtually all industrialized nations begged Ronald Reagan to reduce the interest rate so they could follow suit. Reagan agreed, and the interest rate then began to fall.

At that time people forced to renew mortgages at 18, 19 or 20 percent only did so for one year. By the fall of 1982 interest rates had dropped, and those people who were still solvent were also able to renew their mortgages at much lower rates. So their consumer costs dropped.

By September 1982 the Canadian inflation rate fell below 10 percent. The following month a new finance minister was appointed, and he quickly took the credit for having arrested inflation. Ironically, the Canadian inflation rate dropped in July, August, and September of 1982, the three months of the year that we traditionally get our best government—when Parliament is closed for summer recess and the clowns can't do any damage!

Remember always that politicians try to protect themselves. If Ronald Reagan should raise the interest rate again, in the short run this will automatically signify that inflation is on the rise. Who's going to get blamed for this? You and I, who have no control whatsoever as to what the interest rate is going to be.

Over the last twelve to sixteen months the inflation rate has stayed relatively static somewhere between 5 and 6 percent, owing chiefly to the relative stability of interest rates. Remember, the consumer price index measures percentage changes. If nothing changes, there is no increase or decrease.

There has to be, however, an explanation as to why we still have inflation approaching 6 percent. Let's look at housing costs some more. After mortgage interest, your biggest cost is utilities—heating and electricity.

Remember that government, not only federal but provincial and municipal, is basically bankrupt. Electricity and heating—energy items—are government regulated. Energy prices are increasing at an annual rate well in excess of 8 percent. In some parts of the country the annual increase is still in double digits. Consumers have no control whatsoever over energy prices, but we are blamed when these prices rise.

Real estate taxes are your third largest housing cost. Municipal taxes increase by leaps and bounds. The next time you get your municipal tax bill, try paying exactly what you paid last year, and write your mayor to explain that you're simply exercising restraint. Then see what happens.

I have never tried to prove this scientifically, but I would suggest that about 75 percent of any change in the consumer price index for housing is totally beyond private-sector control.

Let's turn to transportation. For many people transportation means the cost of owning and operating one or two vehicles. Automobile prices have not increased dramatically during the last few years. The average annual increase has been less than 4 percent.

During the late 1970s and the first two years of the 1980s, however, gasoline prices escalated dramatically. From August 1982 to August 1983 alone, during which inflation in general was declining, gasoline prices increased 12 percent. Consumers don't control gasoline prices. In fact, our governments don't control them either. If OPEC increases the price of oil, our costs at the pump eventually go up but, once up, our gas prices don't drop even if OPEC prices fall. Yet, who is blamed in the final analysis for not exercising restraint? Look in a mirror.

For other people transportation means the cost of using public transit, local and commuter. Increases in transit costs over the last few years have been dramatic as municipalities, faced with ever-increasing operating deficits and a need to raise revenues, have raised fares. As with housing, I suggest that 75 percent of any change in the transportation index is beyond consumer control.

Turn for a moment to tobacco and alcohol—the cause of almost one full point in the total CPI when inflation was around 11 percent. What happened here is obvious. Governments have increased taxes on tobacco and alcoholic beverages because, politically, these are the easiest taxes to raise. If you smoke or drink, you won't get much sympathy if you complain about a tax increase. In this area I suggest that almost 100 percent of any inflation can be attributed to government, but let's be generous and stick with 75 percent.

The list goes on. Figure 2–1 doesn't show the figures for the twelve months ended 31 May 1982. Of course, these numbers are now ancient history. But, in May 1982 the CPI in Canada for food took a large jump. The reason is that in mid-May 1982 the province of Ontario brought down a budget in which, for the first time, it was decided to slap a 7 percent retail sales tax on fast foods. And up went consumer prices.

Similarly, look at education costs and medical care expenses. If these go up, this translates into greater pressure on our disposable incomes. If airlines raise prices with government sanction, this tends to cost money as well. Much of our reading material is imported from other countries so, if the Canadian dollar weakens, you can expect an increase in the price of a paperback novel.

Turn to Figure 2–3. If we blame government for 75 percent of the increases in the CPI for housing, transportation, tobacco, and alcohol, and blame it only to the extent of 25 percent in other areas, Figure 2–3 shows you something that you should have known intuitively several years ago. *As early as April 1982 inflation in the private sector was effectively dead.*

The government has been playing mind games with us. I repeat: governments have been saying, "Don't raise your prices!" but have been consistently raising their own; they have been saying, "Don't borrow money!" but have been borrowing every available penny. So far the politicians have been successful, and yet the deception cannot go on forever.

Figure 2–3: Weighted Changes in the Consumer Price Index April 1982, from April 1981

	Estimated % owing to increased interest rates, energy prices, sales tax, and other government levies				% increase not attributable to private sector
All items	**11.3%**				
Food	1.3	×	25%	=	0.3
Housing	4.9	×	75%	=	3.7
Clothing	0.6	×	25%	=	0.1
Transportation	2.6	×	75%	=	2.0
Health and personal care	0.4	×	25%	=	0.1
Recreation, reading, and education	0.7	×	25%	=	0.2
Tobacco and alcohol	0.8	×	75%	=	0.6
	11.3				7.0
Maximum inflation owing to private sector price increases					4.3

The bottom-line number in Figure 2–3 is in the range of inflation to be expected, and tolerated, in a growing economy.

The schedule in Figure 2–4 is an extract from the 29 September 1983 issue of the *Financial Post*. It compares consumer prices as of August 1983 with those of a year earlier. The main offender on the list is fresh vegetables, prices of which were affected by weather, something not regulated by government. Even Pierre Trudeau in his prime could not control climate, and vegetable prices are very much related to the laws of supply and demand. Take a moment, though, and look at the other categories: tobacco, fuels, education, alcoholic beverages, health care—most of the items where the inflation rate exceeded 6 percent were all regulated industries. I'm sure the numbers are no different today.

Figure 2–4: How the Battle Against Inflation Goes

CONSUMER PRICES
AUGUST 1983 VS. YEAR EARLIER

(Regulated prices in bold)		Women's wear	+4.6%
Fresh vegetables	+23.3%	Bakery products	+4.5%
Tobacco products	+18.4%	Food bought in restaurants	+4.2%
Fuel oil and other liquid		Prepared main dishes	+4.2%
fuel	+13.1%	**Poultry**	+4.1%
Gasoline	+12.0%	Clothing materials services	+4.0%
Education	+10.7%	Household cleaning supplies	+4.0%
Piped and bottled gas	+ 9.0%	Home entertainment	
Electricity	+ 8.3%	equipment	+3.9%
Alcoholic beverages	+ 8.2%	Boy's wear	+3.9%
Sugar and confections	+ 8.0%	Furniture	+3.7%
Health care	+ 7.0%	Cereal products	+3.6%
Reading	+ 6.8%	Auto and truck purchases	+3.5%
Rent	+ 6.7%	Fish	+3.3%
Local and commuter		Vehicle insurance premiums	+3.2%
transportation	+ 6.5%	Auto and truck repairs	+2.7%
Telephone	+ 6.2%	Fats and oils	+2.7%
Inter-city transportation	+ 6.1%	**Eggs**	+2.4%
Outdoor recreation		Processed vegetables	+2.4%
equipment	+ 6.1%	Men's wear	+2.1%
Home recreation equipment	+ 5.7%	Processed fruit	+0.7%
Mortgage interest costs	+ 5.7%	Coffee and tea	−1.1%
Dairy products	+ 5.3%	Beef	−2.7%
Girl's wear	+ 5.0%	Fresh fruit	−6.3%
Major household appliances	+ 4.9%	Pork	− 7.4%
Personal care	+ 4.9%	**TOTAL**	+5.5%

Source: *The Financial Post*, 29 September 1983.

To appreciate much of the material which follows, you need to understand what your personal cost of living really is. In later chapters you'll see that people in other countries have come to the same conclusions that I have with respect to living costs— your house and car are key factors in determining whether you will be able to survive, let alone profit, from hyperinflation.

In conclusion, I would like to return again to whether or not inflation is really as bad as the government makes it out to be. Consider that twenty years ago, for example, the average family could live comfortably on $10,000 a year. Today that figure might be $40,000 or maybe even higher. Understand, though, that the $40,000 of today and the $10,000 of yesteryear are the same thing. All this means is that, if inflation is gradual, we adjust to it.

Remember, the words "inflation," "appreciation," and "boom" tend to be synonymous, in their result if not their meaning. If business can count on modest inflation to provide increasing profits, business can afford to hire people.

Modest inflation will solve the unemployment problem. Recognize, however, even at 6 percent inflation, a thirty-five year old earning $30,000 a year will be earning $200,000 by retirement age. It may sound mind boggling, but it really isn't. This doesn't mean that this person will be rich by any stretch of the imagination. If all costs go up by that same 6 percent factor, the individual is merely keeping up with inflation.

If you find it difficult to conceive that you might be earning several hundred thousand dollars a year, here's an example that might bring it home to you. What group in society makes up the highest income earners? You'll probably conclude, like most people, that it's doctors, dentists, or perhaps even successful business entrepreneurs.

Overall, I suggest that the highest paid individuals as a group are professional athletes—the gladiators of the twentieth century. They may not earn large salaries for a long time but, nevertheless, they earn a lot more than most of us do. A professional athlete might have earned $25,000 or $30,000 twenty years ago or, if a real star, perhaps as much as $50,000. That was when the rest of us were earning $10,000.

Today, most executives have caught up to what the athlete was earning ten or twenty years ago. But the athletes are earning $200,000, $300,000 and, in some cases, considerably more. We'll all catch up to what the athletes are earning today, but it may take us another twenty years to do it. Imagine what professional athletes might be earning then.

My suggestion that modest inflation would go a long way towards providing a solution to the economic crisis in North America is, I think, a sound one. I recognize, however, that no single country can set fiscal and monetary policies in a vacuum. For example, if Canada gave in to a 10 percent annual inflation while the United States maintained much tighter controls, the Canadian dollar would plummet. Devaluation would accelerate the inflationary process and put us into the hyperinflation, which I, personally, would like to avoid. What is needed instead is a worldwide agreement to contain inflation at modest levels.

The same concept holds true with interest rates. It is futile to suggest that any country alone can manipulate interest rates for extended periods of time. If every other country moves in a different direction, chaos eventually results.

The point is, however, that governments must act. The status quo won't work, because our deficits will lead us into hyperinflation in any event. If we allow a modest stimulus, instead, in the long run most of us will come out ahead. Of course, today's pensioners living below the poverty line are going to suffer because they did not plan for their financial security. *Unless you plan for your financial security you too will be forced to bear the consequences of living unprepared for hyperinflation.*

In Part Three of this book, the concluding chapters, we will present some ideas to avoid hyperinflation. The most important of these are suggestions on cutting government spending. Sadly, however, this will never happen. Unfortunately, the government has sold too many Canadians on the belief they can have bread and circus without paying the admission price.

A free ride is now seen as a right and, unfortunately, people addicted to bread and circus will vote for the politician who promises them the most—until it is too late. One thing we can promise: The bread and circus won't continue forever, not when government runs out of the money to pay for them.

⁂

Part 2

AROUND THE WORLD FROM NORTH TO SOUTH

Chapter 3

INTO THE INFERNO

T HERE IS SOMETHING to be said about home. Perhaps that it's the nicest four-letter word in the English language. Back in North America, however, I find the warmth and security home offers is overshadowed by concern. After fifty-two days spent examining five countries plagued by hyperinflation and chronic inflation, I understand how hard we will have to work to preserve our way of life.

What we have in North America, despite its faults and our faults, is the best of all worlds and, if we aren't careful, we'll lose it. We will lose it not because someone will take it from us. Rather, through carelessness we'll simply waste it, or let it erode—the consequences of the economic, political, and moral decay that accompany inflation and hyperinflation.

Closing our eyes to reality, pointing fingers at others who are "really to blame," or suggesting it's a problem for our children to face is a cheap way of sloughing off the responsibility each of us must bear if we're to continue demanding, and getting, the good life North America has to offer.

At his seminars on tax, estate, or investment planning for people with enough disposable income to worry about such things, Henry Zimmer always stressed that financial planning is more important these days than ever, because government

58

budget deficits threaten the long-term stability of our economy. Ultimately, he said, we face a return of inflation that will make us nostalgic for the "good old days" of 1981, when the inflation rate was 12 percent, and the attendant prime interest rate was 22 percent.

Henry was saying this a full eighteen months before it became economic gospel that government budget deficits are bad for an expanding, growing, or recovering economy. I point this out because, when we first broached the subject of this book, naysayers insisted we were crazy to consider the return of inflation. "The government has inflation under control," we were told. "Times are getting better. Why look into a crystal ball darkly and project a difficult future? Besides, there are too many historical, political, social, and economic differences between North America and the places you propose visiting to draw any valid conclusions."

Nonsense. That assumes that the desire to survive and prosper is a virtue restricted to North Americans. The will to survive and do well is universal among humans. It's called hope, and it transcends political and economic frameworks.

I was brought up on the notion that the wise learn from their mistakes. But I've learned that the truly wise learn from other people's mistakes. It is pure arrogance to believe we have nothing to learn from other people's experiences.

So off I went to five countries to learn how people coped and prospered in a hyperinflationary world. But why these five countries? Italy and Spain have had long periods of steady slow-growth inflation with spikes that finally forced government action to prevent these countries from sliding into hyperinflation. For more than thirty years Argentina and Israel have lived with what they called tolerable inflation (we wouldn't) which, in the 1970s, exploded into hyperinflation. Mexico, much like Canada and the United States, had very low inflation rates which grew slowly during the 1970s, but which exploded overnight into hyperinflation and has since been brought under a degree of control.

In each of these countries I asked, I watched, I listened, I learned. The next several chapters are my travelogue through a kind of economic and financial Inferno.

The first lesson I learned is that not all in this world is as it appears. Many of the names and characters in this book have been changed, as have scenes, settings and locales. This has nothing to do with protecting the innocent; it has everything to do with protecting the helpful. Many people in many lands opened their doors, their financial books and records, and their hearts to me. They put themselves in potential jeopardy with employers, business associates, and even right-wing or left-wing assassination squads. That may sound melodramatic, but the world out there is tougher than any newspaper will allow us to know.

One economist, a senior advisor to the Argentine government put it succinctly when he was outlining the many problems that country's new democratic government faced. "We will do what we must to repair our problems and settle our foreign debts," he said. "But we cannot do it the way the World Bank and International Monetary Fund want us to. Not with austerity programs like in Brazil."

"Why not?"

He leaned across his desk and held a thumb and forefinger about an inch apart. "Because we are this far away from shooting each other in the streets."

"You mean what happened in the recent past, the junta?"

He shook his head emphatically. "Never mind the past," he growled. "We have many poor, and they suffer terribly from inflation. I am worried about the future."

He would have been one of the first to be gunned down. As much as we would like to turn a blind eye to the realities of this world, Argentina isn't the only country where these kinds of fears are justified.

Of the many things learned, it's especially important to note that *the greater the rate of inflation, the more refined the art of survival becomes.* This means that the need for individual sophistication about money matters, money manipulation, and politics becomes greater as inflation increases. You'll see that the

methods employed are usually a response to government policies to deal with economic troubles. This tends to make life
something of a chess game: taxpayer versus taxman, with no
quarter given and none asked.

In Italy, which has endured inflation for almost forty years,
the populace has developed certain attitudes toward money and
certain techniques for handling finances. Some of these techniques are to be found in Spain but with subtle differences
because, though the inflation rate is similar, inflation has only
been a factor in Spain for half as long. These same techniques
crop up in Israel, Argentina, and Mexico, but with differences
particular to their experiences of explosive hyperinflation.

Also worthy of note is that *the key to survival in inflationary
times is thinking fast enough to hang on to what you have and
turning it to profit, without becoming so clever you lose it all in the
end.* To keep from outsmarting yourself, you have to learn to
gather information effectively, sort it, analyze it, and make the
right decisions quickly.

After the president and comptroller of an Argentine manufacturing firm described cost and management accounting in an
environment where the official inflation rate was 400 percent
per year (a figure most business people dismissed as overly
conservative), I was reeling. It's a confusing spectacle, where
accountants are the real stars of the business world.

"Consider this," the president said, "inflation is what, 5
percent in North America?" He looked for confirmation and got
it. "Fine. Assume our inflation here is actually 500 percent. We
have to think one hundred times faster than you do just to
maintain our capital base!"

It quickly becomes clear that no secret formula exists for
prospering during inflationary and hyperinflationary times. In
fact, the real secret to any sort of success is to be found in
traditional business practices and strategies: *The key to profiting
from inflation and hyperinflation is to be able, first, to profit from
relatively normal, non-inflationary economic times.* That's why
this book is timely. We have time before hyperinflation hits
North America.

The suggestion that you first orient yourself to a normal economy may sound like heresy to those who profited during inflationary times in the late 1970s. Chances are, though, those people played their investments like master poker players. We're not talking card manipulation here because, realistically, very few of us are expert card sharps. But there are things to be learned from the winning poker player's money management techniques.

The player goes into a game with his stake. When the cards are bad, he bets lightly, but folds both soon and subtly enough that no one notices he only bets heavily when dealt a good hand. Meanwhile, when he wins, he quietly holds back a five or a ten per pot until he has re-pocketed his stake. He continues holding back a bit per pot and pockets it, but no one ever notices he's doing it.

He operates by three cardinal rules:
- Never lose your stake.
- Always pocket some of the winnings.
- When you shoot the works, the works are what you have on the table—not what you have pocketed.

Take the same attitude to investment, but keep in mind that each of us has a different level of tolerance for risk. First, know what you're getting into. Bet a little bit of your money or borrow a bit (if you're comfortable doing so) the first time out. You should think of your investment as money you never had. And whatever you do, don't go for the quick killing; it could leave you broke. Instead, think long term, think slow growth, but balance that with a portion of assets put into speculative investments offering short-term profit.

Once you have taken profits, put your initial investment dollars into a portfolio of secure (read: diversified) investments to further spread your risk. Your stake has been pocketed, so now play with, and build up your winnings.

Long-term, slow-growth development of wealth built on a solid financial foundation will always pay rewards. You must also set goals that are reasonable within the limits of the economic climate in which you work and within risk levels you find tolerable. The rewards can be as handsome as your expectations, but hanging on to what you earn is the real test of your success.

In times of inflation, you'll be tempted to build a financial house of cards on the shaky basis of interest-sensitive investments bought with inflated dollars and flipped for quick profits. You'll find that you start thinking you're dealing with "easy money." You'll see, however, easy in—easy out. You will also fall into the fallacy that it will never end.

Eventually, all profitable aspects of inflation are lost to erosion of the value of money, or they become illegal. And, ultimately, the first strong recessionary wind will send the house of cards crashing down. Ask anyone who lost a multi-million dollar empire (on paper), a house, or even a stereo or car to a bank repossession during the recession of the 1980s.

This is not to say that you can't make fast profits in inflationary times. There are, indeed, ways to make quick profits from inflation and hyperinflation. The quick profits of inflationary and hyperinflationary schemes can, however, have offsetting costs. There are legal, quasi-legal, and thoroughly illegal ways of preparing for, surviving, and profiting from inflation and hyperinflation. The illegal ones are few, not particularly imaginative, usually dangerous, and even potentially fatal. As hard-core capitalists, we believe it is incumbent on each of us to prepare for our individual futures. While in the interests of fair and honest reporting we might describe some dodgy methods of doing that, we do not encourage or promote illegality. In fact, we figure if you have to resort to illegal methods of making money, two things have gone wrong: the society in which we live and/or your thinking.

But now join us on a trip to moonlit exotic locales, past historical sites, and some of the finest natural and manmade art in the world to look at the way other people live. There are lessons to be learned that can make our lives easier over the next few years, if only because of the security that comes from the act of planning for the future.

Chapter 4

ITALY: FORGET DOMANI BECAUSE DOMANI NEVER COMES

JANUARY IS NOT the best time of year to visit Rome. It's cool, a wet wind comes off the Mediterranean, and the sun is an occasional visitor. Dawn comes late, sundown early, and daylight pays a quick visit.

But time moves differently in Rome than in North America. Stores open for hectic business at 8:00 or 9:00 A.M., close at 1:00 or 2:00 P.M. for leisurely two-hour lunch breaks, then re-open for four more hours of full commercial activity. Downtown commercial districts, sharing blocks with historical sites, mammoth cathedrals, and ancient monuments, shut down around 8:00 P.M. By 8:05 Rome is quiet.

Except for a few late workers rushing to get home, the streets are virtually empty. There are those Romans who insist that television—five state-owned channels and about thirty commercial channels—has ruined the city's night life. Romans appear to have surrendered the delights of the little cafés and bars, bistros, and restaurants that color our dreams of the romance of Italy for the dubious pleasures of Kojak reruns, rock videos from America, or dozens of other domestic and imported programs.

Some Romans say the city is quiet at night because the locals can't afford to dine out regularly, that the tourists are the only ones who can afford the prices. But January isn't tourist season, so what clientele the eateries have are gifts from heaven.

Perhaps it's the winter. Romans point to the dark skies; the air is dank, moist, heavy with the smell of the last rainfall, thick with the coming rainfall. Rain, after all, does put a damper on Campari and soda at a sidewalk café on the Via Veneto. No, protest other Romans, fear of street crime keeps Romans off the streets.

Though many Romans stay home, the night life does go on behind the silent walls of the city.

"Night life here is restricted to dinner with friends at home, or the theatre, and a good restaurant," grumbles Mario Lambrusco, a New Jersey-born Italo-American who came "home" to retire. "Even then you drive wherever you're going. Thieves have been known to steal the furs off women's backs here."

And this crime? What are its roots?

He shrugs and grimaces wryly. "We're a rich country," he says. "And there are many rich people, but," he pauses for dramatic effect, "there are also many poor people here. Inflation, taxes: Someone is always stealing from someone else—legally or illegally. Someone always has a hand out."

Termini Station is a sprawling railroad and bus complex in one of the many "downtowns" of Rome. When you arrive by train, you descend to one of the many platforms that separate the ribbons of track and walk along the platform into the station proper.

Until you pass through the turnstiles at the end of the platform, you're safe. Then, they descend on you: dozens of men wearing little engraved plastic badges issued by the ministry of tourism certifying them as legal guides and, supposedly, all-around nice guys eager to make your entrance into the city something akin to Caesar's.

"Taxi!" "Hotel!" "Information!" "Change!" The air fills with offers, demands, even threats if you're ready to be intimidated. And they can be intimidating. A chorus of voices assault you, not allowing a moment of thought or reflection during which you can get your bearings and decide on your course of action. They batter you with words until, your guard down, you surrender, nod to one and he claims you as his. The rest back off, acknowledging territorial possession.

"I want to go to Hotel X."

He shakes his head. "Not for you. I can tell…businessman. That hotel…for students. Too noisy."

"Okay. What's your pitch?"

He pulls out a brochure and flips it open. "Nice place, clean." He points to a picture. "Modern."

Why not? Room prices are quoted, then negotiated until a mutually agreeable price is reached.

"Okay. I just want to change my French currency to lira."

"No." He gestures at the exchange booth. "Thieves! You change at bank. Better rate."

On the way to the hotel the guide introduces himself as Mario.

"And that tag. What does it mean?"

"I am certified guide, from government."

"Are you a government employee?"

"Some are, some are not."

"Yes, but are you?"

Suddenly, Mario develops amnesia and forgets how to speak English.

In the hotel he tells the clerk, in Italian, the negotiated price. In Italian the clerk tells him the manager will be in later that afternoon and they'll settle his commission then.

As the clerk takes the bags up to the room, Mario turns to the newcomer, his hand out, to bid adieu. But it isn't quite in the handshaking position. The newcomer reaches into his pocket and pulls out a 10-franc coin. To his mind: very rough conversion—a buck sixty American, about two Canadian. What the hell? He gives it to Mario.

Mario smiles. To his mind: precisely 240 lira to the franc, therefore, 2,400 lira, $1.50 American.

The next day, the newcomer drops his key at the desk. Mario is saying goodbye to a group of Swedes. Krone change hands. Mario knows exactly what he's getting.

"Sure, he took you, no matter what price you got on the hotel room," laughs Signor Lambrusco. "But if you're pleased with the hotel, you got your money's worth. Besides, this Mario was your protection. He knows the score. Rather he 'pick your pocket' for service than you walk out of the station alone and in your confusion really get your pockets picked." He sighs sadly and shakes his head. "Like I said, everybody in Rome has a hand out."

Via Barberini is a commercial street, by day a raucous thoroughfare of noisy cars and throngs of people going about their business. On one stretch of sidewalk a crippled beggar, his mangled legs twisted up beneath him, has his hand out. Passersby ignore him. Occasionally the piteous sight of his wretched legs moves someone to drop a coin or two in his hand.

At night the visitor to Rome, not yet aware that he's risking assault and robbery, walks back up Barberini and stops to look across the street at the crippled beggar he had seen there earlier. Downtown Rome is an expensive place to live, too expensive for a beggar. Where do Roman beggars live? The visitor slips into a shadowed doorway. He watches and waits.

It's 9:00 P.M. The last, late-evening wanderers have scurried home. A wind is blowing up and dollops of rain spatter the sidewalk. The beggar looks around, shoves some coins into a pocket, laboriously lifts himself from the sidewalk onto his crutches, and plods away.

The visitor shadows him down the street and around a corner. Another street. Abruptly, the beggar ducks down a lane. The visitor rushes up in time to see the beggar tuck the crutches up under his arm and walk away.

What is truth when you're trying to survive? The story of the cripple only elicits laughter when it's related to Romans. That spot on Barberini is one of the best in Rome for begging, they say. The rent on it is supposed to be very high.

Rent? People shrug and describe a sort of protection racket among the professional beggars believed to be running the game. All the prime begging spots in Rome are rented, and a good beggar can make a healthy living from a good spot, all tax free. Actually, the rent is protection, to ensure beggars don't encroach on each other's spots. Their only complaint is about the gypsy beggars, who refuse to play by the rules of the government or of the street.

But there is no need for the unemployed to turn to begging in Italy, which operates a social welfare system guaranteeing cradle-to-grave security. It's a system which also contributes to Italy's ongoing inflation problem.

"There are no poor as such. There are no poor," snorts Giuseppe Guerreri, successful Roman lawyer, businessman, and president of the Italo-Canadian Chamber of Commerce. "It is a highly socialist country, where everything is provided for you. For example, everybody who is a resident of this country can get full, free medical assistance." He laughs sardonically. "You register in the municipality and tomorrow, if you need the most expensive operation, you just get it free." Beyond anger at abuses of the system, more awed by the enormity of the abuse, Guerreri shakes his head. "Why, people from North Africa come over here and get free treatment."

Just how this situation contributes to Italy's economic troubles is through the impact on the economy of budget deficits incurred to pay for all the services the government provides. It spends too much money, more than it collects in taxes. To cover the deficits, it must find alternative methods of creating revenue, usually borrowing or printing money.

"But I would distinguish between imported inflation and domestic inflation," Guerreri is quick to point out. "Imported inflation is the one which is provoked and originates from items which we have to pay for in U.S. dollars, which become more and more expensive because of the dollar exchange."

With a population of about 57.5 million, Italy is people rich but resource poor. While possessing coal and natural gas deposits, the country has virtually no oil reserves. To support public, agricultural, and industrial demand, Italy imports somewhere between 75 and 90 percent of her energy needs and raw materials.

The country does produce some hydro-electric power, but mostly in the industrial north. And there are very few nuclear power plants in Italy, because development over the last ten years has been held up by politically astute environmental groups.

Added to the imported inflation is the problem of domestic inflation, blame for which most observers, sophisticated and otherwise, lay at the feet of government. They point to annual budget deficits in the late 1970s and early 1980s, which ran into the range of $25 to $30 billion U.S.

The roots of the Italian deficit problem can be traced to 1968, when the government embarked on a program of calculated deficits.

"It starts because Italy does not have raw materials to trade, so it must concentrate on industry," explains Marco Vignudelli, a soft-spoken economic writer with *Ore 12*, an Italian public affairs magazine. "But the level of demand in Italy has always been greater than our capacity for output."

The problems of demand for goods and services, and the inability to meet the demands, led Italy into deficit financing. To deal with the problems, successive administrations in Italy's revolving-door government funneled funds into public works, rather than offering attractive tax breaks to investors and industry, which might have ensured long-term employment for a growing work force. The solution was based on classical Keynesian thinking: Increased government expenditures cause increased consumer spending, which brings about a further increase in employment. The problem is, however, that money spent on public works isn't necessarily productive—its a purely monetary solution.

While some money did end up in the consumer's hands and roll through the economy, more factories (jobs) weren't necessarily being built, nor were entrepreneurial ventures developed and new jobs created. If money invested or spent doesn't create more wealth by expanding the gross national product—the total input of all goods and services created or performed by members of the society—it is only moving through the society, creating paper wealth, but nothing of tangible value.

Also, because the source of investment is the government treasury, and the outcome is not motivated by the incentives or demands of the profit motive, the possibility of inefficiencies developing is greater than in investments financed by the private sector. When funds run low, government can cover its losses by borrowing or printing money—both inflationary pressures.

If government chooses to tackle the deficit, which all governments are eventually forced to do, the first items to go are government subsidies and contracts. The well dries up. People lose their jobs. A sizable chunk of money no longer moves through the economy. Recession hits certain sectors, generally the ones that were spurred or created by government funding in the first place.

Italy's budget deficit was manageable until 1973 when, like most of the world, the country was hit with the fourfold increases in oil prices called the "1973 Oil Shock."

"After 1973 we imported inflation," agrees Mario Draghi, professor of economics at the University of Florence and consultant to the Italian treasury on matters of public finance and monetary questions. Italy suffers the same problem as Japan, Draghi points out. She has no natural resources to support the industrial base necessary to offer Italians the lifestyle of an industrialized nation. "We have been importing and incorporating all this inflation from increases in the price of oil," says Draghi. "But Japan found a way to re-export the imported inflation."

The technique the Japanese use is very simple to describe, but requires a high degree of social integration to achieve. Though energy costs are high, the Japanese get a high degree of individual productivity from workers, so production costs are low and they re-export to their customers the inflationary factor of expensive energy. Japanese workers see it is in their self-interest to produce at a great rate. In turn, the company rewards them with wage and salary increases, job security, benefits, and recognition of the worker's contribution to society as a whole.

In Italy wage and salary adjustments are made without consideration to individual productivity. A critical component of the Italian economy—and one of the reasons Italians don't rise in mass revolt over inflationary erosion of their earnings—is indexation of those earnings. Incomes are covered to the full extent of inflationary erosion. Depending on income level and job category, indexation can actually surpass the inflation rate. While protecting incomes, indexation also contributes to inflation, because it does not take productivity into account.

If the basket of goods used to monitor inflation shows a 22 percent rise in the past year, that 22 percent is the basis, but not necessarily the top figure, for settlements in the coming year. The range of increases in wage settlements in the country could run from 19 to 25 percent, whether or not there was a commensurate increase in productivity. So, whatever the inflation rate, no one who is employed suffers real privation.

But indexation is a catch-up mechanism that in no way guarantees long-term financial security. If anything, indexation is a pressure dressing holding back the flow of blood from a severed economic artery.

Manufacturers have to compensate for their increased costs by raising prices. These increases are passed on to merchants who, in turn, pass them on to customers. But, if prices to a merchant are raised by 22.5 percent, he adds in the 22.5 percent, rounds it out to 23 percent, and adds on a couple of points "just in case"; inflation goes up rather than down this year. This becomes another inflationary pressure. So, despite indexation, Italians never quite get the better of inflation; they simply manage to keep up with it, or lag just behind it.

In North America, by comparison, when the 1981 inflation rate was 12 percent with no indexing of salaries or benefits, workers suffered a real erosion of 12 percent of earnings. Italy's 1981 inflation rate of 18 percent was tolerable because of the indexing cushions. For example, a pair of Italian-made loafers that in Italy cost $15 U.S. at the end of 1981 cost $18.75 U.S. at the end of 1983, up by 25 percent. At the same time, however, average annual salaries had also risen from about $5,200 to about $6,900, an increase of 36 percent.*

It's no surprise, therefore, to find that foreigners shop in Rome with a calculator in hand and a firm grip on the latest exchange quotation. Survival in a country with an inflationary economy, where the real standard of value is something other than the local currency, depends on developing the art of doing long division in your head and being able to make a decision as you're turning around.

"And there was the mixture of public expenditure—public deficit—accompanied by an accommodating monetary policy in the 1970s," adds Professor Draghi. These government expenditures included transfer payments to subsidize, or nationalize, failing or money-losing industries simply to protect jobs. The result according to Draghi is that somewhere between 15 and 18 percent of the national budget is spent on interest payments on government debt—between $16 and $19.5 billion U.S. on the 1980 budget of $108.1 billion U.S., though actual expenditures were $141.9 billion U.S.

But the deficit isn't only a result of make-work programs, subsidies, and simple government overspending. There's the problem of uncollected money for contributory social programs which, in turn, is covered by government subsidy.

Lawyer Guerreri leans forward in his seat and punctuates the air with his cigar. "The pension system is based on the contributions of people. While you work, you pay; when you retire, you get a pension." He puffs his cigar furiously and speaks around it. "Now everybody says, 'Well, I won't pay my contributions. If they catch me, too bad. If they don't, I get my pension anyway.' So our pension system is bankrupt."

The government still pays pensions to all who claim them, subsidizing the program with income tax money, a value-added tax—a form of sales tax—or by printing more money. Whatever the manner in which government gets its funds, it is a drain on the general public wealth and generally inflationary.

* January 1984 exchange rates. This way incomes and costs can be expressed against a relatively stable benchmark. Consider the confusion if we expressed 1981 earnings in lira valued at 1,100/ $U.S., to compare against 1983 earnings when year-end exchange rates were 1,600/$U.S.

First, there is the administrative cost of collecting money, a cost not only to the government but to the businesses that pass it on to government. This is money that is circulating without creating wealth. Though tax revenues eventually go back into circulation, the value returned isn't as much as was taken out initially. And all printing more money does is dilute the value of what is already in circulation.

What the money pays for is immaterial. Whether it's social spending, the large military and national service establishment, or subsidies to industry to cover ever-rising energy costs, government overspending is the key.

- Deficits put government in competition with business, industry, and agriculture for the consumer's savings and spending money.
- Deficits put government in competition with all sectors of the economy for investment money. Government usually acquires extra revenue through bond issues at real rates of return (above inflation) that have to be higher than private investment offerings, thereby forcing up all interest rates.
- Deficits pull potentially productive money out of the economy to cover unproductive debt—good money thrown after bad, resulting in a loss in purchasing power of the currency.
- Deficits lead to greater scrutiny of public spending by the media and the political opposition. They often uncover stories of bureaucratic incompetence and sloth, administrative and individual corruption, and incidents of cheating, lying, and institutionalized theft.
- Deficits generate a degree of cynicism on the part of all citizens on whose backs these horror stories are financed.

Rome's traffic can play havoc with a car. Giancarlo slammed the horn button and felt a surge of pleasure when the twin air horns bleated their high-pitched warning at the idiot in the Fiat.

He gripped the Alfa Romeo's leather-wrapped steering wheel protectively, possessively, luxuriating in the feel of the material, in the silence and steadiness of the ride, in the sheer beauty of the lines of the fender.

If you want the best, you have to pay for it, he thought, even if it means two years working at a second job. And gasoline.... He sighed and checked the fuel gauge. The prices keep rising. You wake up one morning and yesterday's 1,200 lira liter is 1,300. Damned government! Always taking.

He smiled at the last thought. Yes, the damned government is always taking, but he showed them. He ran his hand over the leather upholstery of the passenger seat, normally occupied by his wife, Angela. The entire car paid for in two years with black money—undeclared income: no taxes, no social security payments, nothing.

Giancarlo wasn't sure what gave him more pleasure, that his car was all paid for or that it was all paid for with black money. Maybe the real pleasure was that he could give up the second job, and he and Angela could go back to a normal middle-class life, living comfortably on their combined earnings.

He did some quick computations—3,040,000 lira per month at 1,600 to the dollar—yes, 1,900 U.S. dollars. Almost three times the national average. Good money for a two-income family with two children.

So, the apartment is paid off, the house by the sea almost. Angela's car is free and clear, and now the Alfa. His smile was smug: Next month we will have money left over.

Better to plan now, play smart, and use it quickly before inflation makes it worthless. Maybe some new furniture for the house by the sea, or that new leather coat. Maybe sneak some money into Switzerland. The U.S. dollar still looks strong, but too many strange things happen in America—too much spending on arms and not enough on new factories. Perhaps the American dollars we already hold should be converted to gold if the interest rates do not rise.

It's so hard to decide, he thought. But I am an economic analyst with the ministry of finance; I should know where to put money! There are too many variables and options, and not all are attractive in the final analysis, no matter how good they appear on the surface. Meanwhile, we just spend. What else can we do to keep value in what we earn? Maybe buy that new Sony video with the remote control.

Giancarlo shook his head in disgust. Inflation of 15 percent. Not much, not compared to 200 in Israel, or 400 in Argentina. But inflation every year since the war; 30 percent after the 1973 and 1979 oil shocks; and even now stable, after a fashion, in the 10 to 15 percent range.

Ridiculous! He snorted, and hit the horn. He spun the wheel, let out the clutch, floored the gas pedal, and took a wide circle around the slow-moving bus full of tourists. He smiled at the surge of power from the Alfa's engine. The money might be worthless and lose its value daily, but this—he stroked the dashboard—this will never lose its value.

Giancarlo's Alfa *will never* lose its value; it's his formal car. He usually drives around Rome in a small, forlorn looking Fiat 850, while the Alfa sits in his garage unused. After all, the Alfa would suffer too much wear and tear in everyday Rome traffic, so it's reserved for special occasions, drives in the country, and holidays.

The Alfa is his pride, something that gives him a reason to continue banging his head against an economic wall, falling further behind the more he consumes simply because of inflation and the hidden and value-added taxes he has to pay. The Alfa is also one of his inflationary hedges. He hopes he never has to sell it but, if he does, provided he takes care of it and makes all repairs as they're needed, he'll be able to command a price, computed in American dollars, at least equal to, if not better than, the original purchase price adjusted for inflation.

Giancarlo and Angela are a fortunate Roman couple. They don't think so; they figure they're just holding their own against inflation, the rising cost of living, and high and ever-increasing taxes. Their combined earnings, from Giancarlo's principal job with the ministry of finance and Angela's teaching position, put them in the mid to upper reaches of middle-class earning and purchasing power in a country where the average annual income in early 1984 was approaching $7,200 U.S. Their earnings make them representative of one segment of the Italian middle class, but the attitudes they adopt to the money they earn make them the standard.

They spend every cent they earn. Sometimes, when they bother to consider the future, they think that maybe they should save a little. But Italy's sustained inflation has created a lack of confidence on the part of the populace in the lira. So Giancarlo and Angela, like most Italians, look elsewhere for a value standard. In the post-war years, until the late sixties, it was the American dollar. In the early 1970s it was the Swiss franc. In the mid-1970s, when inflation in Italy went as high as 30 percent, gold, when it could be acquired, became the repository of confidence. By the early 1980s the U.S. dollar was once again the confidence commodity of choice.

Lack of confidence in the lira reflects to a degree the lack of confidence in government, especially in how it spends taxpayers' money. This, in turn, leads to rampant tax evasion among the self-employed, merchants, professionals, and tradespeople. Tax evasion takes on the proportions of a national pastime, practised with an almost religious zeal by all who can get away with it.

"What they say is, 'The government is not efficient, the tax system is not working, so what chances do I have to get away?'" explains the Italo-Canadian Chamber of Commerce's Guerreri. "Perhaps a good, what...50 percent chance? So, they think, 'Well, I run the risk. And if I am caught, I am caught. But otherwise, I make a good living.'"

If anything, tax evasion is one of the keys to profiting in an inflationary economy. It leaves the earner that much more disposable income to invest or spend. And, on any investment, tax evasion ensures a handsome real rate of return, which is the difference between the nominal rate (what the investment earns) and what you have in hand (what it pays) after inflation and after the tax department takes its cut.

The Italians seem keenly aware of the declining value of their currency. They are loath to part with it unless they have a chance of getting a "real" return, whether from investment or the purchase of durable consumer goods that will hold value. So they run the risks of getting caught for tax evasion because the rewards are worth it: Investments earn what they end up paying. All that an individual earns in a year remains in his hands as cheap disposable income.

Meantime, wage earners (those employed by others who deduct taxes at source) end up carrying the economy, paying 70 percent of the nation's income tax bill.

"But there are examples, striking examples, of people just paying no taxes, not even having a position with the tax office," Guerreri points out angrily. "Or we have cases of people who just declare $3,000 U.S. or $4,000 U.S. per year, and they live like kings."

Antonio Ferraro closed the door behind the last departing worker and crossed the loading docks to the racks of leather jackets. He went through them quickly, taking one last count.

One hundred. Excellent! They will bring a tidy sum in the city. The idea of running this short unofficial night shift was turning out to be most profitable.

He pushed the racks closer to the loading door and peered out the window. The truck should be coming soon to take the jackets to the shop in Rome.

This was a wonderful way of making everyone happy and a little richer—except the tax department. He spit in the corner at the thought of the tax department. Thieves! Drive a person and his family into poverty. For what? To pay for another highway or to hire another tax collector who is a third cousin to the minister's wife.

He surveyed the jackets again. Pay the workers cash. No social security, no tax or pension payments to track down the workers or the extra work. Cash for the jackets. No receipts. He rubbed his hands together in anticipation of the cash he was going to receive. Even the leather for the jackets was administratively hidden in the massive shipments of leather the factory received every week.

Antonio Ferraro felt good. This would give Maria extra money for her studies at the university in Turin. Thought of his youthful daughter led to thoughts of his young mistress. Perhaps a new necklace for her. And perhaps he would get a necklace for Franca, his wife.

Gold jewelry is always a good buy, he thought, and when Franca tires of the new piece, it can go in the vault with the rest of the jewels and gold. It will never lose in value, but.... He savored the memory of the good days of 1981 and 1982, when gold was climbing towards that February 1983 high of $508.50 U.S. an ounce. He had cleaned up, especially when he finally broke down and sold the gold coins his grandfather had given him. Now, again, is the time to buy gold, he thought, while it is cheap. It will rise again. Someday gold will perform well again.

The sound of a motor broke through his thoughts. He looked out the window. Aha, the truck....

The white van pulled up behind Federico Testa's shop in downtown Rome. It was just one of hundreds of similarly painted delivery vehicles plying the city streets.

Testa was already opening the delivery door when Ferraro raised his hand to knock. The two businessmen shook hands and walked around to the back of the van.

"Good quality, like always," Testa grunted while running his expert hands over the jackets.

"Only the best for my clients," Ferraro grinned.

"I will send my man to help unload," Testa said. "Come, Ferraro, some coffee."

In Testa's office Antonio Ferraro riffled the bills in the last of three packets with his thumb and nodded. He lifted his coffee cup and, with a silent "Salut," toasted the business deal.

Testa tossed back his coffee. "When can you bring me more?" he asked.

"Two weeks," Ferraro said. "Another hundred?"

"A hundred fifty," Testa said. "Tourist season starts."

"You never worry about getting caught, Testa?"

Testa smiled and looked out the open door of his office at Ferraro's son carrying in the jackets. "The books always balance at the end of the year. I have paper to cover everything."

"Are you sure. What if they send in an agent to buy a jacket?"

Testa laughed and leaned over his desk, drawing Ferraro into a conspiratorial circle. "Everyone gets a receipt, Ferraro. But my cousin is my printer. He printed three sets of receipts for me. I keep and throw away as I need to."

The profits of tax evasion can be sizable. The downside for Italian tax evaders, however, is facing a predatory tax department. "We have good tax laws," says Guerreri, the lawyer. "It is the application that is wrong. What we have today is just punitive tax collectors," he sighs. "So, if you get hooked, they squeeze you, down to the last cent, with no mercy at all."

It would be optimistic to say that ending tax evasion would put a curb on Italy's deficit, but it would produce benefits. While exact figures on the extent of the tax evasion don't exist, Professor Draghi suggests that it is huge. "It will surely be a lot of tax revenue, but I don't think it can solve all our debts and problems."

The blocks around the Spanish Steps, the location of Rome's American Express office, are a shopper's delight. Everything from a Hermes bag to a washer for a plumbing fixture can be found in the area. So, it seems on a Saturday afternoon, can all the shoppers in Rome, whether or not they're buying.

Dressed in fine furs, leathers, silks, cottons, and exquisite woolens, Romans are a technicolor consumer show. Friends stroll arm in arm, couples cling together, families cruise the shops, all stalking that perfect piece of clothing, crystal, or electronic gadgetry, perhaps a new camera...anything. They are possessed by a quivering hunger to acquire things, a hunger so real the emotions flow from the mass consciousness in waves that assault the senses of the unsuspecting observer.

A mass of modern humanity amid baroque, gothic, renaissance, and classical architecture, Romans flit from window to window, bent on spending everything they have, to get some value for their money, to dispose of the lire that tomorrow may be worth...what?

The lira, constitutionally, is broken down into 100 centessimi. Some people know what "centessimi" means. Others? Well, Tony is twenty-one years old. When asked when last he had seen some centessimi, he wondered if that wasn't Spanish currency. And no, he isn't worried about a job yet. He just spent a couple of months in Amsterdam with friends, drinking and recovering from his bout of national military service.

Where does he go from here? "Maybe university, maybe a job," he shrugs. And if neither, how will he support himself? "My family," he smiles. "My parents, they will take care of me."

It's easy to understand why centessimi are a rarity when, after days of being assaulted by figures like 100,000 lira for shoes, or 192,000 for a jacket, it registers that the price on everything is in multiples of fifty lira.

Admittedly, the area around the Spanish Steps is one of the more chic sections of Rome. Here you'll find shops offering Levi's jeans at prices double the North American or places you would be hard-pressed to call shops, because they are more like artworks sporting designer names, designer prices, and patent-leather sales personnel.

But it isn't the only shopping area in Rome, unless you're a tourist who refuses to venture more than a kilometer from an American Express office without bottled oxygen and bottled water.

Throughout the city, wherever a commercial section exists, people move in phalanxes, darting from shop to shop, looking for something on which to spend their money, just to trade the paper and the coins, for something tangible and durable.

Until the Second World War, Italy's economy was primarily agricultural. Partially industrialized to meet the military needs of the war effort, it was devastated by the depredations of retreating German armies and bombardment by advancing Allied armies. In the post-war years Italy benefited from some of the $12 billion U.S. distributed in Europe between 1948 and 1951 under the European recovery program, also known as the Marshall plan.

Recovered from the war and on the way to modern industrialization by 1955, Italy and the Italian consumer were ripe for North American influences, primarily the exportable elements of American culture: film, television programs, magazines, advertising.

"The consumer suddenly found himself inundated and submerged by American products," says Dr. Renato Musso, of Unione Nazionali Consummatori, the Italian consumer's union. The presence of large numbers of Americans in Italy during the occupation and reconstruction, and the strong links between Italy and the U.S., with about 9 percent of all Americans claiming Italian descent, opened the doors to this cultural cross-pollination.

"Italy has its own way of doing things," Musso says. "But these influences changed the Italian way of life."

For one thing, from a society where the middle class put its faith in savings and owning—free and clear—the homes in which it lived, Italy crept, then rushed headlong into consumerism. The watershed was 1959, when the Italian consumer's psychology went from a savings mentality to an attitude which advocated spending all earnings and even incurring debts to buy new products.

"And ever since this new consumer attitude took hold, those consumers who were relatively well off began to be absorbed by the lower class," says Musso. This slow erosion of the size of the middle class results in basic survival techniques—adjusting to living on less or turning to crime.

Mario Lambrusco, the transplanted Italo-American, is a travel agent. "I had a large car," he explains, "but it was too expensive to drive all the time. So, I did a *redimensione*, an adjustment, or realignment of my finances. I bought a small car for every day, and the other car belongs to the business."

The options to *redimensione* on this scale are not, however, available to all Italians. Our travel agent is, after all, a self-employed professional. Those whose incomes are taxed at source must *redimensione* over whether they're going to have meat once a day or once a week.

"But the unemployed, they become part of the 'submerged' economy," says journalist Marco Vignudelli. "They go into the black market and through other illegal means survive at a very low level." And those means can involve robbery, burglary, kidnapping, extortion, car theft, and other unsavory activities, such as the smuggling that is a traditional part of life in Naples, where high unemployment is the norm.

Overall, the sliding middle class is also a reflection of the old cliché about the rich getting richer and the poor getting children. While the Italian middle class may not necessarily be breeding itself out of existence, Dr. Musso points out that, since Italy's consumer age began, wealth has moved towards the higher economic class with ever-increasing velocity. But that in itself is not an unusual situation.

One way of looking at inflation is as a mechanism by which economies correct themselves after too much government intervention. The idea here is that money tends to concentrate, or pool, and reconcentrate in the hands of those that know how to accumulate and use it, no matter how it was dispersed.

It works this way: The aim of social democratic ideals is to improve the lot of the working class. Social democratic politicians believe the way to achieve these ideals, (and, incidentally, get elected) is to raise the working class to the middle class. After they're elected, social democrats, having defined middle class according to income, redistribute wealth and, suddenly, large segments of the working class move up to the middle class. This redistributed wealth, however, eventually returns to the sources from which it was extracted—the wealthy— because the new middle class spends to acquire the trappings of the middle class. Profits from these expenditures go to those who had the money to invest in importation or production of those consumer goods. At this point a classic inflation situation is created: A large amount of money pursues a limited supply of consumer goods, and the demand forces up prices.

To keep the new middle class earning to its new expectations (and maintain voter loyalty), the social democratic government ensures that salaries and wages keep rising. In turn, prices keep rising.

The classic inflationary spiral is in full cycle. The people with the real wealth, to protect themselves from the effects of inflationary erosion of earnings, become even more wealthy. Meanwhile, the new middle class, dragging some of the old middle class along, slide back into the working class, because they don't know how to manage their affairs to protect what they have.

The problem is that a middle class, from which springs the next generation of aspiring managers, entrepreneurs, and professionals, cannot be created by government edict or legislation. Redistribution of wealth simply creates a group of people who think that because they have the disposable income of the middle class, they are middle class; it also creates at attitude that rewards come whether or not you really earn them. This discourages productivity or creativity in business, research, development, and the flowering of the entrepreneurial spirit.

The essential quality of a real middle class is that it tends to save and accumulate a portion of what it earns. The savings are directed towards the accumulation of durable necessities, such as a house and those consumer items that help a family make a house a home.

Once this home is achieved, expectations and aspirations are to invest outside to protect the home. All further savings, accumulation, and investments are made to protect it from taxation or creditors.

But being middle class, or seeking middle class rewards, is something one must be educated to—through upbringing to want or through privation to hunger after. Either way, one must aspire to the trappings, both material and psychological, of the middle class to invest the time and effort required to earn the goods and security it offers and keep them.

When government creates a middle class through artificial stimulus—job-creating, public works programs financed through budget deficits—the middle-class expectations can only be met during the life of that government or program. Too often that expectation cannot continue to be met when government either finally admits that entrepreneurs, not governments, create jobs, or when it has to enter an austerity phase—as all do eventually—and cut back on programs and services.

"So when we look at Italy from 1971 to now, you'll see the consumer's basic ability to save has been unchanged," says Dr. Musso. "Those who were able to save before, are able to now."

According to the consumer union's figures, the typical family's ability to save averages about 2 million lira per year (in 1984 exchange terms, about $1,250 U.S.). And that only represents the 42 percent of families that actually save anything.

The statistical breakdown of the savings is: 50 percent in real estate; 25 percent in paper investments, such as bonds and savings; 15 percent in investments in small companies; and the remainder in objects of value such as jewelry and metals (gold and silver).

Musso concedes that this kind of investment package, in those proportions, seems as good as any. Because investment policies should be dictated by personal risk tolerance levels, who can say what is the best way to invest in anything except the person doing the investing? But, as for the amounts invested being adequate buffers against future difficulties for a family or individual, Musso shook his head and gravely commented, "Italians, in fact, live day by day...one month at a time," the one month being the period within which Italians must live on their pay packets.

Italian wage and salary earners, business people, and professionals, all know that inflation is a fixed part of their economic lives. Inflation is seen as a part of the cost to be paid for living in a country that is wealthy but has great gaps between the upper class and the middle class, between the middle class and the working class, and between the working class and the dispossessed.

As in all societies wealth in Italy tends to concentrate in the hands of the few. Half of all Italian wealth is concentrated among 10 percent of the families; 30 percent of Italian families hold nothing at all in the way of investments; the remaining 60 percent hold average investments of 112,000,000 lire (very roughly $70,000 U.S.).

Musso points out, however, that half of all Italian families live in a house or apartment they own, often through inheritance.

Until the consumer age hit Italy, Italians would go into debt only for their homes (and maybe for a car after long, agonized thought), making large downpayments against small long-term mortgages at fixed and relatively low interest rates. Those types of mortgages are now history, since interest rates are forced to float to stay ahead of inflation, and high interest rates discourage borrowing.

So people don't buy, or they build illegally on the outskirts of the city or on top of existing buildings. People now get their homes principally through inheritance or through renting low-cost, suburban, government-subsidized housing that equals in ugliness, desolation, and isolation the worst of cheap North American high-rise development.

So, you see, traditionally, especially since the beginning of the 1900s, Italians saved," says Dr. Musso. "They did not like to go into debt, and borrowing for a home was not seen as debt. But after the 1950s they went into debt to buy consumer items." He stops and shrugs. "But now, it is a circle, it's not done. If you can avoid it, you don't buy on credit."

Musso agrees that this flies in the face of what became the North American consumer's psychology, to buy now with credit against payment with inflated dollars. That was a technique that worked in the early days of Italian consumerism, when inflation was still the result of many consumer dollars chasing few consumer goods.

Once the imported inflation of skyrocketing oil and raw material prices began affecting consumer prices, credit-granting agencies adjusted interest rates to compensate for the inflationary erosion. As a result, only those who could afford to, and weren't deterred by the interest rates, would borrow money.

But there's another reason why the offer of credit buying is no longer attractive: Loans do have to be paid back. The average Italian doesn't like to commit to something he can't carry through. Then, of course, lending institutions like to see regular income against which a schedule of credit repayment can be constructed. "And," says Dr. Musso, "not all Italians these days can depend on a stable income, not in an environment where unemployment is 10 to 12 percent."

The stone empire facade of the building is filthy, stained with many years' accretion of pollutants that have risen from factory smokestacks in the Rome region. It looks like any downtown building: a barely tolerable place in which to work, let alone live.

The entrance is set back from the street, a narrow walkway between two shops that enters a small court. Up a flight of steps is the apartment of young newlyweds Carla and Daniel. A modern, cosy place full of new furniture, fittings, and electronic equipment, the interior is a radical departure from the exterior.

It sat empty for years, because Carla's father refused to rent it when the government's fair rent legislation became law. He preferred to leave it vacant and wait for her to marry, rather than rent it and have to go through a complicated legal battle that could drag on for years to dislodge the tenants so Carla eventually could move in.

It had still been an asset, and now Carla and her husband would pay rent on the apartment. No one, especially the authorities, would know the rent was undeclared money that went to a numbered Swiss bank account which, along with the ownership papers for the apartment, would go to Carla upon her father's death. And then only she would know about it.

The apartment had been his family's first home in the 1950s. He had prospered since then, and now lived elsewhere in the city, where the well-off enjoyed the collective security of a neighborhood paid for through high taxes. *La bustarella*— the little white envelope with money—handed over each month to the police officers guaranteed the extra protection from robbers, muggers, and burglars.

And when Daniel, whose income as a lawyer is ensured by the work the family business gives, asked permission to marry Carla, there hadn't been much need to redo the apartment—a little paint, cleaning, some new curtains, and furniture would have done nicely. But Carla had wanted the hardwood floors sanded, the bathroom remodeled, and the kitchen modernized.

Now, they had moved in. Throughout the apartment was the best of Swedish furniture. Carla's father smiled at the thought of the bedroom set—a bed the size of a soccer field. A fine present from him and his wife, so Carla would have a good bed, a fine bed, on which to make strong, healthy grandchildren.

And the Japanese video and television in the bedroom, another television in the living room, along with the German stereo and British speakers.... He smiled proudly. His Carla was starting married life well. He ran his hands over the new walnut paneling. Magnificent work. The kitchen: pure Norwegian design.

The best that money could buy. Nothing was too good for his daughter. And all in a downtown apartment that was increasing in value very year. Carla and Daniel would have had to save for years, or win the lottery, to be able to afford this kind of dwelling.

Better to inherit! And if, Madonna forbid, Carla ever needed money, this apartment would make her much money—if only someone has the money to buy when she wants to sell.

But no need to worry, the father reminded himself. He had made other preparations for his Carla. She would never suffer. He had worked all his life and invested carefully to ensure none of his children would ever suffer. And, barring a war, even with inflation they would have no problems.

Take a walk through Rome. Thousands of years of history are waiting to be discovered. At first glance, they're all familiar. A sense of déjà vu? Perhaps you were a Roman in another life. More likely, you've seen them on postcards or in any of a number of films set in Rome. Maybe that's why it's disappointing to visit and actually see these sites.

The streets are always cleared when the film crews arrive, so you don't expect to see mobile canteens selling authentic Italian delicacies, such as hamburgers, hotdogs, and donuts. They're a gauntlet you run on the approaches to the Colosseum which, even in ruins, evokes images of the grandeur and brutality of ancient Rome. What time and the elements have failed to do—

reduce the glory of Rome to a laughable mess of rubble—is quickly accomplished by the absurdity of multi-colored caravan awnings at the entrances to historical sites.

And for all that it looks like a quarry, the Forum is a quiet place to get away from the bustle and noise of Rome, to gather your thoughts before a climb to the Palatine Mount for a panoramic view of the city.

Dismay greets you at the Trevi Fountain, immortalized in the film *Three Coins in the Fountain*. Once an open courtyard, the area of the Trevi is crowded by shops flogging authentic Roman everything to the tourists who all throw coins in the fountain, in unblushing acknowledgment of the myth that the visitor who throws a coin in the fountain will return to Rome to find love. But no one offers them love (except the girls on the Via Veneto who offer it on an hourly basis) or a movie contract. Instead, street vendors offer roasted chestnuts, fruit, or plastic Madonnas.

Down the road the Victor Emmanuel Monument in Venice Square houses the Tomb of the Unknown Soldier, and today there's some kind of military ceremony going on. Everybody is oblivious to the graffiti defacing the monument declaring the world should be communist, socialist, fascist, or cosmic.

But turn your eyes the other way, drag your attention back from the extraordinary to the ordinary. Play Roman. Make like a shopper. Look in the windows.

The streets of downtown Rome are a thoroughly dedicated consumer's dream. Anything you would ever want in the way of durables is available—for a price. And that price is negotiable, except where the shops indicate prices are fixed, or in the designer shops, where you get the impression they want an irrevocable letter of credit just to let you in the door.

The prices are staggeringly variable. Electronics, usually imports, are even more expensive than in North America—anywhere from 20 to 35 percent more. But domestic products—Italian leather goods, woolens, clothing, shoes—are 20 to 50 percent cheaper than when they are sold in North America as imports.

The shop windows are mirrors of Italian attitudes. Italy has bought a way of life; Italians see it on television and at the movies. They don't want to be Americans, they just want to live like Americans. They want *la vita Americana*—the American lifestyle.

Italians want to have half a dozen suits, wear Levi's, watch videotaped films on color television, and cook with microwaves when they're in a hurry. If the prices get too high, they'll get a second job, or a third job. If they can't get a second job, then they'll hold their ground and pass on the item, or they'll buy it and cut back on consumption elsewhere in the household budget.

Individual Italians who desire *la vita Americana* are quite prepared to pay for it. They don't ask that someone give it to them; they should be credited that. But the country doesn't have the base of raw materials on which to build an industrial establishment large enough and productive enough and independent enough to provide the jobs that would give Italians the incomes to pay for the demand without paying an inflationary premium. Whatever way the Italians turn, inflation occurs.

Italy's major trading partner is the United States, and the country's economic performance reflects the fortunes of the American economy. A thriving American economy and strong dollar makes Italy's products that much cheaper and that much more attractive to the American market. But the strong dollar also makes Italy's imports more expensive, another aspect of imported inflation. And energy imports are inflationary, and the inefficiencies of social spending are inflationary, and so on, and so on.

This is the picture of Italy painted by Italians: a wealthy country with large gaps between rich and poor and all classes in between. Italy's major economic problems are the imported inflation, that results from a lack of raw materials, and the domestic inflation, that comes of government's trying to redress social imbalances by redistributing wealth through bureaucratic means rather than allowing the marketplace to allocate resources.

This brings us to the question that matters: What do Italians see as safe, worthy, and reasonable investments in which their capital base will, at worst, be maintained or, at best, grow?

The answers from the Italian experience may not apply completely to North America, but they do provide valid information that should be examined and adapted to North American circumstances.

"In this high-level inflation country most of us consider it foolish to keep cash or savings invested in anything which may turn out to be cash, such as bonds," says lawyer Guerreri. "So, there has been a policy of many of my countrymen just to invest in immovable estate—land, apartments, shops, development areas, or even in industries such as the poultry or bakery or wine industry."

The types of real estate investments are varied, but the attitude to the investment is what counts. Derek Diab manages a hotel in downtown Rome owned by a group of investors. Most of the hotel's interior is brand new, a few sections are old, almost picturesque, and a few areas are an unoccupied shambles as workers remodel a building whose last renovation occurred just after occupying GIs had gone home.

"We usually don't pay dividends to the shareholders," says Diab. "For the first three, four, or five years, they don't expect any." Instead, during the holding period, income from the property pays for managing, maintenance, and the remodeling.

The point of owning the hotel is that it is a long-term investment looking for appreciation. "And when they sell, if the price has risen, they make their profit," Diab explains. That's one of the reasons for the remodeling.

Remodeled and upgraded, the hotel's rating and, therefore, room prices are upgraded so there's more income to spend on upgrading. Also, remodeled and upgraded, the hotel will be a more attractive investment to subsequent buyers. In the meantime, the hotel pays for its own renovation costs, and the purchase itself provides the investors with attractive tax write-offs.

Management of the hotel revolves around the remodeling,

and it's conducted in a continuing sweep. All building materials are bought immediately, because they will be more expensive to buy as needed. "And we try to do as much as we can in a year without waiting to do it over several years," says Diab.

Budgeting along North American lines really isn't a factor. So, if at year-end the bills are paid and there is a surplus and the expectation of more money coming in, that surplus is spent on something concrete.

It's the only way to deal with the uncertainty of an economy where personal or business financial planning terms are usually six months, and planning for a twelve-month period is considered sheer folly.

Diab shrugs philosophically. "We do it that way because, for the time being, we don't see other ways...unless we get a strong government, or a future that is a little more clear—one that you know you can invest in."

For himself, a salaried employee, Diab sees his best investment as a house or land purchase. "There are people with fur coats—maybe they see them as investments—jewels, paintings. We try to find things with a stable value that goes up with inflation."

From the perspective of the sophisticated professional with disposable income, lawyer Guerreri's investment outline follows a conservative path, which echoes the advice Italian investment counselors and financial advisors give their clients. The advisors favor safe, conservative, blue chip—very blue chip—investments. They're the most attractive, because Italians have no confidence in anything but the safest of havens.

The counselors lean to government securities that offer real rates of return. They recommend mixed portfolios of three different types of long- and short-term government bonds, certain commercial bonds, debentures, and only those stocks that have proven profitable through inflationary and recessionary times. They also fervently recommend regular monitoring of the portfolio with profit taking for reinvestment and realignment of the portfolio every six months.

"And cash, we keep just the minimum amount which may be

needed in any personal emergency," says Guerreri. Operating cash is business income, and surpluses are diverted into a new car for the business or "redecorating the office."

Guerreri waves his hand expansively over his desk and around the office. The desk is huge, a massive modern wooden piece (with a Montreal Canadiens hockey puck resting on one corner) that dominates the office and is complemented by a matching book case that covers one wall. In an intimate corner, a grouping of modernist easychairs clusters around a metal and glass coffee table softly lit by a stand-up brass lamp. The walls are done in a cloth-textured wall covering that underscores the furniture, so the overall effect is soothing, relaxing, and comfortably prosperous without being opulent. Another effect is that the office redecoration and renovation is a deductible expense.

Guerreri, a soft-spoken man with a well-modulated, expressive voice, speaks with absolute conviction when he talks about land. As far as he is concerned, it's the best long-term investment. And he views investment as only a long-term affair.

As he sees it, no matter what happens, land is fixed in supply, immovable, can't be destroyed, and only in the extreme can it be expropriated. And no matter the cyclic downturns that may affect prices, "land will always hold a measure of value. It always bounces back."

Because his business takes him to North America fairly regularly, Guerreri is aware of the recessionary experience with housing repossessions. With the keen eye of the visitor whose vision isn't clouded by the fog of familiarity, he points out that North Americans overextended themselves during the inflationary years from 1973 to 1981. This overextension became debt overload from 1979 to 1981. Meanwhile, people made no real effort to pay off as much as they could with inflated dollars, so they would have real equity in their holdings when the bubble burst.

The tragedies of the inflation of 1973 to 1981 and the recession of 1981 to 1983 are the people who bought the upside of inflation, the free and easy inflated money that comes of an overheated economy, but didn't prepare for the downside of recession. They were the proverbial little guys, middle-class investors caught with too much debt and no safety net while facing wage freezes and wage cuts, unemployment, tight money, and panicky banks quick to foreclose.

There were also the people who were so smart they out-smarted themselves. They were buying apartment buildings, holding them while they appreciated, then flipping them. They figured inflation would keep jacking up the prices of the buildings. Many of them were caught holding buildings they couldn't fill, that became financial burdens during the recession, when people started sharing accommodations or moving in search of jobs.

To explain his belief in land, Guerreri cites the example of Italian agriculture. It suffered a complete collapse during the past five years when the Italian small farmer couldn't compete with other European Common Market producers in the face of high production costs.

"Now," says Guerreri, "I would say agriculture, provided you do it on an industrial scale, a large scale, is very profitable." The same goes for investments in small manufacturing opera-tions or shops. "I don't say you have to manage them," says Guerreri. "They are simply good investments in which you can protect your money and from which you can profit."

Essentially, the Italian investment market is internal because, to discourage the flight of capital into foreign investments, the Italian government has adopted a relatively benign attitude. It's *relatively* benign, because there are no restrictions against Ital-ians purchasing or holding foreign currencies. If prepared to pay for it, an Italian can hold whatever he wants. There are restrictions, though, on what he can take out of the country, especially for business investments.

Should an Italian citizen want to put money into a foreign investment, he must put 50 percent of the value of the invest-ment in a non-interest-accruing deposit with the Bank of Italy for a specified period. So, to invest $10,000 U.S. in France, an Italian would have to deposit the lira equivalent of an additional

$5,000 U.S. with the Bank. Should the term be six months, the deposit would be eroded by the inflation over that period, without any compensating interest.

But, while the Italian market offers a broad range of investments, it is not long on high-flying, high-risk speculative ventures, Guerreri points out. He also agrees, to a degree, with the financial advisors about stocks. "I don't think the stock exchange in Italy is considered one of the main investment shelters," says Guerreri drily, leading to a point that is valid in any country under any economic circumstances. "There is no general knowledge as such of the intricacies of the stock exchange, and it is only reserved, as it should be, to very highly qualified financial people."

As for bonds, he points out certain considerations that are factors in bond investment: A universal consideration is that the real rate of return should be positive after inflation and taxes; and a consideration which is uniquely Italian—*consolidation*.

This is a word that hangs heavily over the Italian bond market, at least in the eyes of the sophisticated investor. Consolidation occurs when the government simply cannot bear the financial strain of redeeming bonds, which Guerreri says has happened once in Italian history. Having happened once, the precedent exists.

To illustrate what some see as a universal truth—that you can never tell what a government will do next under the pretext of necessity—Guerreri recalls one government edict of 1979. "The government said, 'All severance indemnities will be paid 50 percent in government bonds.' So, if you had been working for thirty years for any large company and you were entitled to a severance indemnity of $50,000 U.S., you would get the lira equivalent, half in cash and half, forcibly, in bonds, because the government wanted people to buy bonds."

Bonds fluctuate in popularity in Italy, mainly because inflationary adjustments have only been a recent phenomenon. There was a time when bond returns were flat, or negative. Bonds were still, however, an appealing investment because they offered the best compensation against inflationary erosion while the U.S. dollar was soft and other investment instruments were either weak or too costly.

That still meant, according to Dr. Musso of the consumer's union, that Italian bond buyers lost 10,000,000,000 lira between 1971 and 1981 to inflation. That figure is impossible to translate into dollar equivalents, because it represents a cumulative loss over a decade when the exchange rate fluctuated wildly. The only way to conceptualize this kind of figure is to accept that, to the individual Italian who lost a portion of that figure, it represented a small fortune.

"Jewelry isn't bad," says Mario Lambrusco, the expatriate Italo-American. "At least it looks good on my wife. But would I really sell it?" He ponders the question. "Look, we can buy gold here, if it's been made into jewelry or coins if you can get them. No bullion. But it isn't really an investment. It's something of value." He smiles. "After all, can you eat gold? Remember, you have to be able to sell the gold, or the car, or the video, the fur, whatever. And if it gets really bad, a ring that cost $500 when you got it, might only buy a loaf of bread. But if you're hungry enough," he shrugs, "you'll pay."

The Italian experience of investment teaches one particular lesson: Long-term investment is the key to investment survival. It suggests careful, conservative placement of money in a broad spectrum of assets:

* fluid assets: cash and easily disposable durables that hold their value against inflation, such as jewels, gold, a spare video or television, etc.;

* paper assets: stocks, bonds, securities, debentures, term notes that pay real rates of return, that can be easily rolled into similar, but better performing assets as the investment picture changes; and

* fixed assets: land, real estate, commercial buildings, residential rental units (except where rent controls are as unfair to landlords as the landlords were to tenants to prompt the laws), equity in manufacturing operations, agribusiness.

So this is Italy's economy. This could be North America in two years or five years, perhaps ten. We've had a look at the investment lessons to be learned, but there are many other lessons to be learned, too. They were discerned because no one was able to answer the question: How would you have prepared yourselves had you known this kind of inflation would be upon you?

No one could answer because no one had lived in a normal economy. Those old enough to remember the pre-war years remember the artificial economy of a centrally directed fascist state that was followed by the war economy of 1939 to 1944. After that came occupation and reconstruction until 1955, then growth, the explosion of Italian consumerism, and government involvement in the economy.

Unable to answer the question, people pointed out that inflation in Italy is just another fact of life. Italians have lived with inflation so long, they think of it as they do the weather or geography. Inflation can't be conquered, or controlled; it just has to be lived with.

They did, however, also point out that, like the environment, the inflationary factor in life tends to nurture and force-feed certain thought and behavior patterns. With the aid of 20–20 hindsight, they suggest certain preparations: things to think about, learn, or guard against.

- Buy whatever you want now, today, with the money you have in hand, because the price will be higher later on.
- Buy on credit, if you can get it, at the longest term you can negotiate, because you'll pay back over the long run with progressively cheaper money.
- Buy now, because what you buy will surely hold its value and perhaps even appreciate—and this doesn't apply only to land, or real estate, but to almost any quality consumer durable, from a Sony video to an Alfa Romeo.
- A penny saved is a penny lost to inflation. Saving is a waste of time and money, unless the interest after taxes and inflation is positive. Better yet, avoid the taxes.

The thought processes also lead to certain practices, some of which make sense at any time, but most of which North Americans would recoil from as distasteful or melodramatic.

But, as was noted before, the world isn't quite what we believe it to be.

These suggestions are almost rules for survival in an inflationary environment. They're basic and apparently quite common to long-term inflationary economies. They crop up with great regularity and become more sophisticated as we move up the inflationary scale.

1. Take nothing so seriously or hold it so dear that losing it will destroy you, financially or emotionally. Whatever you do, don't take yourself too seriously. This business of surviving the money game is a game. Be flexible, and be able to take a tumble and still land on your feet.

2. Put no faith in government, even less in political leaders, even if you voted for the party in power. Watch what government does in the way of spending.

3. Watch what government allows its senior civil servants to get away with, particularly manipulation of the money supply.

4. Grab all you can in the way of government subsidies, aid programs, grants, whatever free money or programs and services are available, but don't pay your way.

5. Never trust a civil servant or politician, unless he or she is a relative and owes you a favor, or you, personally, have successfully bribed him or her in the past and have incriminating evidence to that effect.

6. Be prepared to lie and cheat, adopt a flexible morality, and become a good actor to cover up what you're actually doing.

7. Avoid paying taxes whenever and wherever possible, but be prepared, should you get caught evading taxes, to pay the full penalties prescribed by whatever laws are in force at the time.

8. Maintain a foreign currency account, whether or not it's legal, no matter how small (it will build), preferably in a foreign country with a proven record of banking reliability and discretion.

9. Be prepared to do nothing but work all the time and never

get ahead of inflation, bank costs, the tax department, and your own ambitions.

10. Never invest in only one thing. There is no such thing as a sure thing.

10a. Gold is nice, but so is silver; it's cheaper but still a precious metal. It's a bit underpriced now because it's reputation hasn't recovered from Bunker Hunt's attempt to corner and manipulate the silver market in the mid-1970s.

10b. The stock market isn't all that bad, as long as you know what it's about. A hint on finding a good stockbroker: He or she should know your portfolio as well as you do, and know when to pass you the information you might need to make a profitable decision—not insider stuff, but the facts, such as an impending government program that might affect your stocks this, that, or another way.

10c. Work through two or three stockbrokers and at least two banks, so no individual, or institution, has too much information about you in one place.

10d. Look at a broad spectrum of holdings.

10e. If possible, conduct all activities numbered 10 under a variety of identities, so you have a variety of escape hatches.

11. Keep a suitcase packed and your passport current, so you can flee easily, if and when necessary.

12. Have, or learn a marketable skill beyond your primary job, for which you can be paid in cash, kind or services, just in case you ever need an untaxed second income.

13. If a receipt for an item that doesn't have to be registered with a government agency is offered, lose it. Receipts can be as incriminating evidence of a black market sale on a merchant's part as it is an indicator that a purchase was made with black money.

14. Unless a sign in a shop lays down the ground rule that all prices are fixed, or it's a designer shop where everyone takes himself terribly seriously and bargaining is a social faux pas two steps lower than breaking wind in public, everything is negotiable.

15. In business, separate the customer from his money as quickly and profitably as possible.

15a. As a buyer, attempt to negotiate the longest payment terms possible and then be late in payments. A glib tongue and quick mind are helpful in this activity, especially in making up excuses as to why payment hasn't been made as promised.

15b. As a seller, attempt to get full cash payment on the line. Failing that, press for a minimum deposit of 25 percent, bank it, then order the item for the longest delivery time possible, with credit terms favorable to you. Delay payment to your supplier as long as possible. Ensure the deposit is put into a high-yield, short-term investment, and delay delivery to your customer while demanding more money before delivery, claiming your supplier is pressuring you for up-front payment. Then put whatever money you get into more term deposits.

15c. As a buyer or a seller, do yourself a favor and get whatever it is you want to buy or sell on the black market.

16. Above all, trust no one except yourself. Even then, keep an eye on your actions, because you might get cocky or careless or start to take what you're doing seriously. Then you'll become dangerous.

———⌇⌇⌇———

Chapter 5

WHY FEAR FLYING WHEN JUST BOARDING THE PLANE IS A PAIN?

LEONARDO DA VINCI AIRPORT, Rome's air link with the rest of the world, is a hectic forty-five-minute drive from downtown Rome. The airport roads look and sound like any Roman street— crowded and noisy, jammed with vehicles of every sort, color, size, and description.

The international terminal is a dingy maze, full of colorful travelers moving about in a Zombie-like daze, the only appropriate condition in which to face the mind-numbing bureaucratic departure ritual called check-in, customs, and immigration.

The upper floor of the building is the departures check-in area. Airline ticket kiosks, their ranks broken only by the terminal's entry doors, line the wall of the fifty-meter antebuilding—about half the length of a football field. A huge, overhead flight directory also runs the length of the building.

Signs indicate where particular airline check-in counters are to be found. All except for El Al Israel Airlines, that is. The young woman in the information booth, to the right of the main entrance, checks a list.

This morning, 15A.

This morning?

There is nothing to distinguish check-in counter 15A from the others in the airport, except it bears no sign identifying the occupant. At the recommended ninety minutes prior to boarding time check-in, counter 15A is untended; a few people loiter about with luggage, in desultory conversation, reading books or magazines, smoking, impatiently tapping their feet.

A half hour creeps by, then forty-five minutes. An hour becomes history, and two young Italian soldiers in combat uniforms saunter by, submachine guns with magazines in the receivers casually slung over their shoulders. They're young, still boys, wearing expressions too grim for boys.

Suddenly, the area comes to life. A small horde of people, in and out of airline uniform, swoop down on counter 15A, carrying walkie talkies and pushing wheeled tables. Some have conspicuous bulges under their jackets. They get the waiting people to move back, and set up a *cordon sanitaire*—a buffer zone—in front of counter 15A.

Four sharp, ominous "snicks" can be heard, then clicking sounds familiar to anyone who has handled automatic weapons. Above counter 15A, on the mezzanine walkway, two Italian soldiers fiddle with the safety mechanisms on submachine guns. They're loaded. At strategic points on the departures level two more young soldiers check that their weapons are on safe. They're wearing bullet-proof vests.

The young woman at the desk wants to see a ticket and passport. And please put your bag on the table.

"Why are you going to Israel?"

"To research a book."

"Where are you staying?"

"I don't know. I'll get a hotel in Tel Aviv."

"You may not be able to, you know a lot of tourists come to Israel."

"I don't think so. This is the off-season, and tourism in Israel is down this year."

"Why do you not have a reservation?"

"I had work in Rome and I didn't make a reservation because I didn't know when I would be going to Israel."

"Did anyone in Rome give you a letter or package to take to Israel for them?"

"No."

"Who packed your bags?"

"I did. Why?"

"Sometimes bombs, letter bombs, or package bombs have been given to people. Other times, bombs in baggage. Have they been out of your sight at any time since you packed?"

"The big one was in the hotel lobby while I had breakfast."

"But it was locked?"

"Yes."

"Okay. Did anyone know you were going to Israel?"

"The people at the American Express office here."

"Just a moment."

The young woman takes the passport to her superior and speaks with him, gesturing and pointing to the passport, the ticket, and the passenger list.

The four young soldiers are alert. Weapons ready, they scan the passengers, the airport, everything, everybody, looking for signs of trouble.

"What if you can't get a hotel in Tel Aviv?"

"Oh, I have friends and contacts there. They'll help me."

"Why are you coming to Israel?"

"I told you, to research a book. I'm a writer."

"Do you have any credentials?"

Not only credentials are produced but also a general letter of introduction from the publisher and another to the ambassador. She disappears again, only to reappear with her superior. He goes through the same list of questions, then leaves for a conference with a colleague.

All around, people open and close bags, wave identification, communicate information, move around. Confusion reigns. It all happens so quickly, yet it seems everything is in slow motion, like time is suspended.

A moment of panic. What if they don't let me into Israel?

The boss returns. The questions begin again. The same questions; different order.

Finally: "And why are you coming to Israel?"

"To research a book about hyperinflation."

Laughter. "Oh, ho. You come to the right place. So, tell me, are we the worst in the world?"

"Not really. Official figures in Argentina are 400 percent; unofficially, I hear it's more like 1,000."

He shakes his head. "Is crazy. No?"

"Is crazy. Yes."

He returns the passport. "Have a nice flight."

He nods at the young woman. She hands over the ticket and smiles. "Enjoy your visit to Israel."

Indeed.

⸻ ❧ ⸻

Chapter 6

ISRAEL: SHOW ME THE FACE OF GEORGE WASHINGTON

TOURIST INFORMATION DESK, Ben Gurion Airport, Tel Aviv. A young Israeli woman is in attendance.

"Excuse me, is this where I reserve a hotel room?"

"So, what do you want?"

"A single with a shower, please."

"I can't get you a room at the Hilton."

"Did I ask for the Hilton?"

She places a call, speaks to someone and looks up. "Twenty two dollars, with breakfast."

"And a shower?" She nods. "I'll take it."

Outside the airport, while boarding the bus to Tel Aviv, 11 kilometers away, and paying the 100 shekel fare, it dawns on me: She said dollars.

The bus from Ben Gurion Airport stops at a terminal on the edge of Tel Aviv. The country shuts down at noon on Friday in preparation for the Sabbath, and the municipal buses run a very limited schedule. Winter is a rainy season in Israel; today looks to be about day fifteen on a scale of forty days and forty nights. Luckily, a taxi is at the terminal.

Israeli taxi meters are little electronic wonders that automatically dispense receipts when a run ends. They keep duplicate records of all transactions, which must be saved in case the tax department audits a driver. The cabbies who work on the Sabbath don't have to use their meters. At least they don't think they have to. The market is theirs to plumb.

"How much to the Maxim Hotel, 86 Hayarkon Street?"

"Four dollars."

"In shekels, man, in shekels."

"Five hundred."

The exchange rate is 120 shekels per $1 U.S. "Sure, let's go."

The cab splashes its way through suburban Tel Aviv, which is neat, modern, and tidy. The flat-roofed Mediterranean architecture is stuccoed in shades of pink, tan, and buff. They're startling and colorful against blackening skies. The clouds are a brooding presence over the Mediterranean shore, the bearers of quenching rain to this near-desert land at the curve of the sea.

"Is like money to us." the driver comments. "The rain. For the farmers. Precious."

Some things never change, no matter the language.

"Tell me, how do you live with inflation?"

He points to the switched-off meter. "Prices, they change." He raises his hand quickly. "Every month, phhht…up 20 percent. Maybe keep up."

On regular business days, when a meter is used, the first taxi ride leads to the conclusion fares are dirt cheap, and the $4 charge from the terminal to the hotel a rip-off—until the ride ends. The driver reads the meter, 85 shekels, consults a tariff adjustment form, and points out the actual fare: 145 shekels. It sounds pricey, until you convert to that day's conversion; 116 shekels equals $1.25 U.S. Using the chart to convert prices is a cheap and simple method of keeping up with inflation. To adjust the meters monthly would be costly work.

A decent room in a three-star hotel is available during off season for $22 U.S. The lobby of the Hotel Maxim, overlooking the seashore, is clean, hospitable, and dry. The prices on the rate board at the desk are quoted in dollars.

"Why do you do that, post the rates in dollars?"

The desk clerk shrugs. "It is too much trouble to change every day if it is shekels."

When it comes time to settle the bill, the tariff is computed in that day's exchange quotation on the shekel. But somehow, it always comes out to $22 U.S.

On a Friday evening in Tel Aviv, during the first hours of the Sabbath, the streets are deserted. It's so quiet that a person walking alone down a sidewalk is a crowd. Some restaurants are open, catering to the non-religious or visitors who couldn't care less that it's the Sabbath.

At one restaurant the menu is posted in the window; it's plastic coated and the prices, in shekels, are written in water-soluble ink. Three days later the owner sits at the back of the restaurant wiping the menus clean and writing in new, updated prices. No one complains. They know the score: It's his regular price adjustment to accommodate the almost-daily rise in his operating costs to keep up with an inflation rate officially reported at 200 percent.

Down the street a shop sells household goods. Each item is behind a little card bearing two prices: American dollars in ink on the left; shekels in pencil on the right. Prices in another shop are simply numbers on tags. A sign in the window defiantly proclaims they are shekel prices. They are also in pencil. In a third shop prices are in U.S. dollars—no arguments please.

The traveler pulls out a calculator and begins calculating. Suddenly, the impact of what he is seeing and what he is doing stops him in mid-calculation. The shekel devalues against the dollar at about one per business day and loses its purchasing power at a rate of .55 percent a day. Of course everyone would think in dollars! It's the major trading currency for all imports, and it's a stable measure of value.

Arik Dror was still in a daze as he turned down the street to his little house in Rishon Le Zion, south of Tel Aviv.

He couldn't believe his good fortune. He wanted to scream, to shout, to jump up and down, and yell to all the world that he had won the national lottery—80 million shekels.

No! He looked around quickly. Better to control himself. He

walked briskly down the street and turned in at his house. Calmly, he opened the front door and walked in. Carefully, he shut the door behind him. Then he yelled.

It was a bellow of sheer pleasure. It relieved the pressure of the news he carried home. It felt good.

His wife, Yona, and their two children, Ephraim, fourteen, and Yasmin, twelve, rushed into the living room and stared at him. Yona worriedly touched his arm.

"What is wrong, Arik?"

"Wrong?" he smiled. "There is nothing wrong. In fact," he pulled the ticket out of his pocket and waved it at her, "everything is right."

Yona watched the ticket flutter before her eyes, for a moment not sure what it meant. "You don't mean...?" she began hopefully. It was never good to get one's hopes up too high. "We didn't...?" she began again.

"We won!" he exclaimed. "80 million shekels."

Yasmin bounded out of the room and returned with a calculator, working the keys. She looked up. "That's $695,652.17 American."

Arik and Yona stopped hugging each other.

"A good number," said Arik.

"What will we do with so much?" Yona wondered.

Arik paced the living room. "First, we buy a bigger house, move in, and rent this one. Then, another car."

Yona was taken aback. "Another car?"

Arik nodded. "And a video."

"But we have a video!"

"So we'll have two. We won't unpack the new one. Someday, maybe we'll sell this one and use the new one. We'll still make back what it cost us in dollars. Maybe another television too."

"But Arik, this is almost $700,000," Yona objected.

Yasmin played with the keys on her calculator, furiously running figures through the machine.

"No, we have 80 million shekels," Arik reminded. "And it will buy less every day. So we must buy whatever we can that will hold its value and buy all the dollars we can. And if we can't get it all in dollars," he sighed, "we'll buy pounds, and marks, maybe Swiss francs."

"Oh, don't be silly."

"He isn't silly," Yasmin objected. She waved the calculator at her mother. The display was a blur, and the little paper printout flapped like the tail of a kite. "You've been arguing for four minutes about what to do. That cost $16.64." Yasmin ripped off the printout and held it out. Arik and Yona read it while she explained.

"The 80 million shekels is $695,652.17 at today's exchange rate of 115 to the dollar. The shekel devalues one a day against the dollar. So tomorrow, the shekel is 116 to the dollar, and you lose $5,997 dollars. Every day the shekel loses one to the dollar, you lose another $5,997. That works out to $249.88 each hour, or $4.16 a minute. You argued for four minutes." She smiled triumphantly and crossed her arms. "That cost $16.64."

Arik and Yona looked at each other. Yona nodded. "What else do we buy?"

"A new computer for the children." Arik suggested.

"No, one each," Yona suggested. "But the American dollars?" she asked. "How do we get them? We cannot buy them at the banks."

Arik shrugged. "Lilienblum Street."

Yona shook her head vigorously. "The black market is illegal and dangerous."

"Well, I think it is immoral and illegal the way the government has mismanaged the economy so we have such high inflation," Arik asserted defiantly. "I will take the risks, otherwise, at almost $6,000 a day devaluation, we will have nothing in..."

Yasmin busily punched the calculator keys, "...about 116 days."

"Four months," Arik announced. "We must hurry. Yona, you look for the house. Yasmin, Ephraim, the computers."

"And you?" Yona asked.

"I will find out who to deal with on Lilienblum Street, then look at cars."

The only thing that makes Arik and Yona's problem unique in Israel is, not that they have to figure out how to retain the value of their money, but the amount with which they're dealing.

This kind of scene was acted out daily in January of 1984 with much smaller sums. Israelis were beginning to stabilize from the shock they received on what is called "D-Day"—6 October 1983. On that day a fantasy world called the Israeli stock market crashed, and a financial house of bricks without mortar came tumbling down around the ears of most Israeli citizens.

"You know, I think that after the 1973 war this whole country entered what I call a 'crazy period,' says Menashe Grinshpun, a Tel Aviv stockbroker educated in business and economics at Toronto's York University. "It maybe is ending now."

He pauses to look out of the fifth-story window of his office in a converted hotel on the coast and shakes his head. He smiles sardonically, even a touch cynically. "Today, you come at a time of change. You should have been here six months ago—a world of dreams...a world of dreams."

The world of dreams he talks about is a period during which paper fortunes were made on an artificially active stock market in which even the poorest of Israelis participated to the point where everyone could believe he was a "regular J.P. Morgan." To understand what happened, what led to the record 200 percent annual inflation that rose to 240 percent by the end of March 1984, we have to take a quick survey of Israel's economic history.

In 1948, when the leaders of the Jewish Agency declared the independence of the state of Israel, the least of their worries was the economic structure of the new state. They had to finance, organize, fight, and win a war for survival against hostile Arab neighbors. Simultaneously, they had to integrate 600,000 immigrants from the rubble of war-torn Europe into the new state. They needed a future to look forward to—with homes, jobs, the wherewithal to live, and the sense of dignity and self-worth necessary to make a person want to live productively.

The leaders of the new state had no time to tinker with the structure of the economy, so they worked with what was in place: the structure handed over by the British Mandate in Palestine. Part of this legacy was indexing of all sectors of the economy. The indexation structure covered 80 to 85 percent of the inflation rate and was adjusted every six months.

The British had been forced to impose these measures in 1940 to control wartime inflation. Palestine, along with Egypt, was an entry port for war matériel bound for the North African and Middle Eastern campaigns. It also served as a rear-echelon training, storage, rest, recreation, repair, and maintenance center, and supplied much of the vast quantities of food required by the huge mechanized armies that developed during the North African campaigns.

Purchasing of these goods and services resulted in the injection of massive amounts of money into the small Palestinian economy. The economy was overwhelmed and the result was a classic inflationary spiral in which a large, fast, and loose supply of money chased a small quantity of consumer goods. All prices climbed rapidly.

But, as is usually the case when prices skyrocket, wages did not keep pace. To ensure labor and consumer peace in a vital and strategic location, to prevent profiteering, and to keep prices charged to the war effort at some sort of manageable level, the British authorities imposed indexing as a form of wage and price controls. They also imposed strict rent controls. So, when the index of living costs rose every six months, wages and salaries were adjusted for the next six months. This allowed for some recapturing of eroded real earnings and acted as a buffer against the psychological impact of further erosion.

After her "War of Independence" Israel never had an opportunity to establish a normal economy. Hers is still a war economy that is also trying to be a consumer economy and an investment economy at the same time. Part of the inflationary problem endemic to the Israeli economy from the beginning is the massive cost in terms of manpower, matériel, and money that have been diverted from building a productive society into building a large defense establishment. The military costs, however, were the price of physical security and continue to be so today. For example, part of the Israeli economic problem in 1983 and 1984 was the direct diversion from productive activity of the $1 million-a-day cost of maintaining troops in Lebanon.

There were also the costs of ensuring social and economic security during Israel's early history. Those Israelis whose families had settled in the country during turn-of-the-century and pre-war waves of immigration, or who had come to the country with money, were established with their own sources of income and future expectations. But many of the new immigrants had arrived, and continued to arrive, penniless. Yet the government had to guarantee the minimum requirements for survival and establish a framework that, at least, held out the promise of rising expectations to all, newcomer and oldtimer alike.

The government created jobs by building structural redundancies into the civil service and financing public works. Both of these actions developed from the policy that there is dignity in work, dignity and a sense of self worth being major concerns for a populace made up of many concentration camp survivors who came to Israel via Allied rehabilitation camps and British detention camps.

As one Israeli banker who asked to remain unidentified put it, "A system of institutionalized unemployment, where the government allows people to remain without jobs, is immoral. It is a question of survival. You cannot create a class of unemployed and hope your country will survive. The strength of a country is productive people."

At the same time the Israeli government was creating jobs, it subsidized the basics of life—food, clothing, electricity, housing—thereby freeing a relatively large portion of incomes for discretionary purposes, such as investment, saving, or consumer spending. According to Ephraim Davrath, deputy director-general of foreign affairs of the Ministry of Finance, these large government expenditures on the military, job creation, and subsidies, and the overheating of an economy growing at a rate of 8 to 10 percent annually until 1972, created a new cycle of inflation.

The government had provided the prime prerequisite of a developing middle class: surplus income for saving and accumulation. Inflationary erosion of the savings, however, made accumulation as difficult as when the populace had no surplus income. Indexing became the government's tool to keep the promise of rising expectations by protecting individuals from erosion of real earnings. Prosperity did result, despite the fact that Israelis bore, as they still do, one of the highest tax burdens, through a maze of consumer and income taxes, of any Western-style industrialized country.

A foreign diplomat, recently transferred to Tel Aviv from a European posting, was amazed when he began to learn the extent of Israeli taxation. He had driven from his previous duty post to Italy, where he loaded his car and family aboard a ferry sailing for Haifa. At dinner the first night out, he met the chauffeur for an Israeli hotel who had flown to Germany to pick up a new stretch Mercedes-Benz and was driving it home, himself, to save shipping costs.

The diplomat asked what the vehicle cost and didn't believe his ears when told $75,000 U.S. for a vehicle that was no more than $25,000 at the factory gate. He protested to the chauffeur.

"It is not my English you do not understand," the chauffeur shrugged. "It is our taxes."

That same diplomat found it necessary to buy another automobile in Israel. As a foreigner he could buy it without any duty or tax levies. The day it was delivered, his landlord took delivery of the same model car. Out of curiosity the landlord asked what his diplomat tenant was paying; out of professional curiosity the diplomat asked what his landlord had paid. The price differential was $7,000—all taxes—which worked out to about 180 percent of the value of the car landed at the Israeli port of entry.

Through the 1950s and early 1960s Israeli inflation, though regular, continuous, and ranging around 10 percent per year, was manageable. The country developed, the economy grew and individual Israelis prospered with the country. The government had delivered on its promises.

A degree of stability existed in the economy. The defense

budget, while a major expenditure, hadn't yet reached the proportion of the gross national product it achieved in the 1970s and 1980s. Battlefield armaments and computers hadn't yet been integrated, so the Israeli arsenal bristled with guns but lacked the expensive weapons systems directed by sophisticated guidance systems. Besides using cheaper armaments, the Israeli defense forces weren't on almost continuous active duty during those decades.

The turning point was the 1967 Six Day War, after which the defense budget climbed to 15 percent of the gross national product to pay the bills, re-equip in the war's aftermath, cover the costs of maintaining a vigil against terrorist incursions across the borders, and pay for governing the occupied Gaza Strip and the West Bank.

There had always been a black market for foreign currencies in Israel. In an economy as managed as Israel's, strict currency controls had been imposed so government could maintain control. But, wherever currency controls exist, people will find a way around them because, no matter the commodity, if a government forbids its possession, certain members of the populace will hunger after it and pay any price to acquire it. Besides, there will always be people who want a cache of that commodity—gold, silver, jewels, American dollars, British pounds—which is in limited supply and holds their confidence, without the knowledge of the financial authorities.

By 1969 the black market in currencies was part of a flourishing black market trade in just about anything—mainly to sidestep the taxes that made so many consumer goods hideously expensive. The demand for foreign currencies was thriving in response to the inflation figures: the ''hard'' foreign currencies—dollars, pounds, Swiss francs—held their value against the inflating lire (the Israeli lire was converted to shekels in 1980–81).

Five U.S. dollars bought as much at the beginning of the year as it did in the middle of the year; the same could not be said of lire. And English-speaking foreigners, walking along the port road in Haifa or dealing in a Tel Aviv shop or the Jerusalem souk, were perfect targets for the black market currency dealers who offered them a 10 percent exchange premium, with the further inducement that they would also save bank charges and taxes.

Little did the foreigners know that, by holding out, they could have negotiated an even better premium on their money. Even if a buyer paid an 18 percent premium, he or she knew there would always be someone desperate enough to protect earnings, from both 20 percent inflationary erosion and the prying eyes of the economic authorities, to pay a 20 or 22 percent premium for the privilege of holding dollars.

Here we must consider two separate figures and note how deceptive they are. First, the 20 percent inflation is an official national average; as such it doesn't take into consideration regional disparities caused by supply, demand, or transportation premiums on the prices of the items in the goods and services basket monitored for inflationary changes.

Second, the 15 percent of the GNP devoted to defense is also deceptive, as deceptive as the 30 percent it became, officially, after the 1973 Yom Kippur War. It accounts only for direct expenditures on and by the military—the total cost of running the defense establishment. It does not take into account the cost to the Israeli economy of the constant competition between the military, and industry and commerce for manpower, which is a continual drain.

Every Israeli male does two years of national service at age eighteen and after that is liable for thirty days reserve duty each year. The reserve duty and capacities change as the individual gets older, but that thirty-day figure is a minimum. Should an individual be needed for sixty days, he's gone for sixty days. If that individual has a particular skill required by the defense forces, he can be called as often as he is required.

As Syd Dubisky, a Canadian-born recent immigrant, put it, "Everybody here is a full-time soldier, who gets ten or eleven months furlough. If he's lucky." A business person in Canada who had visited Israel and lived there on and off over the past fifteen years before deciding to immigrate, Dubisky muttered:

"Try to imagine what it's like to run a business when, at any time, half of your staff is away on reserve duty. It slows down the economy. Whenever there's a war or a major alert, it stops the country in its tracks."

Allan Green, a British-born architect, shook his head at reference to the war effort. "Travel around the country," he suggested. "Take a good look at what has been done here with swamps and desert and semi-arid land." In a sweeping gesture he indicated all of Tel Aviv, a city with a population just shy of 400,000. "This was all desert seventy years ago. Imagine what we could do, on our own, and with our 'Arab neighbors' if we could work at it full time."

The 1973 increase in the defense budget—the major source of domestic inflation—was accompanied by the 1973 oil shock. Like all countries lacking domestic oil reserves, Israel paid a heavy price for the fourfold increase in oil prices: Israeli inflation headed into the 30 percent range. Added to the rise in oil prices was an overall rise in the costs of all imports, a consequence of the inflation of money and prices in all sectors. By 1977 inflation hit 35 percent.

Also in 1977 popular frustration with the Labor party, which had governed Israel in a series of minority and coalition governments since the Declaration of Independence, led to its defeat at the polls by Menachem Begin's right-wing Likud party. A party that espoused a free-market philosophy, Likud's main economic plank was to open the very tightly managed, somewhat closed, Israeli economy. The experience of 1940 repeated itself with a vengeance.

Israel's economy is a small one, with a very narrow capital base. When Likud opened up the economy ("liberalized" it, as the party slogan went), it also opened an economic can of worms. It allowed foreign money, both as direct investments and loans, to enter the country to take the pressure off Israeli capital markets, hard-pressed to meet the needs of all sectors of the economy requiring credit.

Individuals and businesses alike were allowed to go overseas to seek direct investment and to borrow money; they didn't have to deal exclusively with Israeli banks. Israeli investors were allowed to invest on any one of sixteen approved stock markets around the world, though the daily information available to North American stock market players was only available on a twenty-four to forty-eight hour delay.

Meanwhile, government expenditures continued to increase. Budgets and budget deficits also grew. A very loose monetary policy allowed the money supply to grow drastically to cover increased subsidies, greater military expenditures, and an expensive government-subsidized settlement program in the West Bank. And the income tax collection system seemed to lose its edge.

"Well, the higher the inflation rate, the less willing you are to pay your taxes," observed Menashe Grinshpun, the stockbroker. "And the government wanted to be good to the people, so it wasn't as hard in collection of taxes."

All this was done to fuel a boom. It was a prosperous time, but it was a boom of monetary wealth rather than real wealth. Davrath, the economic ministry official, explained that after 1972 the growth of the GNP dropped from 10 percent to 4 percent per year until 1980, when it dropped to 2.5 percent, took a small climb, then dropped to around zero.

At the same time, inflation climbed in an almost straight line: 35 percent in 1977, 50 percent in 1978, 80 percent in 1979, and 130 percent in 1980. There was an unusual drop to 101 percent in 1981, which Davrath attributes to economic policies that included increased subsidies and a reduction of indirect taxes. But that figure immediately rose to 131 percent in 1982, which Davrath says resulted from cutting the subsidies and instituting new indirect taxes. The figure then skyrocketed to 200 percent by the end of December 1983.

While inflation was growing, the currency was steadily devaluing. In 1979, the year before the Israeli pound (lire) was converted to the shekel, with inflation at 90 percent, the lire devalued by 30 percent (from 17.3 per $1 U.S. to 22.6 per $1 U.S.). The next year the lire was converted to the shekel at a rate of 100 to 1, and the official exchange rate was set at 4.15 shekels per $1 U.S.

The shekel was grossly overvalued, which meant the now freely available U.S. dollar became dirt cheap for a time.

Usually, when money changes hands, people don't stop to think what the paper and bits of metal represent. You want something, it has a price and, if you have enough in your pocket to cover the price, the item is yours. But money, traditionally, serves three purposes:

- It is a medium of exchange.
- It is a store of value.
- It is a numeral, or placeholder, representing quantity.

To the Israeli, the shekel was a numeral and a medium of exchange because the government said so. But, having already experienced a lifelong decline in the lire, the average Israeli couldn't see any domestic currency being a real store of value, given Israel's inflation rate. So Israelis looked for ways to hedge against its eventual anticipated inflation. The American dollar was seen as the answer to the need for the store of value, although the American economy was also suffering about 10 percent inflation.

Stockbroker Menashe Grinshpun explains that what then happened resulted from the cynicism that accompanies a publicly known secret—in this case the overvalued shekel. "Until October 6 [1983, the day the stock market crashed], $100,000 in cash in Israel cost less than $100,000 in the U.S. They had no respect for any currency here. So, as soon as possible, shekels were converted to dollars and the dollars were spent."

Israeli consumers embarked on a massive national spending spree. In the tradition of people afflicted by inflated economies, they put their faith in dollar-denominated investments, goods, and services—foreign bank accounts, stocks, bonds, gold, and consumer durables—which would retain dollar-linked value despite Israel's domestic inflation.

In other countries facing similar problems, governments promote industrialization as the salvation of the country.

Israel has a population of about 4.2 million. For its size and population it is already heavily industrialized. The four most prosperous and profitable export industries are agricultural produce, armaments, computronics, and chemicals.

Despite the country's industrialization, Israel's population is just too small to support industries that can provide a broad spectrum of consumer goods at competitive prices. When it comes to agriculture, though, Israel has some major advantages. Except for a few products that are best imported because domestic cultivation wouldn't be cost-effective, everything needed to feed the population is home grown, and there are sizable surpluses for profitable export.

Despite having some consumer durable manufacturing capacity, however, Israel is a net importer of just about everything that isn't grown.

Ben Yehuda, Dizengoff, and Allenby are three major commercial streets in Tel Aviv. The shop windows are like television screens opening on the world of the Israeli. The time is January 1984; the social condition is shock. The stock market crashed four months ago, and people are still walking around in a daze, counting the costs, trying to decide whether it's worth it to pick up the pieces, tough out the recession and salvage something, or leave.

But where to go? The rest of the world isn't exactly enjoying economic good times. People walk the streets on the Sabbath, discussing what has happened, rehashing with perfect hindsight what they did wrong, what they should have done.

They pause to look in the windows at the state-of-the-art electronics, shoes, clothes, housewares, all of which were theirs to be had only months before. All people had to decide then was which model of what to buy.

Now? The windows stare balefully at the passersby; the merchandise on display is the best of everything manufactured on planet Earth. They bear the names Lacoste, Kodak, Seiko, JVC, Citizen, Hammond, Nikon, Omega, Casio, Cannon, Sharp, Parker, Sanyo, Wharfedale, Moulinex. And there are German, British, and Swiss products bearing names alien to North America.

German and Japanese cars, French and Italian clothes, American appliances, Japanese electronics are everywhere. The occasional Israeli-made product crops up in a window—well made, high quality, but unpopular to Israelis crazy to prove they're prospering by buying imports. The mind reels from the impact of the display, more like a glass-enclosed bazaar than a commercial district, offering everything the consumer's heart desires. All imported. All paid for with American dollars.

Because of the spending spree which lasted from 1979 to 1983 and because of Israel's history of inflation, the country has not developed what economists and bankers call "a mature capital market."

A mature capital market is one in which banks have enough money from deposits to lend out at a higher interest rate than is paid to depositors. In this way the bank actually acts as an agent for the depositor and is investing that money for a fee—the difference between the depositor's interest rate and borrower's interest rate.

A mature capital market exists in economies where currency values tend towards long-term stability. Individuals in these environments hold long-term currency savings as a hedge, not against inflation, but against the proverbial rainy day. The depositor knows full well that after a year, $100 will still buy close to what it bought a year earlier, so there is no incentive to spend cash as soon as it is acquired, and the interest rate is a return high enough to provide an incentive to continue savings. This is real profit.

The players in inflationary and hyperinflationary economies don't save in the long term. They prefer to spend or invest most of their incomes, just to get value for, or protect the value of, their money as quickly as possible before it devalues, and keep a small amount of fluid cash or establish overdrafts.

In the Israeli environment, especially in the 1970s, inflationary erosion was so great the average consumer would pay with credit only for small durable goods. Mortgages were, and continue to be, available for houses but usually with downpayments in the 80 to 90 percent range, except where applicants qualify for certain subsidies. A car buyer puts down 90 percent of the price at the time of ordering, pays the remaining 10 percent on delivery, and also has to give the government a 15 percent compulsory interest-free loan in shekels, repayable in a year in shekels. The loan is simply a government tool to discourage purchases of expensive imported automobiles that have to be paid for in U.S. dollars.

Because inflation climbed regularly, but was only adjusted quarterly, from 1974 on it was futile for a person paid monthly to leave that money on deposit and draw upon it over the month. Opportunities existed to deposit money in dollar-linked accounts, but they were taxed at a 45 percent withholding rate. Another option was to buy American dollars at the beginning of the month and trade them back over the month at the continually escalating exchange rate. A third alternative was to establish an overdraft at 12 percent per month interest. At the end of the month, the individual would settle the overdraft, buy whatever durables the family sought, keep a little cash for pocket money, and use the overdraft for perishables and further pocket money. In addition, people fell into the classic inflationary buying pattern: Buy now, because the price will rise; buy now and pay with inflated shekels; buy now to retain value.

Without extensive pools of depositors' money to meet the credit demand and with a growing demand for credit, banks needed alternatives to expensive foreign money to use as lending capital. So they used bank stock issues.

Israeli banks are full-service operations. They offer stock brokerage services. "But they are also the primary members of the stock exchange," says Menashe Grinshpun. "And with this conflict of interest, they were able to manipulate their stock prices. They made sure that the stocks moved up on a gradual basis every single day." The purpose was to make them appealing as investments. From about 1978 on, bank share values grew steadily with no hint of volatility. They appeared to be safe, healthy investments that sheltered value.

Sophisticated Israeli investors started to buy and regularly trade bank shares and, as is natural with something that is in demand and widely traded, the stock values continued to rise. People bought more, and they kept rising.

"They became the oxygen of the country," quips Grinshpun when describing stocks that increased in value at a real rate above inflation, tax free (because there was no capital gains tax on bank share profits) of 25 percent per year.

Other Israelis watching for safe investments learned of the bank share performance and began to buy in. The action to buy bank shares picked up pace in 1980. After a reported real rate of return on investment (in American dollars) of 53 percent that year, everyone who had spare money started buying the bank shares. But many of the people buying were unsophisticated investors: They did not know what they were getting. All they knew was the return on investment in dollars terms was good and profitable.

The return was, in fact, so handsome that foreign flight capital entered Israel purely to buy bank stocks and take quick profits. "It was better than collecting 9 or 10 percent in New York," Grinshpun says. And the excellent performance continued: 30 percent in 1981, 39 percent in 1982.

Two patterns developed. The sophisticated traded carefully, took profits, and quietly invested them overseas. The unsophisticated spent their profits and reinvested their capital bases. The unsophisticated far outnumbered the sophisticated, and the profits from stock speculation fueled that national shopping spree. It became a binge prior to the 1981 election, when Menachem Begin's Likud government placed a moratorium on existing taxes and duties on imported goods, thereby reducing prices. By an imaginative sleight of hand, the prices were nevertheless raised when a host of other taxes and duties were slapped on, but the result was appreciably cheaper consumer goods.

The national shopping spree became a frenzy of consumption; Israelis spent as if there were no tomorrow. With their experiences of what the government might do, what might happen, and the record of currency devaluations and inflation, today was all that counted. Video-cassette recorder, color television, and auto sales established new records. Tourism figures climbed sky high: More than 400,000 Israelis went overseas in 1981, and that figure climbed to 500,000 in 1982. At that point the chief of Israel's army reserves began to worry publicly when figures showed the numerical equivalent of two full divisions of reservists holidaying outside the country.

"Yes, it was the time of dreams," Grinshpun says, shaking his head. "Everyone was spending, everyone was getting rich, on paper. Everyone and his dog was off somewhere in the world."

The Likud government won the 1981 election but had set a dangerous precedent by encouraging the consumer's passion for durables as a protection for the value of money.

The pace of bank share speculation picked up through 1982. The values of all stocks on the exchange shot up as people bought them too, figuring, if bank shares showed that kind of performance, any share would. This, however, was a reflection of the widespread ignorance that stocks represent an ownership position in a company and normally only hold a value relative to the true economic position of the company issuing them.

In fact, Israelis viewed stocks as commodities with intrinsic value to be traded on their own merits and values. Needless to say, this dream helped escalate expectations to the point where people believed the prices would climb forever. So consumer spending continued apace, financed by the profits from all bank shares.

A variety of schemes to profit from the situation developed. In one, the banks actually lent money to people so they could buy bank shares. The way Grinshpun explains it, for a 6 percent cost of money to the bank, an individual would be lent money at 10 or 15 percent to buy bank shares. The borrower's fears about borrowing would be soothed by reminders of the returns he could expect on his investment.

Another scheme was that a corporation with excess capital would put it into bank shares, rather than use it as working capital, then borrow working capital using the bank shares as collateral.

The bank share picture began to change in 1983. From January to August of that year, share prices only rose 7 percent. That was the first sign of trouble. Two things then happened simultaneously to burst the over-inflated Israeli monetary balloon.

People stopped buying and selling bank shares at a frantic pace because they were too expensive and the prices weren't rising. Then, the government was forced to devalue the Israeli currency.

Israel's government had to accept that it was facing a balance of payments problem. Historically, Israel has always paid its debts on time. But, from the issuing of the new shekel in 1980–81 at the rate of 4.16 per $1U.S. to the summer of 1983, the shekel had already devalued in currency market trading to 34 per $1U.S.; this had occurred as a result of fiscal policy (overspending and deficits), loose monetary policy (printing money), massive foreign borrowing by private interests, and excessive consumer spending.

If Israel didn't act, it might not have the money to pay its debts. Step one was to curb consumer spending through a further, gradual, and official devaluation of the shekel to bring it closer to a realistic exchange rate with the dollar, which would make imports more expensive and less attractive. To stabilize the situation, in August 1983 the government announced a 7.5 percent official devaluation of the shekel and an additional 5 percent per month for the next five months.

Past devaluations had always been more drastic than initially announced by government, and the sophisticated immediately liquidated their holdings for dollars and initiated the widespread capital flight from the country.

As others began to understand what was going on, the pace of liquidation, conversion, and capital flight accelerated. The banks, meanwhile, were buying their own stock at a phenomenal rate to bolster prices and, incredible as it may seem, the truly naive were still buying in.

The banks financed their stock purchases by borrowing short-term money on American currency markets. But by October the truth had sunk in. The banks went to the government on 6 October and asked for, and received, a bail out. The stock market was closed for a week, and all those who hadn't sold out found themselves holding paper that they were locked into until nearly the end of the decade. The bubble had burst.

Most of those who got in early, managed their paper carefully, and got out when all indications were to liquidate made fortunes. The ones who bought in in 1980, 1981, and 1982 made smaller fortunes on a sliding scale. Middle and late comers and those who sat on their paper and never traded aggressively lost heavily. In hard figures, says Grinshpun, *the net worth of 4.1 million Israelis dropped by $10 billion U.S. in ninety days.* And that includes untraceable flight capital.

The shock waves from the 6 October 1983 market crash had barely stopped reverberating in January 1984. Four months after the crash people were living with 200 percent inflation, despite government promises it would abate now that spending had been forcibly curbed by the recession.

During the first ten days of January 1984, one thousand businesses shut their doors for good after the owners declared bankruptcy. No one really believed all of them had gone bankrupt. Many business owners were suspected of having decapitalized their businesses, then declaring bankruptcy, leaving their creditors to pick up the tab.

Crime, mostly burglary, increased rapidly, as the desperate broke into houses in search of the American dollars reputed to be hidden under the floorboards of every home. The biggest selling consumer items in the country were wall safes and strongboxes.

If even a "guaranteed" investment such as bank shares could take such a complete fall, what was a good investment?

"First off," says one banker, "you must think in the long term. Quick profits?" He shakes his head. "Easy come; easy go. Put your money where it will work twice, making profits for you, and in a business or factory that creates jobs. If everyone did that, the economy would be stronger, and the money would be working for you two ways. Because what you really want is a strong economy."

Menashe Grinshpun agrees. "Inflation is not only what happens to your salary. Inflation is what happens to your behavior, to your psychology. And these things in many cases may cause even greater damage than what happens to your net worth."

Israelis, for example, are notorious as the world's most aggressive drivers. After the market crash brought economic uncertainty into an already stressful environment, Israelis began killing and maiming each other in record-setting numbers of traffic accidents.

"As soon as you lose respect for the currency, you start to lose respect for the framework of the society that you work in," says Grinshpun sadly. "The law, rules, police, your courtesy...."

Sam is twenty-three. He just returned to Israel after a year in Australia. He went there after completing his army service, to visit family members and to get another perspective on life.

He operates a small food outlet on Dizengoff Street, Tel Aviv's main drag, a mixture of clothing boutiques, cafés, restaurants, and Israeli fast food joints. This is where the café crowd comes to walk, talk, gawk, and be gawked at. It's a colorful street that's busy with shoppers during the day and street theater at night. Showtime is about 8:00 P.M. when the first couples venture out to strut.

Over coffee Sam points at the passersby. "It makes us so insecure, the inflation," he says angrily. "You grow up, go to the army, then, when you are finished, you just live like an animal, just grab, grab, grab all you can. This is no life."

Sam talks about living what he calls a normal life, what he saw in Australia. A decent job that pays enough so a young person can hope someday to own his own home and a small car. "But this. It pushes you to do what you can, the black market, to cheat, to get what?" He shrugs expressively. "A bigger car than you need? Two videos, a television in every room? This is crazy."

He laughs too cynically for a twenty-three year old, no matter what part of the world he calls home. His anger is the anger of a young man who wants things in life, but who doesn't want to play the games that corrupt the soul to get them. "Look, you know when we had peace with Egypt, you could fly there for $50. When we travel, we can take $500 American cash, and $1,500 in traveler's cheques, so people would buy tickets for the whole family and not go, just to buy the travel allowance of dollars."

Sadly, he shakes his head. "I can stay here, maybe take home $250 or $300 each month from what I make, maybe $400. And what is home?" He sniffs loudly. "A mousehole I share with two people for $250 a month."

He looks out to a couple striding arm-in-arm down the sidewalk. "Or maybe I should steal, or play with dollars on the black market on Lilienblum Street.

Lilienblum is a narrow, nondescript street just off the street named for Allenby, the British general who liberated Palestine from the Turks during the First World War. Nothing distinguishes it from any other side street in Tel Aviv except that when you walk down it, there's an air of furtiveness about some people you pass. They're the ones who are desperately trying to buy American dollars. The ones with dollars to sell stride confidently along the street. It's a small community of dealers; they pause to chat with each other and confirm the quotation of the hour. They're all there for a purpose: trying to retain some value in their money. They don't look like criminals but, according to the new currency control laws, they are.

"And if you want to buy a house, $100,000, more. And you pay cash for most of it," says Sam. "Where do I get that money when it takes all I earn to stay alive?"

Sam figures his only hope is to start a business with his brother. At least with a business you can always hide some income, beat the newly invigorated tax authorities, and have a storefront through which to circulate black money.

"Or I leave, like the others who left to make something of their lives. Maybe I will go back to Australia."

Sam's sentiments are echoed by Maria, an Argentine-born,

thirty-three-year-old widow and mother of three. Her husband came back from Lebanon in a body bag. If she could, she would return to Argentina. "I know it is worse than here," she says. "But at least my family is there. I would have help with my children."

Her friend Shoshana is thirty, and she just wants to get out. But she doesn't know where to go. "Who will let me in?" she wants to know. "I have given so much here. I did my army service. I work and barely have enough after food and rent to get by. And I lost one boyfriend in 1973, another on the Suez in 1978. The government wants me to take less. Give something to my country! I have given enough."

Sam and Maria and Shoshana are among the ones who have lost hope, or profess to have lost it. But they don't necessarily represent the majority, who have cooled off. When the going was good, everyone who could cashed in; when things got tough, they voiced their grievances with screams and shouts. When the dust settled, many of them sheepishly admitted they had been party to a giant scam, and it was time to get back to work. But the government would have to pull in its belt too.

Davrath, the economics ministry official, tapped a report on his desk. "I have it here," he said, "Hard survey data. The people of Israel are ready to do what has to be done to straighten out this mess."

What they have to do is simple in the saying, but painful in the doing. In January 1984 there had to be a 5 percent cut in government and consumer spending. Industry had to become more productive, especially the export sectors. Everyone had to cut back on spending.

And that costs, because the government is the major player in the economy. Construction contracts were cut; construction companies shut down. Garages wouldn't service government vehicles, because they weren't getting paid.

"The damned country's shut down," commented a dazed sales representative for a British-based heavy construction equipment company. The company's Middle Eastern representative, he had gone home in the summer of 1983 after writing up orders worth a million pounds sterling with the promise of more in December. He returned to find no one wanted to speak to him and, when they did speak to him, they had only one thing to say: no business!

"I've driven all over this country," he said. "And there isn't a construction site that's operating to capacity. Most of them are just idle. They have no money to work with."

Many of the construction companies had started, grown, and prospered because of government work. And when the government cut back in the development areas—a significant portion of government spending—the contractors were asked at a special meeting to continue working without pay. They laughed all the way back to the office.

So it turns out that, while having one's own business and operating it cannily provides a means for protection and hedging, there's no guarantee of survival if the business is heav'ly tied in to something as fickle as government contracts.

There's always the consideration of traditional investments. "If your government allows you to buy and hold gold bullion or coins, do so," says one banker. "But spread out your risk. Diversify."

Diversification on the North American model has meant buying into anything durable—art, for instance, and antiques. Borrowed from Europe is the even more exotic, but more stable, area of coins and stamps.

"With coins and stamps, you can learn what is valuable. There are books," explains one Tel Aviv coin and stamp dealer. "And if you can find a buyer at a price you can live with, your stamp or coin is then a real investment. And stamps are more portable than coins. Most customs people, they don't know what a stamp means."

Art and antiques, however, are a different story, say Israeli collectors and advisors. Unless you're in possession of a certified rare find (and how many people can look at an item and tell the real thing from a fake or forgery?) art and antiques could cost you a fortune, rather than make you one. The consensus among

Israelis was that art and antiques may be good hedges in terms of return, but there are no guarantees. The risk of getting stung is out of proportion to the return, no matter how high.

The business of investing for the future comes down to a very simple notion: There is no magic secret. Investing in anything is one of the most personal activities in which a human being can engage, because it involves risk, and every one has a different risk tolerance level. Leaving decisions for your investments up to the advice of others leaves you as open to loss as to profit. Research the range of investments, choose something you can live with, and become an expert in that field.

"You never know what some shark of a government is going to do next that affects your money," says Allan Green, the Jerusalem-based architect. "I don't plan. I live from day to day, month to month. I'm one of the few Israelis that doesn't have a color TV. I eat, I drink, I buy books and records. If I can, I buy a good bottle of whiskey. It all comes down to government. You can't trust what they'll do. And when I've finished my bottle of whiskey, the bastards can't get that from me."

Somewhat less free spirits who think traditionally about saving, despite what governments do, try to find havens for their money. While Israelis take their money out of Israel to foreign tax havens, Israel itself is a tax haven for non-Israelis.

The administrator of the foreign currencies department of one Israeli bank is regularly asked by his clients for investment advice. "I tell them all the same thing. Investment performance, no matter what, is irrational. We have no control over how anything behaves. Gold goes up sometimes; sometimes it comes down. Stocks, bonds...." He stabs at the air. "It is what you believe in. Nothing is guaranteed. These days, with communications the way they are, a plane goes down in Lebanon, a soldier is shot on the China–Russia border, it could change the whole story everywhere."

He points to a Reuters news and financial services monitor on his desk. "There's where it happens. I show that to my clients and tell them, 'if you think the world is going to be a peaceful place, with no pressures or problems for the next two years, put

your money into the hard European currencies and the yen.' "
And if not?

He shrugs. "If you feel in your heart that the world is going to suffer crisis and trouble, with more and new wars, put your money in the American dollar and American-dollar investments."

If there isn't a definite answer to be had about investments, perhaps pushing to have indexing institutionalized as a part of every economy is the answer. But Ephraim Davrath has worked with an indexed economy all of his professional career, and he dismissed the idea as a way of providing protection for the individual from inflationary erosion of income.

"Indexation should be avoided, as long as you can afford it," he says. "If you can avoid it at all, even better. The first effort you should expend is to combat inflation. But you must understand inflation is part of an economy that is growing."

All indexing does, says Davrath, is complicate the structure of the economy if it runs too long. It also creates an impression that things aren't really as bad as they seem, because, when prices go up, everything goes up.

Some people profit by this, but others lose drastically. Indexing is a very delicate mechanism. It works best when inflation is steady, no matter if it's high or low, because there is minimal loss of real earnings between adjustments.

When, however, the inflation rate leaps from 30 percent to 120 percent almost overnight and adjustments are made only every three months, indexing fails. The salary and wage earner is caught with a real 90 percent erosion of earnings during those three months. When it comes time for adjustment, even through indexing to compensate for that 90 percent, the wage and salary earners are only playing catch up over the next quarter. No one ever regains what they lost during the previous three months and, after all sectors of the economy have been adjusted, they could well lose again over the next quarter.

As in Italy the merchant is also adjusting with a "built-in hedge." As long as inflation continues and there are free-spending consumers, the cycle continues. When a recession occurs, prices no longer move upwards and, if anything, the merchant is forced to drop prices to attract customers and generate some cash flow.

There are some very important lessons for individuals to learn from the Israeli experience when it comes to surviving and profiting from hyperinflation.

The first is to maintain a stance of skeptical self-examination and not to let your ego obscure reality. By illustration: A fellow bought a house in a booming real estate market for $120,000. At the height of the boom, after a four-year period when inflation went from 5 to 9 percent, he could have sold it for $220,000. Along came a recession and, suddenly, inflation was 4 percent. When he sold his house, he obtained $130,000.

"I lost $90,000," he laments.

No, he didn't. The $90,000 had never been in his pocket or bank account. The profit existed only in his mind.

So never take today, and yourself, so seriously that you forget tomorrow is another day, and a whole new ball game.

The second lesson is that value—an understanding of it and an ability to assign it accurately to anything—is the key to smart management. In broadest terms it means that, when spending money, you honor it and remember what it cost you to earn, because the money is only a means of exchange. It represents compensation for the time and effort you invested in a job or business. So, when you buy something, you're buying it with time you expended, and time is the most precious commodity individuals have—it's irretrievable.

In Israel, though people get paid in shekels, the currency doesn't mean to them what it should, because it devalues too quickly.

What does mean something? Pull out an American $1 bill.

Show me the face of George Washington.

———— ∿∿∿ ————

Chapter 7

POLITICS, DOLLARS, AND UNCOMMON SENSE

ONE OF THE ARENAS in which financial institutions are involved which their clients rarely see, let alone know about, is the dealing room. It's a high-pressure environment that guarantees an ulcer to any of the players or employees.

The main feature of a dealing room is a large desk in the center of the room. Depending on the size of the operation it could be anything from a triangular, three-station affair to an eight-station operation. The really large rooms run series of desks. Each station is usually equipped with a video monitor, at least two multi-line phones, and possibly a Telex terminal. The ultra-modern dealing rooms also have computer terminals at each station.

Once the work day begins, a dealing room goes from active to hectic. When time zones coincide so that certain European, North American, and Asian money markets are open at the same time for a few hours, the action is frantic. It is sometimes described as a shoot-out that begins and ends on command.

Currency dealing rooms are dedicated to one activity: trading money on a bid and offer system. The operations make money on the exchange spreads, in the simplest manner possible: buying currency when it's cheap and selling when it's dear.

The dealing may see one block of currency—any kind will do,

as long as it's negotiable—that starts as $100,000 U.S. at 8:00 A.M. traded thirty-six times over four hours through ten different dealing rooms in six different countries. Groups of dealing rooms may underwrite large exchanges of currencies for very expensive international deals. The object is to profit, so the $100,000 U.S. opening position is worth more at the end of the day.

Adrian Alba runs a small dealing room in Madrid, a three-person operation for a multi-national bank. In 1983 his dealing room, one of the smallest in the city, netted a $2 million profit for his employers.

Adrian starts his day by reading the bank's overnight confidential internal wire service, the Reuters news and financial wire, the European edition of the *Wall Street Journal*, and any reports that may have come in the mail. He assesses the information, has a short talk with his superior and decides, from early reports from London or the late ones from Hong Kong, where the action is likely to be. He plans his strategy and dives in.

The factors he has to take into account are the fickleness of other money traders and how they react to the news—political, business, and general. He has to consider the previous day's closing exchange rates, the Dow Jones average, the gold index, and Amsterdam spot oil prices.

Adrian is something of a cynic. He suggests his cynicism is born of working in this crazy business where people react to the slightest indication, real or imagined, of trouble. If a U.S. president sneezes in public and looks pale and drawn, the dollar could take a nose dive; a new offensive in the Iran–Iraq war could make the pound sterling, now a petro-currency (a hard currency backed by oil export revenues) rise.

Adrian suggests that he would read star charts, have an African witch doctor throw bones, and consult his horoscope if it would make his decision making any easier. He's convinced that is how other traders make their decisions. As a result of working the currencies market for some years, he sees the conventional wisdom the media use to describe and analyze currency markets as just so much wishful thinking.

Three days in February 1984 were unusually active ones on a world political scene that is anything but quiet.

Day One:
The phone rings.
"Hello."
"Adrian here."
"How's it going?"
"Rough. The Americans announced they're pulling out of Beirut."
"What's happening?"
"Everyone is dumping American dollars."
"Is it critical?"
"No. They're only panicking...a momentary drop in confidence in the U.S., so the dollar is dirt."
"So why isn't it critical?"
"No one's buying gold after dumping their dollars. If they were buying gold I would worry. That means they're thinking long term and figure the dollar's going to begin a long-term slide."
"Then what are they doing?"
"Playing with the yen, the Swiss franc, and the mark.
"So how are you taking things?"
"Badly. My boss didn't like that I was selling American last week, so this week I've been buying."
"And?"
"I've lost $80,000 on the price drops, and I'm holding dollars no one wants."

Day Two:
The phone rings.
"Adrian here."
"What's up?"
"There's a rumor that Andropov is dead."
"So what's happening?"
"The Russians came on the market this morning like storm troopers, dumping all their American dollars."

"Hold on now. The Russians?"

"Yeah, the Russians."

"But why would they dump American dollars?"

"They're scared. If Andropov really is dead, there's going to be a lot of edginess about international relations. The rest of the market will dump dollars and go into gold. They don't want to be caught holding American dollars on a down curve."

"That doesn't make any sense. I would have thought that kind of uncertainty would make the dollar attractive."

"Sure. But they're so paranoid they figure if the Americans think Andropov is dead, the Russians are in disarray, and the Americans can put pressure on the Russians."

"Pressure?"

"Sure. While the Russians are busy trying to get their act together, the Americans could maybe convince the Syrians they're better off being in bed with the Americans than the Russians."

"Are you serious?!"

"Of course."

"Is it valid?"

"Know any good oracles or tea-leaf readers? No one knows what's going to happen tomorrow."

Day Three:

The phone rings.

"Adrian here. It's official. Andropov's dead."

"So what's happening?"

"Everyone's buying American dollars."

"But you said...."

"Hey, I only run one dealing room. The market decided it wants to stay fluid. Gold isn't as easily, or speedily negotiable as American dollars."

"This is crazy.

"Of course it is. My ulcer is killing me."

"Then why do you stay in this business?"

"Why do junkies shoot heroin when they know it's killing them? When you win big here, the charge is incredible."

"So how are you doing?"

"My feet are about six feet off the ground. I made back my $80,000 loss, and the day's only half over. I'll clear another $30,000 pure profit."

———❦———

Chapter 8

SPAIN:
PARANOIA STRIKES DEEP

S PAIN, a country of 504,750 square kilometers, supports a population of about 38 million in an economy that is based on agriculture. The country does have an industrial and mining sector and is rich in many mineral resources. But Spain has minimal oil reserves and imports almost all of her oil supplies. The major supplier is Saudi Arabia, whose oil sales trade represented 11 percent (about $3.5 billion) of Spain's total imports in 1981.

In 1983, despite being on the barest edges of recovery from a deep recession, Spain's inflation rate was running at 15 percent, down from a 1977 high of 28 to 30 percent.

At the turn of the century, Spain was ruled over by Alfonso XIII, a Bourbon king who, in 1886 ascended the throne of a strictly class-regimented society. The country was technically a constitutional democracy until 1923, when it became a military dictatorship. In 1931 Alfonso was deposed and a republic was declared. A moderate, middle-of-the-road, and somewhat ineffectual government was formed, but it was always hampered in its work by opposition from conservative rightists who wanted no change, and leftists and separatists who were agitating for sweeping economic and political reforms.

The problems came to a head in 1936, when a leftist govern-

137

ment was elected and the right-wing opposition, led by General Francisco Franco, rebelled against the government. By 1939 the ensuing civil war, a kind of dress rehearsal for the Second World War, had left 2 million Spaniards dead, much of Spain in rubble, and Franco—*el caudillo*—dictator for life.

During the Second World War Franco gave aid and sustenance to Nazi Germany and Italy, which had aided him during the civil war, and incidentally used Spain as a testing ground for the new weapons and tactics of total war. Franco did not, however, take Spain into the war; he was too busy rebuilding the country. In the following years, social stability was established and maintained by the military dictatorship.

The late 1940s and early 1950s were years of increasing prosperity for Spaniards. Inflation was almost non-existent, and poverty was restricted to the most primitive of isolated mountain villages. Relative to most other western European countries except, perhaps, Portugal, Spain had a small and poor economy. It was also an insular one, divorced from the rest of the world, having for years shunned most advances from would-be investors.

By the late 1950s Spain had reached the point where, if her economy were to continue growing and the standard of living to improve, the country would have to industrialize. In 1959 the Spanish economy was opened to direct investment from outside the country.

Spain's economic troubles were about to begin.

The sad thing about visiting some cities is that your first conversation with resident foreigners usually includes the warnings:
• Don't drink the water.
• Drink the water but not the coffee.
• Don't drink anything!
• Watch your wallet.
• Beware of pickpockets.
• Don't look prosperous.
• Don't go out at night.

This is depressing, because a city does not reveal itself only during the day, nor does it stop being interesting when the sun goes down. The warnings tell you things aren't right with the world; they also serve to raise your ire if it's a city you cherish, because it's a place of fond memories, dreams, and fancies.

Long leisurely walks along the main streets, side streets, and alleys are required to understand any city; and becoming reacquainted with one of your favorite cities means prowling those routes that were most impressive the first time around.

Parallel to Madrid's Gran Via, a major downtown street, runs the cobbled mall that hosts the centerpieces of Spain's major department store chains: Galerias Preciados and El Corte Ingles. The Galerias Preciados is a red brick tower that dominates the entrance to one end of this outdoor mall. The Corte Ingles stands sentry at the other end, where the mall opens onto a square called Puerta del Sol—just call it Sol—one of the stops enroute to Madrid's magnificent Prado museum.

This square is home to pastry and sweet shops selling treats so rich they guarantee instant tooth decay and shoe stores, most notably Los Guerrilleros, a shop whose owner should be in North America giving small business seminars. It's the base from which a prosperous chain was built, offering quality shoes at amazingly low prices for the person paying in pesetas, and *incredibly* low prices for the buyer carrying dollars.

There are many new features to Madrid these days: McDonald's, offering a Spanish innovation—beer with McFood—and an internationally recognized tradition of slow fast food service; Wendy's; and Pizza Hut. Just off the mall, on a little sidestreet to the left before you enter Sol, is one of the other new features—slot machine parlors. The neon sign says *Jugueteria*. Transcending language, the music says fun and games. Inside, harmless-looking electronic boxes with hypnotic lights and cute electronic jingles seduce people into dropping coins in the slot. It doesn't seem like gambling; it's the cheapest (for a short time) light and sound show in all of Europe. For 25 pesetas a throw it's an electric circus, with fruit and symbols rolling around on drums, lights flashing, electrons whizzing around a sound chamber, and monkeys climbing vines.

The decor isn't quite haute Las Vegas, and the garish lighting makes skin look pallid. Gamblers everywhere have the same looks, some desperate, some serene, all lost in their world of hope for the easy pickings that come of hitting the jackpot.

The instructions are simple. Put your money in the slot. Twenty-five pesetas might get you two hundred; it might get you nothing. You pay your money and take your chances. So start with a handful of twenty-five peseta coins—a stake of ten is about two bucks. Time slows as a coin drops in the slot. The drums spin, lights flash. A liquid melody plays.

Nothing. But it doesn't hurt too much.

Again. Two twenty-five peseta coins return. Even. Hit it again. Nothing. And again. Twenty coins! Automatically, the winner counts out ten and pockets them.

Mesmerized, the winner drops in more coins in the smooth rhythm of a well-oiled, well-tuned machine. He wins; he loses. But he's winning more than losing, and every fifth win is twenty coins. He counts off enough from each win so he's always holding ten coins, his playing money, his stake. The rest is pocketed.

A quarter hour later, one trench coat pocket is weighed down, bulging with coins. A crowd has gathered and cheers and applauds every twenty-coin win. The winner looks around sheepishly, almost apologetically. No matter what he does, the machine keeps giving him money. Something's wrong here. No one else is winning like this.

An attendant, Carlos, son of the owner, comes over. He points to two lit up monkeys on the slot machine's multi-colored glass and metal breastplate and explains. Sometime during his early play, the winner had advanced the monkeys up their respective vines to the top, which opened the door to the jackpot run.

Carlos hands him a bucket for his winnings and smiles, tolerantly amused by his customer's ignorance. "Play, señor, until the machine turns off."

The winner shrugs and puts another coin in the machine. He acknowledges the watchers' applause for his win with a tip of the hat. A quarter hour later the machine gives up the ghost. With a rumble in its workings, it surrenders twenty more coins, coughs, gasps, wheezes, and the lights blink off. Rest in peace.

Carlos leads the winner to the counting room and runs the coins through a counting and sorting machine. At 4,500 pesetas he stops and stares at the winner. He explains that the jackpot only pays 4,500 pesetas. He points to the bin; there are still at least 2,000 pesetas in there. This is most unusual. The final count is actually 2,200 more pesetas. When the counting ends, Carlos pulls out a wad of bills and hands over 6,700 pesetas. He congratulates the winner, who pockets the money and walks out to the applause of other players.

He walks towards Sol, exhilarated. *Winning is fun.* Never mind that he hadn't known what he was doing or what it took to go for the jackpot. He had won. Why, he had never seen a slot machine before except in movies and on television, let alone play one. But he had 6,700 pesetas in his pocket—$42.95 U.S.— that hadn't been there an hour earlier. He had won!

Then it struck him. He had been puzzling over one bit of information from his last stop in Israel, still trying to understand how an entire country could have bought into a stock scheme when the buyers didn't understand the meaning of stock certificates.

He had just done what the Israelis had done, walked blindly into a situation where he had won first time out. And winning is fun, especially when you win money. So that's how the game worked in Israel. All else had its price but, in the heyday of the bank share prosperity, profits were essentially free; winning was an added attraction.

He pondered that idea as he looked in the windows of the shoe stores, wondering how to spend his winnings quickly, before he started to take them seriously and begin to think he could win at the slots every day.

The next day, the winner discovered that people were amazed he made it back to his hotel without any trouble because muggers cruise the parlors watching for winners, so they can "liberate" their winnings; because his winnings represented approximately 15 percent of the gross monthly wages of a Spaniard; and because, since his last visit in 1981, Madrid's crime rate had risen substantially. This was attributed to a national unemployment rate of 19 percent (in a population of about 38,000,000) projected to climb to 24 percent before leveling off.

In 1959, when Spain opened her doors to foreign investment, the economy was overwhelmed by the amount of money that flowed in. An underdeveloped country, Spain set about building a modern industrial infrastructure overnight. The resulting development created an overheated economy that grew by leaps and bounds, and carried with it an annual inflation rate of 6 percent. While a high rate by European standards, it was not dangerous at the time, suggests one economist working for a Spanish bank.

"It was stable," said the economist, who declined to be identified.* "But it was planting the seeds for higher future inflation."

The key was a problem built into the wage and salary system—they were indexed, across the board, at 102 percent of the inflation rate. That is, at an inflation rate of 6 percent per year, wage adjustments were 6.12 percent per year.

"The economy could accommodate those rises," the economist said, "because productivity rose quickly, and prices of consumer goods—perishable and durable—were controlled."

This growth in the economy, along with its 6 percent inflation, 102 percent indexation, and price controls continued until 1973, the great turning point for the economies of so many countries of the world.

The fourfold increase in oil prices struck the Spanish economy just as hard as it did any other economy, except at the beginning the consumer didn't feel it. Government policy, still dictated by the aging Franco, was that the price of energy to the consumer, to agricultural producers, and to industry was to be

---

* No one interviewed in Spain, except one government official, would consent to be identified for fear of being fired, reprimanded by employers, or becoming a target of tax officials.

supported by massive transfers of public funds to the state oil entity and private corporations.

The reason was fear of the social consequences of choking off expectations that had been constantly rising, and met, for thirty years. Management of the Spanish economy had been directed towards turning a volatile, fractious populace into a middle-class nation that would have too much to lose from political unrest, violence, and revolution.

These government subsidies were paid for through a loose fiscal policy—free-handed spending—and deficit financing, because the government wasn't collecting enough in taxes to cover the bills. The bulk of government tax revenues was paid by employed workers, from whom it was most easily collected. Landowners, the self employed, and professionals, however, were avid tax evaders, using every ruse available to avoid paying taxes.

The major source of revenue became indirect taxation, those taxes paid on the purchase of consumer items, from cigarettes to cars. And in Spain just about everything is taxed. The taxes vary according to the type of product being bought, and whether the item being taxed is of domestic manufacture or is an import. As inflation began to eat into real earnings, consumers cut back on consumption, and indirect tax revenues began to drop.

Farm products received heavy government subsidies to appease the conservative landowners, some of Franco's staunchest supporters. The government also subsidized a large pension program that isn't all based on contributions. Many veterans of the civil war, and other citizens who never contributed to a pension program, receive pensions. At its peak the pension program deficit has been as large as the government's budget deficit. Also, a vast amount of public money is spent to subsidize the Catholic Church in Spain.

By 1974, inflation was rising and the value of the peseta was beginning to slide. Depreciation of the peseta made imports, especially oil, much more expensive and worsened the impact of imported inflation. The government had also by this time freed price controls, so farmers and manufacturers could pass on their rising costs to consumers. Consequently, the indexing factor which compensated for the impact of imported inflation was almost obliterated by price hikes throughout the economy, which worsened domestic inflation.

At the same time Spain began to suffer the beginnings of a lower, slower growth trend in exports as other countries, also suffering from higher oil prices, diverted growing portions of their import dollars into oil purchases and cut down on other import expenditures. The problem worsened when Spanish industries proved unable to increase productivity to reduce unit costs. They could no longer hang on to what market shares they had, because the rapidly built-up industries of the 1960s were already becoming obsolete. This was occurring in shipbuilding, steel, and some sectors of the textile industry.

The economy suffered an abrupt transitional period. From a period when gross national product growth had averaged about 5 percent a year, it dropped to about 2 percent.

The Spanish labor force, accustomed to high wages, continued to get them, along with large indexed increases. But, with the economy not growing quickly enough to accommodate the continual wage demands, and Spanish labor practices being highly restrictive (it is virtually impossible to fire an employee in Spain), unit labor costs on manufactured goods continued to climb. Obsolete industries became even less competitive.

The result was stagnation of output. Many manufacturing companies became non-productive money losers. To forestall closures and protect jobs, massive government subsidies and takeovers by the state holding company ensued.

By 1975 the inflation rate was a critical factor running in the mid-20 percents. But, as Alfonso Carbajo Isla, deputy director-general of foreign finances for the Spanish economics and finance ministry explains it: "General Franco died, and the government priority was the transition to democracy. The economy was not of primary concern."

It took from 1975 to 1977 for King Juan Carlos and Adolfo Suarez Gonzalez, his appointed premier, to steer Spain down the difficult road from military dictatorship to a constitutional monarchy ruled by a democratically elected parliament. The king and his premier not only had to re-educate the people of Spain politically, they had to lay the groundwork for change to the internal workings of government, society, and the economic system.

Until 1975 as a military dictatorship, Spain's government hadn't made any attempt to operate within the limits of a budget. As money was required to pay the bills, it was taken from the revenues from indirect taxation and bond income. If that wasn't enough, it was printed.

By 1976 Spain was well on the way to the transition to democracy. The changes in political and economic orientation no longer allowed Spain to act as if the country were independent from a world economic order. Along with democracy, Spain was forced to use budgeting as a guideline, rather than as a mere show of organization, and the first serious attempts at enforcing incredibly lax income tax laws were made.

This, however, coincided with the period when, despite government subsidies to shield consumers and indexation, the impact of the 1973 oil shock was beginning to reverberate through the economy. Spanish democracy was in a rudimentary and vulnerable state. To protect the new-born democracy from any social unrest that might result from widespread unemployment and economic dislocation, the interim democratic government pursued an open-handed policy of subsidizing or nationalizing industry to protect jobs.

By 1977, when the first democratically elected government in Spain in more than forty years took power, the inflation rate was 30 percent and still on the rise.

The situation at that point was critical and the government reacted by again tightening up on price controls and devaluing the peseta (already devalued by 10 percent in 1976) by a further 20 percent and leaving it to float on world exchange markets.

Unfortunately, this resulted in a further jump in unit labor costs and a rapid increase in agricultural costs. The government was again forced to step in with further subsidies and price supports.

This loose fiscal policy and the budget deficit it created could have been very damaging to the already fragile Spanish economy. Spain could have been pushed into a hyperinflationary spiral, but a tightening of monetary policy and a squeeze on private sector credit counteracted the effects of the deficit.

In the process Spanish authorities succeeded in containing the 30 percent inflation rate at the cost of high unemployment. In fact, inflation was cut to 15 percent by 1979 and was poised for a greater drop when the oil shock of 1979 occurred, and prices were again raised. Spanish authorities acted more quickly and sensibly and didn't shield consumers. The subsequent round of consumer price increases, nevertheless, kept inflation hovering in the 15 percent range.

The tight money policy was the major, and virtually only, weapon at the disposal of Spanish officials to combat and contain inflation and rising unit labor costs. Very simply put, the tight money and credit policy meant very little money was allowed to the private sector for expansion. Some sectors of the economy just shut down.

Spanish labor laws make it virtually impossible for an employer to lay off employees to cut costs, but they can't stop him shutting down and throwing *all* his employees out of work. In some cases that is exactly what happened during this period of shrinking revenues and ballooning labor and operating costs. In some industries and regions 25 percent of a manufacturer's costs were contributions to Spain's social security system—unemployment insurance, pensions, and health programs. But people, employees and management, still managed to survive.

Jaime Azana looked sadly out his office window over the production floor at his employees. He was the fourth generation of Azanas to own and supervise this factory, and it was his sad fate to have to shut it down.

He sighed and turned away from the window. Slowly, shoulders drooping, he walked to the desk. No longer would

Azana shoes be sold in Spain. And all those people who looked to him like a father, to keep them working.... He hated the prospect of throwing them out of work.

But what could he do? Costs were rising every day, and he was not making enough to keep the factory running. And there was no way he would put any of the family fortune in the business simply to protect jobs. Mortgage the vineyards? The ranch in the south? Never! The way the government wastes money—that is part of the problem!

There was a bold knock at the door. It opened a crack and his son Ramon looked in. Azana motioned him in, his shoulders drooping even further. And what would he leave Ramon?

Ramon entered, his step light. He didn't appreciate the gravity of the situation, Azana thought angrily. Maybe it is good he will not get the factory. It takes a man to be responsible.

"So, Papa, you have decided to close the factory?"

"Si. There is no other way."

"No," Ramon shook his head. "There is a way."

"To stay open?"

Ramon smiled. "No, to stay in business."

"Explain, please."

Ramon took a cigar from the humidor on his father's desk. He lit the cigar and began to pace while his father seated himself.

"Our business is shoes, Papa. And people will still want Azana shoes but not at the prices we have to charge, correct?"

"If we could cut prices, we are saved. But our costs are so high because of the social security, and they..."

"Can be avoided," said Ramon, "or completely cut."

Azana leaned forward eagerly.

"This way, Papa. We close the factory and put the workers on the unemployment. Then, we sell them the machines and the materials to make shoes. They make the shoes, as they do now, but they work for themselves at home. Then they put the Azana label in the shoes and sell them to us. We sell them to the stores as we always did. They will not be our employees, so we pay no social security. We do not pay wages but buy piece work. We have no overhead...the workers will make the shoes at home.''

Azana thought a moment, his mind racing. "It will not work. The authorities will know we closed the factory and will want to know where the shoes with the Azana label come from.''

"True," Ramon agreed. "But all we do is say we are now designers and distributors of shoes, and contract out work to one of the other shoe manufacturers. We will have invoices to show that a legitimate manufacturer is making shoes for us. And we do not have to invoice all of our customers. You know as well as I do all of them lie about the number of shoes they sell to cheat the government.''

"But..."

"And even you, Papa, you have been under-invoicing for years and taking part of the payments in cash. Think of it. Azana shoes will be price competitive once again.''

Throughout 1978 and 1979 little more than maintaining a tight monetary policy could be done to tackle either inflation or the high unit labor costs that left Spanish industry languishing. With businesses begging for, and receiving, government handouts, more government deficits piled up, serving to worsen a deficit that hadn't been much of a problem until 1976. From being a negligible factor in that year, the government's deficit grew to 16 percent of the gross national product by 1983. As a percentage of the GNP, this still wasn't critical because monetary policy had been tightened considerably. The fiscal laxity was, in effect, cancelled out as an inflationary influence by tight monetary policy. But all this did in the final analysis was keep the economy in a tenuous balance from 1979 to 1982. Inflation couldn't effectively be reduced below the 15 percent range achieved in 1979.

Government policies to reduce prices were partially successful, however. Unit labor costs were forced down by reducing the indexation of wages from 102 percent to as low as 50 percent of inflation, but wages were still not dropping fast enough to have an appreciable effect on the domestic inflation factor. At the same time price supports for agricultural products were not cut, despite the fact that in 1981 Spain's agricultural sector produced bumper crops that did not need subsidizing.

The gradual depreciation of the peseta as it floated on the world exchange markets, coupled with price controls, forced cutbacks in consumer demand for imported items. Fortunately, oil prices were beginning to soften, and these factors combined to bring Spain's overall inflation rate for 1983 down to 12.2 percent. This gave the government hope that its 1984 goal of 10 percent was attainable.

The problem that remained to plague Spain's fragile economy and social stability was the high unemployment rate resulting from the recession that began in 1978. At 19 percent Spain's unemployment rate was of the kind that, in some countries, leads to shooting in the streets. Projected to go as high as 24 percent in 1984, the unemployment rate should have excited fear in everyone but, as one Spanish business person put it: "There are too many people alive today who survived the civil war." He smiled and looked out over Madrid, a mixture of every architectural influence to sweep Europe, including art deco and glass-and-steel modern. "They know that, if only the economy is bad, they will lose much but not everything." He shrugged. "If the shooting starts again, they know they will lose everything, including maybe their lives."

Adrian Alba, the dealing room manager, interpreted the situation differently. "The Socialists, who are very moderate, were elected with a 5 million majority over the conservatives," he said. "Their policies are very reasonable and sensible. Their priority is to reduce monetary growth, inflation, and the deficit and make Spain more competitive in the world market. They will probably meet all their goals, and the people will be patient with them." He hesitated a moment. "The only problem is whether the people will be patient with the unemployment problem."

A banker in a management position akin to the North American executive assistant had a different explanation for why the country was able to survive. "Many of the unemployed, they can get social security money if they lost a job. Others, they go back to the family. But..." He paused, tapped the side of his nose, and smiled, "if you want to know the truth, many of these officially unemployed survive, and even do well, by work on the black market."

Emilio Cadena looked at the blue jeans spread across his desk. He fingered the material of one pair and smiled. He pulled another from the pile, grabbed the material on either side of a seam and pulled with all his might.

The seam held. He laughed, a cackled, broken laugh of triumph. The best thing that ever happened to me was losing my job six months after coming to Madrid. Ten years ago they closed the factory, but I, Emilio Cadena, he thought triumphantly, tailor, son of a tailor from the south, I survived, and now ten years later I am an important clothing manufacturer.

And it had all started with one pair of slightly worn Levi's in 1974.

He remembered his poorer days, when he had wandered Madrid looking for work. He had supported himself by buying and trading at his flea market table, bargaining for everything, sleeping on his cousin Armando's couch, saving his money, watching for a way to make his fortune.

One day an American teenager, hungrier than he was, offered to sell him a pair of Levi's for enough money to hold him until a money order arrived from his parents in America. Emilio bought them for next to nothing, $25 U.S. He hadn't even folded them up and laid them out on the table before they were sold for $45, and he almost had a riot on his hands as Spanish youths descended on him after hearing he had jeans to sell. He knew then how he would make his fortune.

He acquired another pair of Levi's, carefully took them apart, and sketched out patterns. For weeks he worked on the patterns until they were perfect, until no one could tell the difference between the cut of his jeans and the real thing. Then he experimented with cloth and thread and, when he was finished, he had the perfect replica down to the wisps of orange thread on the right back pocket, so the pants looked like Levi's with the label torn off.

Working at Armando's apartment, with Armando's wife and one sewing machine, he turned out fifty pairs the first week. The fifty pairs sold in two hours for $30 each, no questions asked, at the flea market that Sunday, and he had orders with deposits for one hundred more.

The second week he had two seamstresses do the work, and by the third week he had ten working full time making jeans. After a month he had to buy a small van so he could drive around the city to the homes of his seamstresses to collect the jeans they made. He paid them cash, no questions asked. Every Sunday he sold out his entire stock at the flea market for cash, no questions asked.

Oh, it had been wonderful, dizzying, exhilarating as he grew and expanded so quickly. The money poured in, almost all of it black money. Then he opened a shop to sell from all week, then another shop, and another. Then a line of shirts to go with the jeans, and jackets, and shoes. And he didn't even have to open a factory. Half of Madrid's seamstresses and tailors, it seemed, were working for him, banking what he paid them, and living on their unemployment. All they produced was hidden in the production run he contracted out to the factory in Madrid and the other two in Barcelona.

Despite certain financial arrangements with officials, he had profited and had been able to spirit away some money, slipping it into a gold account in Switzerland and a dollar account in New York. And there was the house for his parents in Seville and his new apartment in Madrid.

Cadena lit a cigarette, English, and looked at the jeans again. He laughed delightedly. Spain is indeed a land of opportunity, he thought. He opened the door and looked out over the designing room as if reassuring himself this was all real.

Casa Cadena was now an empire. Five designers worked for

him, designing clothes for the European market. And there were no problems about his designs selling everywhere in Europe, not with factories in the Common Market countries making his own Cow Country label clothing on contract and royalty arrangements.

He shook his head. The Americans might have grown bored with Western clothing, but Europeans…romantics, all of them. All crazy to be John Wayne. And all to my profit, and to the profit of many unemployed tailors, cutters, and seamstresses.

Madrid is not typical of all life in Spain, because it's the capital of a country where the population is well distributed among agricultural and industrial regions. The first difference between country and city is that Madrid has a large portion of the middle-class population. Middle-class aspirations are, to a degree, raised and met by living in that city.

Secondly, Madrid is the epicenter of one of the two major areas of development in Spain. The other development area has grown inland from the coastal city of Barcelona.

So a typical middle-class city dweller in Madrid has different worries than his counterpart in the country.

Jaime and Francisco Guerrero walked out of the house and across the yard to the barn. Francisco paused to look across the fields he and Jaime had roamed as boys when they headed to their favorite fishing spot among the trees.

"It is still beautiful, Jaime," Francisco said, following his brother's gaze. "I will tell you a secret. Sometimes, I do not go to the church on Sunday, but I take Alejandro, my oldest boy, to the river and we fish. It is not like your city."

"True," Jaime agreed. "But we all give something up when we want something else."

"But you give up so much. You work too hard in the city, for what? A million pesetas each year ($6,410 U.S.)?"

"One million, two hundred fifty thousand ($8,012 U.S.)," Jaime said indignantly.

"And what do you have?" Francisco demanded. "Do you own your home?"

"No, but..."

"A car. You own a car, and you have new furniture and color television. What else?"

"We have a video machine, and the trailer. And the children are in fine schools."

"You work like a slave so you can have the money to pay through the nose for everything."

"But I have all that Madrid has to offer."

"And that is so important? When do you see your children? And to own your own home, you will have to work at two jobs, and Maria will have to work. No," Francisco shook his head. "You were born with all the brains in our family, Jaime, but it looks like I was the smart one."

Francisco opened the door to the barn, entered, and waved Jaime over to a stall housing a chestnut mare. He entered a stall with a large coal-black horse.

"This farm has been in our family one hundred years. It is all mine after you took your share as money for the university. And it will be in our family another hundred years," Francisco said as he led the horse out to the yard. Jaime led out the mare, and they saddled the animals.

"I work on the farm, and the government makes sure I am paid enough for what I produce. The church school is good enough for the children, and it does not cost as much as the fine city school of your children with uniforms and snobs meeting all the right people."

"I have what I want."

Francisco looked at him sardonically. "You do? Little brother, your wife and my wife grew up together. They are still best friends and speak together. You are deeply in debt, and you barely get by on your salary the way the inflation and growing children eat it up. You have a part of what you want, but you will never get all that you want."

Francisco jumped into the saddle. He leaned over and grabbed the fishing rod leaning against a fence post. "I do not have everything that I want, and I work as hard as you do, but you have to deal with the jealousy and greed of people scared about their jobs and losing everything. In the city they are crazy." He waved the fishing rod. "Here, when I want to forget that life is never easy, I at least have my fishing rod and that spot under the trees where time and the world leave me alone."

The solutions to Spain's problems are the same solutions voiced in Israel and Italy. "The government is maintaining its tight money policy," says Alfonso Carbajo Isla, the divisional deputy director-general from Spain's economics and finance ministry. "And this after already substantially reducing the rate of growth of the money supply. As for the deficit, it is trying to keep that at the same level."

He shrugs, almost apologetically, and knits his fingers together. "So that makes for problems in the modernization of all industry. If more money goes to make government-controlled industry competitive, the deficit grows. A large deficit forces up interest rates, which means private industry cannot afford to borrow money to become more productive."

The challenge is to make Spanish industry more competitive, return it to a profitable position without increasing spending, and dispose of or privatize government-controlled industry to relieve the state of its role as major player in the economy. As long as the person who is responsible for the bottom line is prepared to dole out more money, rather than tighten operations, when the bottom line reads red, there is no incentive to make the operation profitable and self-supporting. Industries then become holding pens for the otherwise unemployable.

"This is a highly pragmatic government," points out one observer in the financial field. "The time its members spent at the Harvard business school is paying off for the country. They're going to the roots of the problem and dismantling the inefficient businesses; in the process they're finding it's easier to create jobs that are productive than to maintain the ones that aren't."

The sources of Spain's problems are known, as is the means by which they can be sorted out. The situation was described by one Madrid investment banker specializing in international finance: "The sickness is the same in all countries in the world. It's only a matter of degree—we all live beyond our means and spend more than we can afford. The solution is to live within our means. It will hurt in the short term but will ensure we have a long term to look forward to."

So, in the face of this kind of uncertainty and its social and economic ills, where do Spaniards, who in the past have experienced losing it all, invest?

"Real estate," says one. He has a high-profile, upper-middle-class managerial job and works within a corporate policy that forbids interviews. But he's an amiable, talkative sort. Besides performing to the best of his ability in the job, he also has to maintain a certain image, because image is a big part of life in Spain.

"So, there is a large flat in Madrid, about 11 million pesetas ($70,000 U.S.)," he says as he smooths down the lapels of an elegant, hand-tailored three-piece suit. "And there is the country house no more than forty or fifty kilometers away from the city, another 11 million ($70,000). There is the small house or flat by the sea to send the family to for the summer, 6,250,000 ($40,000), and the flat in the Pyrenees for skiing, 4,700,000 ($30,000)."

But how does someone afford that kind of lifestyle in a country where the average monthly income—the median between the highest and the lowest salaries—is about $600?

"Well, there are many ways," he smiles and brushes his hair back. "Income taxes are low and regularly evaded. It is estimated that about $12 to $15 billion U.S. (the peseta figure is virtually incomprehensible) of black money is drifting through Spain's internal economy, much of it in foreign currency—dollars, marks, pounds—and perhaps just as much is on deposit in foreign banks."

What is the government doing about black money?

"The government has said that it will crack down on implementation of the tax laws."

But that will only combat future frauds.

"Well, there's also the treasury bill, which incidentally is an excellent investment."

He was talking about the new security sold weekly by the government as a means of financing public debt. It's a promissory term note with an interest rate that is positive after inflation adjustment. It's also untaxed, can be traded without any controls, and is an untitled bearer security—redeemable by whomever is holding it on the day of maturity.

Because there is no way of identifying who owns what in the way of treasury bills, black market money holders see them as excellent investments which allow them to use their black money profitably. Such investment also serves as one means of easing an estimated $25 to $50 billion U.S. from the black economy back into the legal one.

"But the large figure is, I think, optimistic," the talkative Spaniard said. "The money outside the country will stay there. You know it is not unusual for people in this country to inherit numbered Swiss accounts."

But how do you get that kind of money out of the country?

"Well, it has been going on for many years, don't forget. Understand that no one here really saw inflation coming, or saw it as a threat when it arrived. It is Spanish tradition to hold a portion of wealth somewhere the government cannot touch it. And since the economy opened up, trade has been in the billions, in and out, to the point where the trade flow is now $60 billion annually."

The favored mechanism for getting money out of the country, despite strict controls on acquiring and holding foreign currencies, is in rigging invoices and juggling. If the Spaniard involved is an importer, he arranges for his New York trading partner to over-invoice on a falsified set of duplicate documents.

Assume the deal is for $100,000 U.S.; he is invoiced for $125,000. The Spaniard presents these documents at the bank, which has no reason to suspect the amount has been padded, so he is allowed to buy American dollars, usually in the form of a draft, irrevocable letter of credit, or electronic transfer.

The trading partner receives the transfer, and ensures that the *true* amount of $100,000 owed him, as shown on his books according to the real invoice, is transferred to the company's credit. The Spaniard then pays him a "commission" for helping him spirit the extra $25,000 U.S. out of Spain. The money usually goes into a savings account, and the Spaniard has what he perceives as a secure deposit in American dollars gathering interest.

Meanwhile, that $25,000 gets written into his books as a business expense, deductible when he pays his (likely crooked) income taxes, and it's also built into his pricing structure. In effect, the Spanish consumers subsidize his financial machinations through their taxes and the inflated prices they pay for his goods or services.

The scam also works the other way. A North American who wants to get money out of the country without the tax authorities knowing simply arranges for a Spanish supplier to over-invoice him. Because Spain's central bank authorities have to be given all foreign currency proceeds from business transactions as soon as they arrive, the payment for the reverse pipeline has to be remitted first to a Swiss holding company. This way the padded portion of the payment can be skimmed off for deposit before the final transfer on the true cost of goods comes through the Spanish banking system, which converts it to pesetas before paying it over to the Spaniard.

"It's quite an old system, effective, proven successful, and very difficult to find upon investigation," said the Spaniard. "Then of course there are the very crude traditional methods: yachts and fishing boats traveling the Mediterranean, small planes over the Pyrenees, suitcases full of dollars on the train to Paris. Most times it works, but there's always the risk of that one time when you might be caught."

The income tax system in Spain before 1977 was a complex one. A government that suspects, or knows about, widespread tax evasion, usually institutes a double-tiered tax system, a flat-rate income tax (in Spain's case, 12 percent) and an assets tax. The assets tax is levied against items such as land or cars that have to be registered with a government office. For Spain that became a complicated system which, in its complexity, offered many opportunities for tax evasion. No opportunity was left unexplored or unused.

In 1977, along with democracy and budget deficits, the Spanish people were presented with a revamped taxation structure and a modernized, but still bureaucratic system of tax collection. It offered new avenues for tax evasion. But even if a Spaniard gets caught evading taxes, there's always a way to escape prosecution.

"It's called *sobrecito*," said a Canadian-born Spaniard, who remained in Spain after finding he liked the lifestyle. Possibly he enjoyed the lifestyle because he is an overseas-recruited executive paid in American dollars, the modern-day Spanish aristocrat. "*Sobrecito*, that's why this country will never get anywhere. It means little white envelope, and the little white envelope is usually full of money."

Mention *sobrecito* publicly in Spain, and you'll be shunned as if you had dragged in something odious or unpleasant on the heel of your shoe. That doesn't deny that it is a fact of life in Spain.

"It results from this being a very rigidly class oriented society," explained Adrian Alba, the currency dealer. "On the one hand, everyone is encouraged to become middle class, but the obstacles are incredible. You need education—that costs money. You have to present a certain kind of image—that costs money. And a Spaniard on a Spaniard's salary can't do it."

So what happens?

"Well, I've seen it in restaurants. They're all monitored by the government for pricing. So an inspector comes in, has a big meal, free, and gets a little envelope with his napkin. Or a tax inspector comes into a shop to check the books, and the envelope is between the pages of the ledger. And you have to understand, this hasn't been going on just since Franco's days. It's always been like this." He laughs cynically and points down the hall to his boss's office. "Why, if I leave this job someday, there's a line of people out there waiting with envelopes to hand to the person who does the hiring. Need I say more?"

Spanish investment practices, besides buying into land and real estate, are generally restricted to savings, paper investments, and durables. The mix, however, is much the key. According to one investment analyst, the Spanish attitude advocates saving toward purchase of the home first, unless it has been inherited, which is the pattern in rural areas.

With the critical matter of the home in hand, the next step is the acquistive phase: furniture, fridge, stove, stereo, television, video, and automobile. At the same time, people attempt to save money. Even though the return on savings tends to be flat, the interest is at least high enough to compensate for inflationary erosion. This protects the purchasing power of the money.

Government securities provide some protection: Treasury bills are quite profitable, since the interest is untaxed; bonds provide protection, but no real profit; and the stock market requires a lot of information and a lot of guts because it's an insider's game, with restricted access to playing positions.

One way of providing against inflation, pointed out by an economist who specializes in consumer patterns, is that Spaniards buy durable foodstuffs in bulk and replenish them as they are used. In the long run it can mean large savings in family food costs.

Unfortunately, food hoarding can also lead to problems when buyers purchase from less-than-reliable suppliers. The most notorious incident occurred a few years ago, when thousands of liters of tainted olive oil were sold by disreputable operators to people overjoyed to get their cooking oil at one quarter the normal price. A large number of people died before the operation was discovered.

A debate exists over whether gold is a worthwhile investment. On the one hand, interest rates tend to move hand in hand with inflation, so purchasing power of savings is protected. Gold is very speculative and, at the prices quoted for it these days, the only way to make a small fortune in gold is to start with a big fortune and be lucky enough to buy cheap quantities that you sell at high prices. This way, you at least profit on volume trading.

But gold is too unreliable. It doesn't always perform as expected if you are looking for quick profit. It is, however, a different situation if you are looking for long-term security. Then, a rousing chorus of voices says to buy gold, and not let anyone know you have it until you're ready to sell.

As for the exotic investments, Spaniards believe in buying jewelry, by all means, but not in estimating it has any greater value than what can be negotiated for it when it comes time to sell.

If you buy antiques and art, Spanish investors advocate you buy what you enjoy; don't look at art or antiques as an investment, unless you've managed to acquire the originals of Goya's *Maja Nude* and *Maja Clothed*.

There is much more support for buying coins and stamps than any of the other exotic investments. Across the board— Italy, Israel, and Spain—the explanation has been the same: These items have true, easily defined values to collectors and do tend to appreciate. They are extremely portable, stamps more so than coins, and most times the authorities don't see them as being of value so they can easily be transported across international boundaries.

Before leaving Spain, we should highlight a few points.

First, tax evasion and exportation of a portion of assets and wealth form a long-standing tradition in Spain. This tradition developed out of a history that is not noted for political stability, so that those with money always hedged their bets. As such, providing against losing wealth to war, civil war, dictatorship, expropriatory governments, or whatever life can offer is a part of the Spanish behavior pattern. Inflation is simply another of the many misfortunes of life.

The Spanish adapted. As required, they adjusted their spending habits to the new predator eating away at their money. The family structure is one bulwark upon which they count heavily, families being somewhat extended and interdependent. Otherwise, the Spanish counted upon their wits to survive inflationary erosion of their earnings and still find ways to survive, and prosper, despite the grim unemployment figures and attendant problems.

Unfortunately, the greatest predator of earnings is government. Between inflation and government, it's easiest to beat government. So it still comes down to tax evasion and accumulating black money as the key to survival: *The higher the inflation rate, or the longer it has been a factor in the economy, the less tendency there is on the part of the populace to pay taxes willingly.*

When caught between inflation and erosion, the citizen will fight whichever obstacle he or she can beat. A moral flexibility creeps into the thinking. You can't beat inflation, but there is a way to beat taxation: Work hard, maybe too hard, and don't let anyone know you're working.

———❧❧❧———

Chapter 9

THE BUCK STOPS HERE

THE GRACIOUS CHEERINESS of the Aerolineas Argentinas ground staff at the check-in counter at Madrid's International Airport is infectious. Unlike their co-workers assigned as cabin staff, the ground personnel are among the most charming and helpful people in the airline industry.

The Argentinian behind the counter handed over the ticket and boarding pass. "Have a nice flight," he said in Oxford-accented English.

"Thank you. Tell me, is there any place around here where I can exchange some dollars for Argentine pesos?"

He looked over the counter, puzzled. "Why?"

"Well, I like to have airport money, a little change for the bus or a coffee."

"Oh, I see." He laughed, quite amused by the request. "You can't get any here. It's a controlled currency. The government decrees it exchanges at..." He thought for a moment, "almost 28 pesos to the U.S. dollar, but no one outside Argentina carries pesos." He laughed again. "No one outside Argentina wants them." He stopped and chuckled merrily. "I'm not sure anyone in Argentina wants them either."

"Why?"

"You'll see. You have dollars?"

"Traveler's cheques."

"Better for you."

"What does that mean?"

That quizzical look again. "You really don't know?"

"Know what?"

"You are better off carrying dollars to Argentina. And you are better off carrying dollars in Argentina."

The international airport in Argentina is called Ezeiza. When you disembark and move through the building to the immigration area, you pass a government-run duty-free shop. All prices are quoted in American dollars.

A sign indicates the rate at which pesos are accepted in payment against the dollar prices. Today the quotation is 42 pesos per U.S. dollar, a big jump from the 27, almost 28 quoted the night before. Inflation here is more than 400 percent per year, but to change that much overnight?

The ever-present calculator comes out, and after some calculations total confusion reigns. An inflation rate of 400 percent per year means 33.3 percent per month. That means adjusted monthly they should only be demanding 36 pesos. But even so, 33 percent? Overnight.

After immigration, where business is conducted in no less than six languages, you go down to the baggage claim and customs area. Argentina uses the "something to declare; nothing to declare" customs system. It doesn't matter. Whichever way you go, the officer will check your bags.

Sight of a Canadian passport and the sound of French-accented Spanish elicits a look of dismay from the customs officer.

Just past the customs desks is the exchange counter, where the dollar is traded at 27.8 pesos. Confusing? The first lesson learned in the first thirty minutes in the country: Argentina is synonymous with confusion.

There's a desk outside customs at Ezeiza Airport where you buy tickets for the bus ride into the city. The fare is 120 pesos. The attendant hands over a ticket, and a mix of crisp new bills and a handful of ragged old ones with very large denominations.

"What's this?" The outstretched bill reads 1,000. But 1,000 what?

"The old money, from before devaluation last year." The attendant takes the banknote and puts a decimal point before the one. "It was 1,000 old pesos. It is now 10 centavos. 100 centavos makes one peso."

Calle Florida is a cobbled mall in the center of the sixteen-square-block section of downtown Buenos Aires that is the heart of the city. The Hotel Eibar is one of many little hotels on the street with entrances tucked between clothing stores, gift shops, and galleries full of shops. The reception desk commands a view of the lobby and the street. A fellow named Roberto is on duty.

"Excuse me. What is the peso worth here."

"Pardon?"

"I said what is the peso.... Wait a minute." His interrogator pulls out a wad of bills, leafs through them, and drops a new one-peso note on the counter. "What will this buy?"

Roberto shrugs and sniffs. "Nothing." He reaches over and pulls out two more one-peso notes and a pre-devaluation thousand-peso note and lines them up on the countertop. "This will buy you a token for the *subte* (subway) or a ride on the bus."

Now, the moment you have been waiting for: the tip on how to make a quick buck from hyperinflation. You are going to play the black market.

The Argentine peso is a controlled currency; if a financial institution outside Argentina offers a correspondent institution in Argentina a bundle of pesos for exchange, they won't be accepted. They are only negotiable and exchangeable in Argentina.

The government sets the exchange rate for the peso, which is a purely arbitrary statement of what the government decides the peso is worth relative to whatever currency you choose to exchange. All are accepted, but the U.S. dollar is the standard against which all currencies are judged.

There is a thriving currency black market in Argentina. A currency black market is one in which currencies are traded as if they were commodities. In simplest terms, money is bought and sold at whatever prices people are prepared to pay, according to supply and demand. The demand these days is for American dollars. In mid-February 1984, when the official rate was 27.8 pesos per U.S. dollar the black-market rate was 39.5 pesos, a premium of about 42 percent. Some ten days later, after a government decree that interest rates, which averaged about 148 percent per annum for a *three-day* term deposit, were to be dropped, demand for the dollar rose appreciably. The black market exchange rate rose to 45 pesos, a premium of about 60 percent over the official rate of 27.8 pesos per U.S. dollar. This was the figure for selling American dollars.

The reason the duty-free shop at Ezeiza demanded 42 pesos for dollar purchases, when the official exchange rate was 27.8, is a beautiful piece of Machiavellian thinking. The posted rate is the black-market exchange quote for the buyer for that day. It's one way for the authorities to get a bit back from those tourists who have been merrily playing the black market, planning to buy duty-free items at super bargain prices.

Here are the mechanics of profiting handsomely from hyper-inflation. All you need is larceny in your heart, loose cash, a lot of nerve, acting ability, and a friendly disposition. Patience, while not necessarily a virtue, might come in handy, but only in a small dose.

Get on a plane bound for Argentina carrying a suitcase full of American dollars. You'll have to figure out how to get them into the country, past hawk-eyed customs officials. Hint: Make sure $50 U.S. is neatly, and discreetly, folded into your passport before you go through customs. This will ensure that you go trouble free.

If you haven't already done so, book yourself into a hotel in the downtown core. Nothing like a Sheraton; you want to blend in, and be near the financial sector, which revolves around the intersection of Corrientes and San Martin. You want to be near the financial sector, because you want to be able to move quickly; two days at best, three days at most, should be the length of your stay.

The three-day limit is important. It's your critical path to getting away with this scheme. The Argentine financial system is bogged down under a mountain of paperwork because of all the controls on currency. It will take a minimum of three days for the paperwork from your financial machinations to begin filtering into the Central Bank. You want to be out of the country before enough paper shows up to make the curious suspicious.

Assume you have $22,000 to play with.

Day One, Morning:

Go to the nearest bank and exchange $2,000 for pesos at the official rate. You're going to need documents that show you have legally acquired a large amount of Argentine currency.

Later that morning check the day's *Buenos Aires Herald*; the black market exchange rate is usually on page two or three. Please, don't ask questions. This is Argentina.

There are two ways to meet a buyer. One is to walk down Florida to the block between Avenida Cordoba and Paraguay. Stand around, peer into windows, look confused, and frantically work a calculator. A tall blonde fellow will approach you and ask: "You need help? Exchange?"

Knowing the quotation, and presumably being brave enough to contemplate dealing with a street buyer, negotiate.

The faint of heart, conservative, or more discreet are better off asking a hotel bellboy, or the desk clerk: *"¿Por favor, dónde puede cambiar una billete de veinte dólares Americano?"* (Please, where can I exchange $20 American?)

Chances are he will miraculously produce a business card. Seek out the individual named thereon and deal with him...discreetly. Don't barge in announcing you have a bundle to trade. Negotiate.

For large amounts of currency, he'll need time to make arrangements. Don't trust anyone, no matter how honest they look or act. Count every bit of currency you get. Greed and panic make it easy for you to be fooled by cut up newsprint.

Day One, Afternoon:

The hard part begins. Assume your $20,000 U.S. at 45 gets

you 900,000 pesos; you also have $2,000 U.S. × 28.7 = 57,400, so your total is 957,400 pesos. You want to trade these back at the official rate (buying American dollars) of 29.3, which will give you $32,675.77 U.S.

Divide the money into packets that will return you no more than $1,500 U.S. at a time. Start hitting the exchange houses and banks (don't worry, there are more than enough), buying U.S. dollar traveler's cheques. Move fast, but not so fast that you draw attention to yourself. Don't act nervous or suspicious. Dutifully produce the papers you were given when you legally exchanged currency so you'll be covered against embarrassing questions about where you got the money in the quantities you're trading.

Also, you're buying dollar-denominated traveler's cheques because the strict controls on foreign currencies don't apply to traveler's cheques.

Day Two, Afternoon:
Assuming you have completed your transactions, pay your bills, take a taxi to the airport, and leave the country. Once you've made it out of Argentina, allow $2,000 for expenses and congratulate yourself for your ill-gotten net profits of $8,662.11 U.S.

Your balance sheet would be:

Opening balance	$22,000 U.S.
Legal conversion $2,000 at 28.7	57,400 pesos
Black market trades $20,000 at 45	900,000 pesos
Total legal and black market pesos	957,000 pesos
957,000 pesos reconverted at 29.3	$32,662.11 U.S.
Gross profit $32,662.11 minus $22,000	$10,662.11 U.S.
Gross profit minus $2,000 expenses	$8,662.11 U.S.
Closing balance: net profit	$8,662.11 U.S.

Now all you have to do is figure out how to beat the tax people at home. If you are larcenous enough to adopt this plan, you probably already have a way to launder your money.

The sum of $8,662.11 U.S. may not sound like much, but for two days work? Well, if you're really ambitious, syndicate with some friends and pool your resources.

One warning: if you get caught, kiss your ass goodbye.

Chapter 10

ARGENTINA: DON'T CRY FOR ME

IN 1516 Spanish adventurers led by Juan Diaz de Solis arrived on the shores of what is modern-day Argentina. They were met by Indians who roamed the pampas, the huge prairie that stretches through lower South America. By the late 1880s the Argentines had killed off most of the Indians and all of the Blacks descended from slaves brought to work Argentine plantations.

Buenos Aires was founded in 1536 by Pedro de Mendoza, an explorer seeking an overland route to Peru. The city was abandoned in 1541, after five years of continuous Indian attacks, but was re-established in 1580 and made capital of the Spanish vice-royalty of South America in 1776.

In 1810, when Spain's South American colonies revolted, Buenos Aires was the first Latin American city to declare its independence. The war of independence continued until 1816, when Buenos Aires declared itself an independent city, but a civil war raged in the interior until the 1829 dictatorship of J.M. de Rosas, who ruled, except for a three-year break, until 1852.

An American-style constitution in 1853 created the Republic of Argentina, and in 1862 Buenos Aires joined the republic, becoming the capital.

A railroad-building boom, financed by Britain, swept Argentina in the late 1800s, bringing with it a wave of English immigrants. The railroads connected Buenos Aires with the interior, supplementing the river transportation network that linked the city with neighboring Uruguay, Paraguay, and Brazil. As a result, Buenos Aires grew rapidly as a port and service center for the cattle and grain-producing regions of the pampas and the Gran Chaco, the northern prairie.

Large waves of immigration from Italy, Spain, and Germany occurred between 1880 and 1914; the period is called the Golden Age of Argentine growth because of its stability and the explosive development and modernization that made Argentina the most European, prosperous, educated, and industrialized country in Latin America. By 1919 Argentina was the standard for development in the early twentieth century; other developing countries, such as Canada and Australia, fared badly when compared to Argentina.

The population of Buenos Aires at that time tended to be upper-middle-class administrators and upper-class absentee landowners—the "educate them enough to operate the machinery properly" type of conservative liberal. Settlement and landholding practices were based on the Spanish land grant system, and ownership of large properties concentrated in the hands of a small number of families created a rigid social hierarchy. Most immigrants either worked for the landowners, or in the factories of the growing industrial cities of Córdoba, Rosario, La Plata, and San Miguel de Tucumán. These workers became the rural and urban blue collar, lower, and mid-middle classes.

The moneyed classes tended to spend their money or invest it overseas, rather than invest heavily in the country. Any industrialization was financed by overseas interests, but even that was for the primary industries characteristic of developing nations. Essentially, the profits produced by Argentina were taken out of the country. One lament of Argentines is that, between the two World Wars, most of Argentina's domestic profit was deposited in French and Swiss banks.

A series of military coups beginning in 1930 lasted until 1944, when a group of army colonels, led by Juan Domingo Perón, seized power. In 1946 Perón, now a general, won a presidential election and established a popularly elected dictatorship. His second wife, Eva Perón, who effectively ran the labor and social services ministries, built great support for Perón's regime. Her death from cancer in 1952 accompanied an economic downturn, and by 1955 a dissatisfied military ousted Perón from the presidency.

Governments for the next eighteen years were unable to establish any real consensus in Argentine politics because of the influence of Perónism. More an attitude than an ideology, Perónism encompassed the full spectrum of political belief from left to right, all age groups, the military, labor, and the church. The core of opposition to Perónism was the somewhat liberal element of the landowning, entrepreneurial, and administrative middle classes concentrated in Buenos Aires. Perónism combined the ideas of Marx, Hitler, Mussolini, and Al Capone.

In 1973 a Perónist candidate took the presidency and held it until Perón, who had been invited to return from exile, arrived in Buenos Aires. In a new election Perón and Isabel Martinez de Perón, his third wife who ran as his vice-presidential running mate, won with a 61 percent electoral majority. Perón died ten months later and was succeeded as president by Isabel.

At that time the annual inflation rate was 40 percent. Isabel Perón proved totally incompetent as president, ruling with economic policies that forced inflation up to 335 percent in 1975 and saw political violence and terrorism become an everyday affair. She was ousted by the military in 1976. The ensuing governments, ruled by juntas of senior members of the army, navy, and air force, set new lows in abuse of human rights to bring the violence under control. Their initial success in bringing a semblance of order to the Argentine economy and forcing inflation down to about 175 percent in 1977, then 100 percent in 1980, was transitory. By 1981 inflation was creeping upward. After the fiasco, and the expense in lives and money, of the 1982 Falklands/Malvinas War, inflation skyrocketed to a 1983 high of 400 percent.

The deteriorating economy and loss of prestige over the Falklands/Malvinas defeat forced the military to call free elections. In December 1983 the military relinquished power to a democratically elected Radical party government, which was immediately faced with the task of bringing inflation under control, bringing the military under control, bringing the $45 billion foreign debt problem under control, and re-educating the Argentine public in the ways of democracy.

That's the official history.

Buenos Aires, Saturday, 18 February 1984, 10:30 P.M.

The obelisk, a hundred-meter-tall monument to Argentine democracy in the center of Avenida 9 de Julio, is bathed in light. The neon signs adorning buildings all around this white marble erection, the biggest in the southern hemisphere, are technicolor billboards flashing the names that apparently make the good life so good: Marlborough, Hitachi, Mercedes, Philco, Coca Cola, JVC, 7Up, Nestle, Philips, Fiat, Bulova, Seiko, Citizen.

Cars, thousands of them, race up and down the sixteen lanes of Avenida 9 de Julio. At 144 meters wide it's really a huge racetrack disguised as a city street; it's so bewilderingly wide, the north side is called Cerrito and the south is called Carlos Pellegrini (just so you know where to find places), and center sections are municipal parking lots.

People walk everywhere, amid the tables of the sidewalk cafés on Cerrito and Pellegrini, on the streets, and around the two semi-circular plazas flanking the obelisk, which is at the intersection of ten different streets.

It's a kind of Latino chaos, jovially anarchic. Everyone is well dressed, well fed, and complacent looking.

The stores in the throbbingly busy heart of the city are crammed with consumer gadgets. Santa Fe and other side streets crossing Florida are a dedicated consumer's dreamland, a fairytale collection of storefronts and galleries—cell-like shops housed in the basements of buildings. They're all selling the same watches, radios, shoes, leather goods, jewelry—real and costume.

Some of the clothes are so beautiful in design they're breathtaking but, after the thirtieth window displaying the same merchandise, they become just the same old rags. One woman, then two, some of the most beautiful in the world, pass by wearing such clothes, and they're interesting again. But, after looking around and seeing a parade of fashion clones, it dawns that conformity in the unusual is the norm in Buenos Aires.

Over it all, Michael Jackson sings about "Beating it" to the counterpoint of an across-the-street tango, while Paul McCartney and a host of foreigners are the warm-up acts in the background blaring from the speakers of music shops. And the score invariably leads to Irene Cara's version of "Flashdance," or a French, Italian, or Spanish cover of the same song. As soon as the song is heard, passersby pick it up, hum the tune, then invariably mouth the line, "take your passion, and make it happen," complete with Latin inflection. And when it happens, you expect John Travolta to appear, reprising, along with the locals, his strutting scene from *Saturday Night Fever*.

Where it is being conducted, business goes on at a frantic, almost desperate pace, albeit at prices that stagger the imagination, until you convert to dollars. Leather goods are inexpensive, the lustrous, luxurious Argentine woolens are incredibly so, and food is as cheap as the dirt in which it's grown. Pay in dollars or black-market pesos and you'll find the price on everything so small, in no time you'll go broke saving a fortune.

But the cars, videos, and televisions—imports or items manufactured on license in Argentina—are outrageously costly.

The *Portenos,* the name residents of the city give themselves (derived from the Spanish for port, which is what Buenos Aires is), walk, race, run, cavort, play, commit adultery and criminal acts, and conduct their daily lives through everything—more than 400 percent inflation, daily revelations of debasement of human dignity under the military regime, massive foreign debt, and political infighting in the new democracy. They appear oblivious to everything except the signs, the hot, muggy night air, the craftwork that artisans have laid out on tables in the plazas, the smells from the restaurants, and other people jostling and chattering on the streets.

How can they be oblivious to a $45 billion foreign debt? How can they behave as if this were the 1920s when Argentina was rich, prosperous, and relatively well run, when Buenos Aires was the Paris of the south? All around them this once-beautiful city, designed to service its official population of 3 million, has gone to seed in the effort to accommodate more than 9 million. Where is all the misery and privation that is supposed to accompany hyperinflation? There haven't been any reports of hungry people eating a fat capitalist or black market profiteer.

But they must suspect something. Despite all the outward signs of wealth and despite their being, overall, among the most physically beautiful people in the world, the scarcest items seem to be genuine smiles.

It's a Friday afternoon. Buenos Aires is sweltering under a burning sun, steaming its occupants like clams in 33-degree Celsius weather with 80 percent humidity. That combination makes for dense, moist air, the only kind to expect of a place like Buenos Aires, which is in the estuary of the Río de la Plata and where, in summer, the prevailing wet winds are offshoots of the Southeast Trades blowing in from the Atlantic.

You simply accept the kind of soupy atmosphere that engulfs you when you leave an air conditioned building. But, at one point, a fine mist drenches everyone and everything in the street. If you look up, row upon row of air conditioners grow out of walls of buildings everywhere, and all of them have drain tubes that feed out onto the street and spray passersby.

But, in looking up, another sight, a most incredible one, greets the eye—a startling confusion of telephone wires hanging every which way. They come out of windows and holes drilled in the sides of buildings. They're wrapped around vent stacks and hooked onto nails driven into bricks and concrete. They're bunched up in four-inch bundles and tied to balcony railings. Some just drop from the twenty-fourth floor of a thirty-two story building, loop down, caress the tops of light standards, cross over other suspended phone lines, and dangle, unconnected, above the street. No wonder placing a telephone call in Buenos Aires can drive anyone to tears. If you make your connection, you hurriedly identify yourself, hope the person at the other end caught your name, and shout your message. When the line drops, you call again. On a rainy day, don't even bother taking the phone off the hook.

All over the city, the streets are strewn with the paper litter of careless passersby. There are traffic lights in which the signals work, but the lights are burnt out and the city can't afford the cost of replacement bulbs. There are sidewalks in some downtown sections which are guaranteed to cripple. After observing all this and after observing everyone apparently on the take and the make, black marketeers and daily reports in the *Buenos Aires Herald* of the body counts from the recently uncovered graves of unidentified victims of the military repression and the suburban detention and torture centers, two questions cry out: How is the country run, and how is it made to work?

"We are eating at our guts," replies Armand, the Argentine-born manager of a foreign bank's Argentine operations. He spends most of his time these days rescheduling the international debts of Central and South American countries. "We are not living or progressing."

He looks out the window of his twentieth-story office at Buenos Aires, once the jewel of South America, commiserating over how the setting has become tarnished. "We know we're chewing up the country. It's because we aren't a nation anymore. Maybe we never were. But now, everything is *cuenta propismo propio*, on my own account, only for me, everyone for himself."

It was the start of a four-hour monologue, unbroken by interruptions except calls for more tea and coffee. It ranged across Argentine history, economics, finance, morality, corruption, and misery. Here was a man who loved his country telling a foreigner of the anger, frustration, and pain he felt over its debasement at the hands of thieves. He spared no one but himself, but that's to be expected; it's human nature. What follows is taken directly from Armand's monologue, for he tells

Argentina's story better than an outsider ever could.

"This is what developed in Argentina in the last years. Visit the neighborhoods, from the best to the worst, and you will see in every block one house has a garage that is sealed off and is now a kiosk. A member of the household runs it. A truck comes by and drops off twenty cartons of cigarettes, biscuits, candies— no one knows how much of anything. The money...it's black mostly.

"And maybe in that house, as in many houses, the woman is making something, maybe sixteen pullover sweaters a week, or pants, or shirts, or something. It's all black money whatever she makes.

"And the father, maybe he's a bank worker. He finishes at 5:00 P.M., grabs a sandwich, and goes to another job, and works until 1:00 A.M. He gets no real sleep and isn't productive at either job. It's a bad life. He's a vegetable, unhappy, embittered. But it's the only way he can survive. He's the kind we say is always five centavos short of a peso.

"How does this happen when, in 1945, at the end of the war, Argentina had $5.3 billion U.S. in gold in the Central Bank? These were payment from feeding everyone beef and grain during the war. The vaults were so full we couldn't accept any more.

"We had more money than you could imagine. But, if you wanted a spade, there were none to be had. Fix a plough? No steel. Why? Argentina wasn't industrialized past the basic levels. We never had to; our cattle and grain and sheep made us wealthy, and we traded for manufactured goods from Europe and America. But they were rebuilding and retooling after the war. They had nothing left for us to buy.

"So Perón said, 'Fine, we industrialize.' You see, he had discovered the gold in the Central Bank, and that paid for industrialization. And how did we industrialize? We bought all the war surplus machinery and equipment Perón's agents could find.

"But a truck that was $200 in a surplus lot in San Diego became $20,000 by the time it landed in Buenos Aires, and

Perón and his agents, and the seller, and officials all along the way got a piece. And Perón and his buddies... 'Here's one for you and one for me, and one for you and two for me, and one for you and four for me.' You see?

"Until 1941 you could take the Argentine peso anywhere in the world and exchange it at four to the U.S. dollar, and everyone would gladly accept it. After 1945 Perón and his friends set up exchange controls, so they touched the money first. And they used licenses and permits to rob the country, and they expropriated his enemies where they could, and after a while the peso was to be laughed at.

"Perón fed Argentina his brand of fascism. He was the military attaché in Italy and Germany, and he learned from Hitler and Mussolini how to mobilize the masses with a mixture of nationalism, socialism, and ignorance.

"He ensured the military put up industries—so what if they had built-in inefficiencies?—all to bring in blue-collar workers from the interior to Buenos Aires to offset the conservative white-collar anti-Perónist class. He organized fascist-style mass rallies in the city and arranged free train rides from the provinces to the city.

"The workers came with their wives and families and stayed after the rallies. There was no housing for them, so they built shacks, what we call *villas miserias*, shanty towns. They worked in these inefficient industries and were Perón's power base. And at Christmas he would send them truckloads of cider and gifts. It was sheer demagoguery.

"He industrialized the country as an excuse to bring to the city what he called the *descamisados*, the shirtless ones, those whose expectations were raised but never met by the old conservative intellectuals of Buenos Aires. But the *descamisados* were never shirtless until they came to Buenos Aires, where they truly had nothing.

"So Perón created them, made them shirtless with the left hand, and handed them a shirt with the right, to have a city population that could outweigh the anti-Perónist vote. He would actually redraw electoral boundaries to cut across enclaves of these anti-Perónist voters and consequently never lost a district.

"The moral condition of the country and government became laughable. You see, what most people miss or forget, everywhere, is that the government, by setting the example, has the moral authority to create and enforce all attitudes and behavior. Perón was in power for ten years. He was completely corrupt and set the tone for the country.

"So, in that kind of climate, do you think anyone would willingly pay taxes? Do you think that, after the stories of planeloads of bullion being shipped off to Perón's personal accounts in Switzerland, that the people would have faith in any government, any law, anything but corruption?

"But delinquent behavior hurts. The body adjusts to pain; it becomes inured, and so does the soul. So Argentina and Argentines became inured to pain ... the privileges of the military, the corruption of the tax inspector, the customs inspector, everyone. It's done in places like Spain, but with decorum. Here, you pay off the policeman on the street rather than go to court to fight a speeding ticket you don't deserve, because it takes so long and costs so much.

"Here, you don't dare to believe. People know they're being lied to. Like on the road job, when specifications are published, people know one quarter of the bags of cement are stolen. They hope the bridge or road will not collapse.

"You become anesthetized to anything and everything. So we have corrupt authoritarian governments. The civic preoccupation is to keep to ourselves, nose clean, pipe down, turn away.

"And that's where they want you. If they have political impunity, they have moral impunity. And you get what happened here in the last seven years, the killing, torture, the *desaparecidos*, the missing ones.

"It works this way: You lose respect for the money, you lose respect for the law. You can buy your way out of anything. So the law is cheapened, as is responsibility and accountability. When law is cheapened and laughed at, what is the cost of one life, or a hundred, or a thousand, or two thousand?

"Look, one of the leaders in the first junta, an admiral, took a fancy to a woman, and quite the beautiful one she still is, but there was the problem of her husband. The man was arrested on a trumped up charge, and shortly afterwards he died in prison. The admiral consoled the widow, his way.

"That was his attitude to a life! Imagine what he was doing financially.

"In Mexico, there's *mordida*, the bite. The person in power, or a position to skim or steal money, has to leave behind at least something more than what he stole. There's some dignity there. Here, the immorality is total and absolute.

"And what is [President Raoul] Alfonsin facing? There is no civic responsibility here.

"When Perón was in power, he was president of the republic, commander-in-chief of the armed forces, and president of the Conference General de Trabajos (CGT), the general labor confederation. When he coughed, the rest of the country coughed with him. He controlled the military, political, and union machinery.

"The other 25 percent of the population...they were the *anti-patrias*, the ones Perón said were oligarchs who were against the country because they were against him. And there had been no unions before Perón. So he created unions. The leaders, they were thugs he put in charge to keep the workers in line.

"Alfonsin has to dismantle the unions and start over. But where do you start? Come, I'll show you something."

At this point Armand jumped up and stormed out into the hallway. He threw open a door facing a catwalk along the side of the building. Two men were working at a telephone cable junction box that looked like a bowl of spaghetti. Wires came in from every direction, some into the box, others to be wrapped in a tangle around it. Armand pointed to the worker using a circuit-testing tool to find out what circuit was what.

"You see that man? If he dies, I'm in trouble, as is every other businessman in the 122 offices in this building. He has been working on this building for sixteen years. He is the only one who knows what's what in our phones."

Armand snorted and pointed to the tangled phone lines as they converged on the junction box from every neighboring building. He turned into the hall and pointed to a wall panel.

"That's where my phones are hooked up. I paid him 100 pesos for a sketch of how it is done. It's survival. You see, the phone company is corrupt. There was a time you could order a phone, and it would be delivered within a half hour. Now you can wait—and it has happened—twenty years!

"So, my landlord, who needs more phone lines, can't get any. He comes in on Saturday and switches the wires. And I come in Sunday and switch them back.

"Look at the sewer system. It was designed and built by the British seventy years ago to serve a city of 3 million. The system hasn't been upgraded. The city is officially 3 million. The officials forget the other 6 million around the city. So there are not enough sewage pipes and plants. But we have one of the finest storm sewer systems in the world...or it was once. Now everyone diverts raw sewage into the drainage system, so there's human waste flowing into the harbor.

"And when it rains, the sewers back up into the drainage system, which can't handle the water, and it floods underground switching stations and short-circuits the phone system. Nothing works and that repairman, poor fellow, he gets sent down there to fix it. The boxes are all corroded and need replacing, so he goes back and puts in a requisition for new parts that goes to purchasing which puts it in a pile and says, 'No!', because they have no money."

Armand re-entered his office and pointed to a window ledge. A phone line came through it.

"I needed an extra line. An influential relative interceded at the phone company. That guy out there came to put it in. He couldn't find a spare line here. So he threw this one from across the street. See?"

He pointed out the source line and sighed.

"Where do we start to sort things out? This country is suffering from forty years of neglect, from corruption. The middle manager who runs the show is corrupt. He takes bribes or bows to pressure to give you a phone and has the repairman running around like crazy. He remains forever. He's the guy you have to shoot, and I'm sorry for the waste of lead.

"And the smart boys who come in to clean things up can't take the strain of working with people like the middle manager. When they get an offer from the World Bank, or Citibank, or whatever, they run.

"So, what happens? Nothing ever gets done, because the one guy at the phone company who does any work, my repairman, is running around dealing with the urgent. The important is always neglected.

"Just look at our history and you'll see our problems. In the last fifty-four years we have had thirty-one presidents of which twenty were from the military, and only one, Perón, completed a term. We've had fifty-six ministers of economy and fifty-two of education.

"Those are our two worst problems—education and the economy. Because ministers have been in the job on average nine months each during the past fifty-four years, there is no real stable infrastructure.

"Look at this building. It was put up in 1932. The wiring conduit is one-inch galvanized steel, the hinges are on ball bearings, the doors are solid wood, everything is top quality. That's the way the country operated in those days. The best!

"Now? The subway was built in the 1920s, and you ride in the original cars. The telephone system? In this building alone, it was designed to meet the demands of, at most, six hundred people. Now, it somehow has to serve the six thousand who work here.

"And inflation? The pensioner in this country is kaput. Many of them, the ones who don't have families, live together, and they live like animals. The others, they live with their families. That's one way to fight inflation, if all family members live and work together for a common goal.

"But look at our education system. The system is universally free and available, but 40 percent of our children don't finish primary school. They have to go to work to help support the family, and without an education they have no real future. And 70 percent of the secondary school students don't complete their schooling—more who end up on the junk pile. Ultimately, only 5 percent of all university students complete their education.

"Then, the ones with brains and talent leave, because there is no opportunity for them here. The world is full of Argentine technicians and mechanics and scientists and researchers. They leave because there is no investment here in building the country and the economy, so they aren't needed.

"Instead 50, maybe 60 percent of the economy is underground, and the greatest minds in Argentina are the financial ones.

"And yet, this is a wealthy country, rich in raw materials and human resources. The people of this country, when they have a sense of direction, can stand shoulder to shoulder with the people of any industrialized country in the world. There's no drug problem here, no alcohol problem. We never, at the worst in our history, had the kind of human rights monstrosities that occurred in the past seven years. That in itself is real evidence of the decline.

"But now we have democracy, and it has brought freedom, but it is a freedom without responsibility. It's some sort of magic, and Alfonsin is going to perform miracles. Here it is, sixty, seventy days since he took office, and already people grumble that nothing has changed. They think that thirty years of damage can be repaired overnight.

"And Alfonsin is committed to economic growth of 4 percent and real salary increases of 10 percent. He's going to reduce inefficiency, reduce the deficit, and reduce inflation to 100 percent by the end of 1984. And he's going to do this without sacrifices, without unemployment, without imposing monetary and fiscal restraints!

"Hah! We have $45 billion in foreign debts. No foreign reserves. No credit. No credibility. He wants to turn the clock back to a time when Argentina could go its own way, selling grain and beef to the world, and being left alone.

"Maybe someday, but not now. Our freedom is precarious. His policies might work; more likely the troubles will start again but not from the military. It will be organized, violent, destructive rioting orchestrated by the Perónists.

"Yes, it is almost like the conditions before the Spanish Civil War. But we have a saying here, why Franco could keep the peace in Spain and how Perón kept it here: Franco had 2 million *muertes* (dead ones) behind him; Perón had 2 million *vivos* (live ones) behind him. But *vivos* is also slang here for wise guys, thugs, toughs, the kind of people that would break your arm so you would see things Perón's way.

"So Alfonsin has his hands full. He has to change things, but his talk is unrealistic. He must tell the truth, but he must also act upon the truth. You preach with example, and you speak with moral authority.

"And that is the biggest problem here now. Not the inflation, or anything else, that's all an outgrowth.... The real problem is that everyone is lying here. Mostly to himself, then to you and me, then to the world.

"You talk about beggars here. It starts on the street with the beggar. He's lying. The guy in trouble doesn't have time to beg, he's looking for work.

"Businessmen are afraid to talk about real costs; they're worried about price controls.

"The government is afraid to face the truth and tell the people the truth.

"Demagoguery is so entrenched, honesty is looked upon as foolishness.

"Everyone is hiding something, living in shame, because, despite the inflation, life is good, and they're doing it with tax evasion and black money. And the unions say there are 2 million unemployed out of 5 million. Yes, people are poor, but no one is starving. But where is all the crime, the violence? This is still one of the safest cities in the world in which to walk the streets without fearing for your life, except from traffic.

"Everyone is lying to themselves and others. We live a fantasy here. Like the guy who buys a new car, but never drives it to work, for fear his boss will see it and wonder how he can afford a car on what he is paid.

"Oh yes, it has been hard to be an Argentine in the last few years. Consider the individual moral costs of inflation.

"In March of 1976 inflation that month was 50 percent. Compounded annually that's 17,000 percent per annum. That is mind numbing. So you develop a thick skin. You don't care. You enjoy what you have while it lasts. But once in a while, you look at your children and wonder what kind of country you're going to leave them. I don't want my children to grow up like this, to inherit this madness.

"I'm fifty-five years old. For twenty years I have resisted offers from my parent company to move to the head office in North America. Argentina is, after all, my home. But now, for the first time in all these years, I'm seriously considering the latest offer.

"But where do I go? Canada? You think things are so perfect there? You think what happened here couldn't happen there or the United States. My business takes me there often. What about the new poor, the ones who lost everything in the recession? Or the ghetto dwellers in the United States. All it would take is someone who is totally corrupt and can mobilize them politically, so he can get into power. It doesn't take much, just a lot of unhappy people and someone who listens to them."

Four hours had passed by this point. Armand checked his watch and apologized profusely. "I'm sorry for taking so much of your time. But if anything, this was better than going to a psychiatrist. I didn't have to lie down, and it was free."

There's a story told in Buenos Aires about the young boy who comes home from school and talks with his father.

"Papa, what is ethics?"

"Ethics? Why it is...." The father screwed up his face and thought for a moment. "You are a partner in a leather shop on Florida. A man comes in and buys a suitcase. He pays and leaves and forgets his wallet, full of money, on the counter...."

Eagerly his son broke in. "And ethics is returning the wallet with the money when the man comes looking for it?"

"No, no, no," the father said, looking sadly at his son and wondering if the boy would ever learn anything on his own. "Ethics is whether you tell your partner about the wallet."

There's another story told in Buenos Aires about the couple who, each payday, split up the husband's pay packet and go shopping. Nothing unusual there, except they go shopping with walkie talkies and are in constant contact, to ensure they get the best prices.

They do it this way because comparison shopping on the North American model just doesn't work in Argentina. Prices change radically and drastically from month to month. An inflationary environment of 440 percent per annum averages out to 36.6 percent per month, a figure which applies as brutally to income erosion as it does to price erosion.

So, if a merchant puts an item on his shelf on January 1, priced at 120 pesos, against his purchase price of 80 pesos, and inflation in January averages 37 percent, he has to raise his February selling price on that item by a minimum of 37 percent to 164.40 pesos. But he adds in a bit, as a hedge against the coming month's inflation. This way, when he sells the item, he makes a profit and earns enough money to pay the replacement price of new stock. And the figure simply builds and compounds.

"But it gets crazy," says one foreign business person located in Buenos Aires. "There have actually been days when I've tried to buy something, and the shopkeeper won't sell it until he gets the new manufacturer's price list for the coming month so he can confirm costs. He would rather lose the sale than lose money."

This method of setting prices can result in some wild variations in pricing. If, for example, a merchant bought a large quantity of item X in August, and still has a sizable number of Xs, he'll have stock priced at an August cost base. Someone in a new shop, or who only recently picked up that item for sale in his shop, would have stock bought in December, four months later, and his prices will work on a different cost base. So, the same item might vary in overall price between two shops by as much as 20 percent.

This doesn't make comparison shopping easy, which is why the couple shops with walkie talkies—deals seen become sales made immediately. This economic environment makes Argentine attitudes seem like nothing but rampant consumption.

"If you see something you like and you want it, you get it today. You don't wait for tomorrow," explains one Argentine-born senior administrator in the local division of a multinational corporation.

"I've waited for tomorrow and seen prices double! I saw a tie I wanted, I didn't have the time, and I said I would get it next week, and next week it was twice the price. Here," he tapped his head, "you have a calculating machine here, and no matter what you are doing when you walk around, you are pricing, in pesos and dollars, keeping a tally. When you see something that was $250 that is now $128 U.S., because of exchange differentials or sudden devaluations, buy it! Even on credit. Especially on credit."

The credit system is called the bicycle. As one financial whiz—in a country where it's easy to think there are 28 million financial wizards—described it: "You're constantly pedaling it, trying to throw payments out ahead of time so that, when you pay them, your cost is less than if you paid cash for the item today."

If the consumer side of business in Argentina is a simple case of buying when the price is right, and buying on credit while getting the maximum payback period possible, the management side of business is somewhat more complex.

For one thing, the merchant selling on credit, or accepting credit cards, is adding 15 percent to his prices to cover the erosion his revenue will suffer from the date of acceptance of the card to the date of payment of the bill. Cash commands a 10 or 15 percent discount.

Management of Argentine big business, however, is a convoluted affair that appears to be a sophisticated refinement of the art of management and cost accounting to compensate for hyperinflation. In fact, it's like a downhill race against an avalanche, a frantic race to keep ahead. It simply protects a capital base from erosion and tries to get a decent return.

When you first come to Buenos Aires on business and contact embassy trade officials or any foreign business people living in Argentina, they say: "Watch the velocity of money here. It will have your head spinning in no time."

It's a confusing kind of warning, because North Americans don't generally think in terms of the velocity of money—the number of times and the speed at which money moves through the economy. Money simply changes hands, and everyone seems happy. In Argentina, an inflation rate almost one hundred times that of North America means Argentines have to think one hundred times faster than North Americans to maintain their capital base. Argentines also have to move money around a lot faster, and it has to change hands a lot more often if it is to retain its purchasing power and contribute to the growth of the gross national product.

Ernesto is thirty. Technically he's a criminal—a black market currency trader. A year ago, when the economy was open and currency trading was freely allowed through the legally sanctioned exchange houses, he was a prosperous businessman. Now that currency controls have been reinstated, he's still a prosperous businessman, but his business operates differently.

"If you walk in my front door and I do not know you and you are Argentine and you want to buy American dollars, I will sell them to you at the official rate and with much paper work." He tosses samples on the desk. "But, if you come in and I know you or you are a foreigner," he shrugs, "we can do business. No trouble, no paperwork, but much different rates of exchange."

So if someone has referred you to Ernesto, you go in and introduce yourself.

"I have dollars to trade. What's the rate?"

"Forty pesos."

"Okay, I'll be back in an hour."

"It may be different then."

"In an hour?"

"Señor, there are days when the quote changes every thirty minutes. One day last week, the busiest ever, it changed thirty-six times."

"But how do you set the price?"

"It is offer and demand, the only true free market. Many of us, we talk, we negotiate, we set prices."

Ernesto freely admits that people on the black market make too much money. But he shrugs off the windfall nature of black market profits and wealth. "In 1979, 1980, and 1981 there was free exchange, and I made a good living, but the risks are twenty times what they were before."

There are legal ways to get money out of Argentina, but they're strictly controlled by the government. There are also illegal ways, and they're somewhat expensive. Both methods of transferring money can be arranged through the exchange houses.

If an Argentine wants to get money out of the country, officially or unofficially, he brings it to someone like Ernesto. He accepts dollars, pesos, marks, pounds—it doesn't matter: money is money.

"Then, I call my banker in New York and ask him to take the equivalent amount in U.S. dollars from my account and credit it to my client's account. The client feels secure, so he is happy. I make profit; my banker is happy. Everyone is happy, including the Central Bank, as long as they do not know what we have done." He sits back in his chair. "They know it is being done, but they do not know when, or for whom, I am doing it. And many times," he laughs cynically, "they help me do it...for a price." He rubs his fingers together and smiles cynically. "It is *acomodación*...ah, accommodation? Si. Accommodation."

Moving up the scale of business, the picture becomes even more complex. In North America these days the stars of the business world are the entrepreneurs. Business people want to know how they do what they do. What are the secrets of their success? How do they attract capital, and then how do they make money grow?

In Argentina, the stars of business are the accountants, the brightest of whom become corporate controllers. As corporate controllers they wield as much power as the president of a North American corporation.

At forty-two Juan is at the top of the world, or at least the world that his company, which does $200 million U.S. annually, has staked out. When he comes in to work each morning, he is at the very center of every flow of corporate information, each senior analysis session, and all decision-making processes. In fact, he tends to make the real decisions about the most critical factor in the company's financial health: Where to put cash reserves and surpluses to ensure that, when needed, they have held their purchasing power?

"It works this way. I have certain physical assets to work with. They do not lose their value. But money, at 36 percent monthly erosion...." He throws his hands up in disgust. "We must compensate for last month's erosion in the coming month. But we are still looking for our profit. And we cannot leave money idle or it loses its value."

So what happens is that Juan is examining, on a daily basis, every piece of information. If it appears most attractive to put every available penny into raw materials, that's where it goes, and perhaps money will be borrowed to buy more. But, while the price is being negotiated and a decision seems some days away, he'll put the surplus into a three-day term deposit at 148 percent. And, even when it matures, there's still a day or two of lead time until the irrevocable letter of credit can be drawn to pay for the materials, so maybe the money will be rolled over into another three-day term.

There's always the possibility of taking some of that currency and looking for quick profits in the currencies game. Most business people will deny they ever do that sort of thing. Armand, the banker, and certain of his colleagues in the national and international banking community slough off corporate protestations of honesty with cynical laughter.

"If only we could mention the name of the two multi-nationals that each made $25 million profit here in the last few years on currency speculation," Armand sighs. "Their currency dealings made more profit than their operations did, and one of them then closed its plant, throwing hundreds of workers out of jobs, and left the country."

While Juan looks at where to put money, he also has to examine pricing adjustments to accommodate the new prices of the raw materials. He has to plan salary adjustments for the non-unionized staff. They don't get government-directed indexed salary settlements the way wage-earning employees do. He has to keep track of import restrictions and currency regulations, any government schemes to allow for conversion of American dollar loans into peso loans to take the strain off foreign exchange reserves, transfers to the parent company, or loans from the parent company, and resolution of accounts—all done with compensation for 36 percent erosion.

The pace would wear out a North American workaholic, but the Argentine has lived with it all his life.

Juan pulls out a pad of paper and begins sketching. "We budget here, make no mistake about that, but it is a guideline because our inflation in one month is the same as some countries have in one year."

The result is: at the end of each month, the average Argentine corporation undergoes an accounting exercise that North American companies perform each year; at the end of each week, the average Argentine corporation undergoes an accounting exercise that North American companies perform quarterly; at the end of each day, the average Argentine corporation performs as many financial operations and resolutions as North American companies perform monthly.

"Remember, this is a big game where there are winners and losers," explains another Argentine business person. "And we want to be winners. That is why we have to move so fast. If people are not on the ball, they can lose, and they can be wiped out quickly."

From the time an Argentine business person makes a wrong

decision to the time the business has to close its doors is, minimum, thirty days, maximum, sixty days.

Antonio, an Argentine banker, leans back in his chair and thoughtfully blows a smoke ring. He sits up and fiddles with his cigarette pack. "You see, it is like this. The government announces that inflation last month was 20 percent, and next month it will be 16 percent. Well they originally predicted 14 percent for last month, so they were wrong by 6 percent. The businessman says 'they were wrong by 6 percent, and I believed them and made a 2 percent error, so I have to raise next month's prices 16 percent, plus the 2 I was wrong, plus the 6 the government is surely off, so that's a 24 percent jump.' But if the government is off again, he is falling behind too quickly, running and losing speed, to catch up to inflation, which is picking up speed. He must shut his doors. End of business."

The essence of Argentina is at once exhilarating and frightening, exciting and debilitating. The fact that the country is trying to drag itself back to a semblance of freedom in the face of a fascist tradition is a fascinating exercise to observe. You want to help the Argentines who, individually, are open, friendly, gracious, and energetic.

And it is easy to marvel at Argentina, a country in an unique and enviable situation. It has abundant agricultural resources, and output could be tripled or quintupled with no strain on the land or manpower.

It has great reserves of natural gas, is almost totally self-sufficient in oil, is rapidly developing its already extensive hydro-electric power sources, and has invested heavily in the future of nuclear-generated electricity. The geography provides every type of climate from tropic to antarctic, and the Argentine prairies—the Gran Chaco and the pampas—are respectively, as Argentines wryly observe, incredibly fertile and fertile. Argentina has some of the best, most productive land in the world.

To top it all off, by South American standards, Argentina is underpopulated, is not experiencing explosive growth, has relatively low unemployment, and has a relatively high literacy rate.

Its problems are straightforward. For years a regime—not political, but psychological and social—of corruption ruled and made corruption the norm. This corruption of all levels of Argentine society had its price—a government that spent the national wealth feeding a myth, created during the Perón years, that Argentines had a special place in the sun and didn't have to work for it.

The price was paid by a government that in 1983 printed 68 out of every 100 pesos it spent, meaning that 68 percent of government spending was done with worthless paper. The rest was revenue from what was laughably called government tax collection.

The money the government spent bailed out inefficient industries or went towards social spending or a military too large and preoccupied with expensive armaments and a pointless war. It was money that ended up in the pockets of graft artists and *piolas*, skimmers who demanded payoffs or diverted monies intended for one purpose into their own bank accounts.

The money was spent wastefully, inefficiently, and added nothing to the economic welfare of the country. To add a further measure of economic insanity, the situation was worsened by foreign borrowing that resulted in a $45 billion foreign debt, a good quarter of which is estimated by the government to have been skimmed and deposited in foreign currency accounts in the United States, Paris, Switzerland, and various tax havens around the world.

Alonzo is twenty-four years old. When he speaks about opportunities the future holds for him in Argentina, he speaks in a manner that is disconcertingly common to many people you meet there: He talks about the opportunities Argentina offers him *to get out*.

Though Argentine-born, and a citizen, he spent his childhood, boyhood, and early teens in the United States. He wants to go back. "At least there, even when it's tough, if you're ready to work, you can get ahead, earn, make things happen for you," he says, almost wistfully. "Here too you can get anything you want, but it's too hard. It costs you the work of a lifetime."

To explain, he spoke of his desire to own a car. "I make 5,700 pesos ($204 U.S.) a month. It costs me almost that much to live, and I live at home. In the U.S., with the skills I have, I could make enough to live well and buy a good, late-model car on a couple months salary. Here a twenty-year-old Ford Falcon would cost me 40,000 pesos ($1,429 U.S.) and an even older Fiat would cost more. That's eight months earnings for me, if I could put that away. And to borrow? No way. Not at 20 percent a month. I would be paying the rest of my life."

As Alonzo sees it, a person with ambition has no chance, unless he has a second job, and Alonzo has experienced the two-job life. He's been putting away American dollars against the day when he goes to the United States. Because of restrictions on buying and holding dollars in excess of certain amounts, and because he didn't want it on the record that he has American dollars (in case the government might decide to expropriate them) he bought most of them illegally. And he needed a second job to have the spare money to buy dollars, legal or otherwise.

"I finally quit. But do you know what kind of life that is? It's no kind of life! I would be up at 6:00 A.M. to go on shift at my second job at 8:00 and work until 3:00 P.M., then I would go to my main job at 3:30 and work until 11:00 P.M. and be home by midnight, maybe 12:30. You call that living?" He shakes his head angrily. "I couldn't even see a doctor if I got sick."

Alonzo admits that maybe he has a distorted memory of the United States that colors his feelings about Argentina, or maybe vice versa. "After all, I did return here when I was about fourteen, so my attitudes had been formed in the States." He shrugged. "Maybe I don't fit in with the mentality here, even if it has a lot more to offer in the way of living. But the problem is that, once you work hard all your life to build something, at the end you don't have anything to show for it. You have to go outside and earn money to invest when you come back. But even then it isn't safe, the way the government devalues the currency whenever it feels it has to."

When asked about investments, Argentines point to two items first: land and American dollars.

"Dollars, because they're fluid and easily exchanged," said one businessman in an observation that was echoed by everyone else who answered the question. The rationale goes back to the three ideas of what money represents: placeholder, means of exchange, and repository of value. In Argentina, by law, the means of exchange is the peso, but it does not retain value. Nor is the peso much of a placeholder, because it inflates so rapidly. For example, before the spring 1983 devaluation, the prettiest Argentine banknote—1,000,000 pesos—would buy five packs of cigarettes of indifferent quality.

After devaluation, the 1,000,000-peso note became a 100-peso note and would still buy those five packs of cigarettes. Rather than call in the currency on one day or during a particular period to replace the notes, the government left the old notes in circulation and just fed the new ones into the economy while bleeding off the old ones. This left a large amount of currency circulating, actually fueling the inflation rate.

(One similar historical experience of devaluation that effectively capped inflation occurred in Japan at the end of the Second World War. Fiscal authorities decreed that on a particular day all old yen notes were to be exchanged for new ones, and from that day old yen would not be negotiable as currency. The limited supply of currency choked off spending and forestalled inflation in the scramble by Japanese to buy what they could in the wake of the country's defeat and collapsing economy.)

So the dollar immediately springs to the minds of people in all levels of Argentine society as the safest investment. But even then Argentines are cynical. They ride the investment of the moment.

"In the early 1970s they bought Swiss francs, then later gold," says Ernesto, the black marketeer. "But when you have to run, gold is heavy, so it is on deposit in Switzerland, or Uruguay. Now it is dollars. Tomorrow, who knows?"

Property is seen as the real investment for those who can afford it. "But it has its problems," points out one banker.

"First, it's registered with government, liable to taxes and all. And it isn't fluid, not in this economy. Prices and interest rates have gone so high, unless you already own property, stand to inherit, or are filthy rich, you have no chance of owning. And rents to Argentines are controlled, so there's no profit in renting unless you rent to a foreigner."

The tradition amongst the more affluent residents of Buenos Aires has always been to own a large family apartment and several other ones as rental properties. Perhaps the most telling sign that hyperinflation takes its toll, even on the propertied middle and upper class, is that people are moving into their lesser apartments and renting their prime properties to foreigners at high rents, quoted and paid in foreign currencies.

In the list of investments, antiques, art, coins, and stamps have prominent places, but only among the upper classes and only among the knowledgeable.

Ultimately, the answer to survival in Argentina's hyperinflationary environment is heard in one loud, long chorus of "give me American dollars." At least they're stable and hold their value. For the time being.

———∿∿∿———

Chapter 11

ONCE BITTEN, TWICE SHY

ARRIVE IN MEXICO CITY early on a Sunday morning, when the interminable din, clatter, and congestion that passes for traffic has been switched off. For a few hours that day the pollution count lowers enough that Mexico City can be seen through a gauzy haze, rather than an oppressive smog.

The drive into the city from Benito Juárez Airport will awaken even the most exhausted traveler. The Valley of Mexico is ringed by mountains draped with snow that will bring tears to the eyes of anyone who lives in the shadows of the Rockies and is recovering from the disorienting view of Argentina's flat pampas.

To get to where you can appreciate the sight, however, you have to make it out of the airport. The most convenient method is a Setta bus to your hotel. But first, a side trip to have some money changed. Watch while the clerk shortchanges you.

"Uh, that's 200 pesos short."

"Tax!" the clerk snarls.

Now the thing is, they'll skin a *turista* for all they can in Mexico City, but it's one of the few places in this world where the banking system still doesn't charge tax or commission to cash, or exchange, a foreign-currency traveler's cheque. But, for a buck and a half at 7:00 A.M. after a ten-hour flight, why bother arguing? But pause and look back as you walk away. The clerk pockets the 200 pesos.

The Setta desk is fifty meters down the concourse, through a pair of glass doors. Just beyond are chromed-steel security barriers, upright steel posts set one foot apart in the sidewalk. On the other side of the barrier are Setta's red VW microbuses.

The ticket is 1,100 pesos. While money changes hands, the driver grabs the handle of the "wheels"—the little fold-up baggage-handling contraption carrying one typewriter and a two-foot-wide bag packed for a trip that goes from sub-zero to tropical climes and back. The grunting and groaning draw the new arrival's attention away from the ticket booth to the driver trying to drag the two-foot wide load through the one-foot space between the barrier posts. Before anything can be said, another driver helps him lift the whole affair over the barrier and into the microbus. A bent wheel hangs forlornly at a new, but definitely not improved, angle.

Later, the microbus pulls up in front of the hotel. The driver insists on taking in the baggage. By the time he deposits it on the floor at reception, the support bar has been ripped out of its mounting, the handle has been pulled off, and the wheel is broken. And he's hanging around, smiling toothily, waiting for a tip.

Those wheels survived cabbies, impatient bus drivers, hotel attendants, and the streets of Amsterdam, Paris, Rome, Tel Aviv, Madrid, and Buenos Aires. This guy has managed to have them in his hands for a total of two minutes and they're a mangled wreck. And he wants a tip!? Fat chance!

At the desk, the clerk asks if the new arrival has a reservation.

"Yes. It was made ten weeks ago and confirmed last week."

"Were you to arrive last night or this morning?"

"This morning."

"No, I cannot find it. But it is all right, Señor, we have a room for you anyway."

"How kind of you. Could you check for any mail for me, please."

"No need, Señor, I checked only one hour ago. I would have

remembered your name. Maybe they no longer love you at home?"

He laughs at his little joke. (Two days later, the same clerk produces a letter time-stamped as having arrived at the hotel three days before the guest did.)

In his room, exhausted, the traveler shuts the drapes, glumly tosses the mangled remains of his wheels in a corner, and turns down the bed. It's 8:00 A.M. He undresses and climbs wearily under the covers. Blessed sleep takes over.

The ringing of a phone is a rasp drawn over already frayed nerve ends! Who the hell is calling in the middle of the…? Confused, he peers at his watch…day! Right, who's calling at 2:00 P.M.?

"This is housekeeping. When will you leave your room, so we can make your bed?"

"I was asleep. I'm still in it. Don't make the bed. I want to go back to sleep."

"I am sorry, Señor, we must make the bed."

"I just want to sleep. Forget the bed."

"I am sorry, we cannot do that."

"Why?"

"Because we must make the bed."

The logic is inescapable. Ridiculous, but inescapable.

"Give me a half hour. Uh, it's okay if I take a shower, isn't it?"

"Of course, Señor. You are our guest."

The television doesn't work properly. The desk clerk is told on day two of the guest's stay. "Right away, Señor. Someone will be up to fix it within a half hour."

A small self-service bar in the room is stocked with soft drinks, hard drinks, bottled water, ice, snacks, and cigarettes. When the people in charge unlock the bar, the ice tray is frozen into the freezer by an inch of ice. Complaints are registered. Promises are made. A week later, the guest checks out. The television still isn't working, the ice tray still is locked in by an inch of ice, and the guest is presented with a bill for cigarettes he hasn't smoked.

On the third day of his visit, the guest sends a telegram home through the hotel giving details of his arrival. That evening, during a long-distance phone call from home, he hears: "…and all I got was your greeting, a garbled line, a date, another garbled line, your name, and your address in Mexico City."

In the hotel coffee shop, a grinning Boston doctor says, "If I didn't have to come down here to settle up an investment that got frozen in 1982, I wouldn't be here. This is my fourth visit to Mexico and, for every story you have, I've got a few more. I have no patience with this place."

In a business office across town, as an interview is ending, the writer is asked, "So tell me, how are you getting along in Mexico City?"

"Well, I find it a bit frustrating. I'm trying not to judge by Canadian or American standards, but I keep wondering how things get done here? How you manage to make things work?"

"Hah. Often, nothing works until *la mordida*—the bite—is taken. Then anything is possible. But only if you have the money. If you don't have the money…. Well, frustration is free."

La mordida is the lubricant that makes the wheels of business, industry, government, and life in Mexico move. In plain English it means graft. In its most common form it is money, but it can also take the shape of goods or services. Its most common characteristic is that it can make things that were impossible to move suddenly go. Like justice.

—————❧❧❧—————

199

Chapter 12

MEXICO: MAÑANA REPUBLIC

MEXICO CITY is situated about 2260 meters or 7,400 feet above sea level in the Valley of Mexico which slushes through on the central Mexican plateau. The city is a sprawling metropolis with a population estimated officially at about 10 million and unofficially (probably more accurately) between 16 and 18 million. Known as Mexico City D.F. (Federal District), the city is the national capital, the hub of the country's political, cultural, agricultural, and industrial activities.

To the north and west of the city are the pyramids of San Juan Teotihuacán, remains of the Toltec civilization, which abandoned the site between 700 and 900 A.D., when the migrations of the Chichimecs, a warlike tribe new to the Valley of Mexico, forced them to move north. Before leaving, the Toltecs buried Teotihuacán. Until 1909, when the area was excavated, two mounds dominating the site were believed to be just another pair of hills in the valley. During the excavation two pyramids, temples, and a road were uncovered and have since been restored.

Though there are tunnels and chambers in the pyramids, they weren't built as monumental tombs as were the Pyramids of Gizeh in Egypt. These Toltec pyramids were the foundations upon which temples were built.

The squat 150-foot high Pyramid of the Moon broods over Teotihuacán's main road, the Avenue of the Dead, staring straight down its cobbled surface. The avenue, lined by short, flat-topped open temples, runs to the 210-foot tall Pyramid of the Sun, which stands at right angles to the road. The original road ran on for miles, but only a portion of it has been restored.

Teotihuacán is about an hour's drive from Mexico City. The brave (maybe foolhardy) will rent a car and drive. Friendly Mexicans will warn you, however, that you might get lost, and there are *barrios*, neighborhoods, in Mexico City that should only be visited by foreigners in armored cars. The venturesome take special buses to the site. Friendly Mexicans also warn you to watch out for the pickpockets who cruise the Mexico City transit system.

The weary traveler who wants to let someone else take care of the arrangements will forego the inverse snobbery of not wanting to behave like a tourist and book into a guided tour. Chances are you'll be booked into a small group of half a dozen or so traveling in a red VW microbus. The driver/guide will take you the long way around to the pyramids, showing certain sites of the city and environs while trying to avoid the slums. It's hard to do; the slums are everywhere on the edges of the city. So the guide drives with his foot to the floorboards, trying to get past the slums quickly, which makes the ride a white-knuckle special: You grab on to anything solid in the vehicle and pray you'll reach your destination alive.

Despite the driver's attempts to approximate a rapid transit system, his passengers sometimes manage to see the realities of Mexico City.

"What's that?" a nervous woman from Washington state asked her companions as she stared out the van window at a motley collection of crude huts and shacks made of tarpaper, tin, and bits of salvaged wood.

"A slum," a New Yorker replied laconically.

"Oh," said the woman, staring intently. "People actually live there?"

"If you call that living," the New Yorker replied.

"Did you see that?" the woman asked indignantly, shaking her head and staring in wide-eyed wonderment at the truck that had barely missed running into the van. It is, after all, amazing to see the way Mexicans manage to fit three lanes of traffic onto a two-lane roadway.

"It is nothing," laughed Manuel, the guide.

"Nothing!?" the woman demanded. "I've been here three days, and most of the cars I've seen look like wrecks. Accidents must happen all the time."

"Many accidents, yes," shrugged Manuel. "Everyone is in such a hurry."

"Doesn't it make you afraid?" she demanded.

"Driving here," Manuel shrugged again, "is like politics. If it looks like you will have an accident, you cover your eyes. If you are not hit, it did not happen. And it was not going to. So why worry?"

"Does that mean you only see what you want to see?"

"Sí!"

Sunday in Mexico City is a lazy day, honored by Mexicans for religious reasons. It also happens to be the only day of the week they don't have to work. Sunday is a day to visit friends and family, drift off to the bullfights, stroll in parks such as Chapultepec Park (also a national shrine), or listen dreamily to band concerts in Alameda Park on Avenue Juárez, a ten-minute walk from the Plaza de la Constitución.

The rest of the time Mexico City teems with life. People are always on the move, going somewhere, rushing about, noisily moving from point to point, honking horns, bashing fenders, hawking wares. But no matter how much Mexicans rush to get where they're going, they're either losing ground, or arriving to find out whatever they came for isn't there, or worse, is there but slips from their grasp much too easily.

One Mexican, an American-trained accountant, explained it one day when he helped a confused visitor puzzling over a map of the city. He pointed out the visitor's destination, shouting over the din of car horns, racing engines, and grinding gears.

"Is it always like this . . . a noisy rush?" the visitor asked.

"Yeah."

"Why?"

"It's a rat race," the accountant grimaced. "And everyone wants to be number one rat." He paused to eye a feature unique to Mexico City, the low-flying white Volkswagen Beetle taxi cab. "The thing is, though," he shouted, "even if you get to the front and win, you're still a rat."

Mexico City is a city of marked contrasts—Spanish colonial, moorish, Mediterranean, rococo, baroque, art deco, ultra-modern, slum and shanty architecture (though the slums are only allowed to flourish where they aren't in plain view).

Walk through Chapultepec Park, and a rat the size of a large kitten scurries across your path. Look at the sky through pollution-reddened eyes, and it's a gray haze of smog from vehicles unencumbered by pollution control devices. The middle class rub shoulders with the urban poor.

And, though everything is costly, everything is spiritually cheap.

Walk out of your hotel at 11:00 P.M. and stand on the stoop for a quick look at Avenue Juárez, Alameda Park, and especially the marble and gilt Juárez Memorial under light, and a shill will offer you a cab. Refuse, and he'll offer "a girl, Señor?" Before you can answer, he'll look you up and down and say, "No, for you, something special. Two girls, Señor!" Refuse again and he'll offer you a boy, or anything else that strikes your fancy.

Survival is such a cunning word; it implies a whole set of sliding moral values. The closer you are to the edge, the broader the scope of acceptable behavior. Once the slide begins, the skids get greasier, and it's a downhill run at an ever-increasing pace that's virtually impossible to slow down, let alone stop.

So, walk the streets any time during the day right through to late evening, and harness your own cynicism at sight of the beggars. They've been a common sight for weeks now, and we know they're all fakes and flakes. They put on interesting shows—like the "Tiny Tim" beggar. Mama has her hand out, while a little boy bops around on his crutches. Or there are the "kneebiters," little girls that kneel with Mama, hands out; when you pass by, they jump up and prance about in front of you, hands out as you try to walk down the sidewalk without stumbling over them. Suddenly, as if they had run into a glass wall, they stop in their tracks, shrug, and prance back to Mama. You look back, knowingly, and watch as they repeat the performance, stopping at exactly the same spot. Well trained. They're all alike.

But you look a bit closer. The eyes don't look right. The pride has been starved out of them. Naw, can't be. There's no such thing as a real beggar.

They crouch forlornly on the sidewalks of Mexico City, and look pitiful and wretched, despair etched into their faces. Naw, it's just an act.

C'mon, these are the organized poor, right? Like Rome and Buenos Aires. These aren't really poor people. They don't exist; this is the twentieth century. This is Mexico, part of North America, the richest continent in the world. They're just professional beggars, right?

A foreign banker whose busiest moments are spent trying to salvage something from his bank's exposure with Mexican debt, corporate and government, looks pensively out the window of his office.

"They're real," he announces quietly. "But they're used to it. They never knew anything else, so they don't complain. Life never changes for the really poor in Mexico. But you know what the real problem here is?" He doesn't wait for an answer. "The middle class. They're the ones who are really suffering. They keep getting a taste of the good life, then it gets taken away. They get slapped down and become the new urban poor. They're the ones that frighten me."

At the end of Paseo de la Reforma, the broad tree-lined avenue that cuts through downtown Mexico City, is Chapultepec Park. At the entrance, just near the foot of Chapultepec Hill, are six marble shafts, stylized flaming torches set in a semicircle around a small plaza.

The torches represent the boy heroes, six cadets who in 1847 wrapped themselves in Mexican flags and jumped off the ramparts of Chapultepec Palace rather than surrender to attacking U.S. marines. Statues around the palace and brass plates in the walls where each one jumped commemorate the actions of these six young nationalists in defying the *Gringos*, a word thought to be a perversion of "green coats," which is the tunic the Marines wore.

The palace was originally built for colonial administrators during the 1780s and was used as a military academy during the early republic. The building was renovated to house the ill-fated French-installed Hapsburg emperor, Maximilian, between 1864 and 1867, after which it was the presidential palace until the 1940s. Chapultepec Palace now houses Mexico's Museum of National History.

From entrance to exit, the museum is set up in chronological order, from the arrival of the *conquistadores* to the present. While celebrating the heroes of the hard-won Mexican republic, the museum inadvertently recounts the history of the Mexican middle class.

Unlike traditional middle classes, which were entrepreneurial and administrative and developed as a side effect of industrialization, the Mexican middle class was allowed to develop by a government that needed a middle class to aid in developing the country. Members weren't brought up to expect that, through hard work, dedication, and perseverance, they could save, accumulate things, and build a financially secure future. Instead, in the early 1800s, the best and brightest of the mass of peasants were educated to become the middle class.

Political influence, however, escaped the Mexican middle class. The odd exceptional one reached dizzying heights of achievement—such as Benito Juárez, an Indian boy from a small village who became a lawyer and the rallying point for liberal Mexican republicanism. In 1855 he helped overthrow the dictatorship of General Santa Anna (remember the Alamo?) and set limits on the powers of the church and army in Mexico.

Juárez led liberal forces during the civil war known as the War of Reform. As president from 1857 to 1865 and 1867 to 1872, he was instrumental in shifting power from the control of the Creoles, pure-blood Spanish Mexicans, to a broader base, including the Mestizos (mixed Spanish and Indian) and Indian Mexicans. He also led the Mexican resistance against the French-supported Maximilian.

Overall, however, the theory that the middle class had a bright future was the social myth that kept the middle class working, shoulders to the wheel, noses to the grindstone; their noses were kept clean, and out of politics, so the leaders—after Juárez invariably military dictators who ruled for the benefit of the landed gentry—could rule with impunity. Because they had the most to lose during troubled times, the middle class could always be counted upon to work to maintain political stability.

That's what makes the mural about the dictatorships of Porfirio Díaz (1876–1911) and Francisco Madero (1911–13) so poignant. What stands out is one scene in which a peasant, a *campesino*, is being executed. The landed gentry, looking rather piggish, hovers discreetly in the background, a soldier guards the scene, and a wolfish-looking functionary, representing the middle class, directs the execution.

It was the sad fate of the middle class to be the functionaries of government, administrative intermediaries between the rulers and the rest of the ruled. When the shooting started during the many post-Juárez uprisings, the middle class were the first targets of the revolutionaries. They were also the ones whose wealth and property was expropriated whenever someone with the power to take it decided he needed or wanted it.

Nothing has changed much for the Mexican middle class, whose fortunes have risen and fallen throughout the history of post-colonial Mexico (1815 to the present). The pattern has been to get ahead, lose most of what has been accumulated, then start over. In the short-run the economic events of the 1970s most benefited Mexico's middle class. In the long run when the boom went bust, the Mexican middle class also lost the most.

"I used to know a banker," muses Denis, a Belgian-born Mexican businessman. "In 1979 he was earning the peso equivalent of $75,000 U.S. a year, plus two cars, plus I don't know what other benefits. Since that time, he has moved up in the bank. He has a higher position, he still has his two cars, one of them new, and I calculated that his peso income in U.S. dollars is $23,000. He is a good example of the middle class. Where has he gone? He has gone upward to nowhere.''

In 1929, after years of revolution and civil strife following Francisco Madero's assassination, the National Revolutionary Party was established, took power, and ruled under the authority of the Constitution of the United States of Mexico. Renamed the Institutional Revolutionary Party (PRI) in 1946, the party has ruled Mexico virtually unchallenged since 1929.

Mexico operates under a form of republican democracy that could be called a constitutional presidency, managed from the top down. This means that the republic is structured with an elected congress, a judiciary, and the presidency. Unlike the American republic, where Congress, the judiciary, the presidency, all act as checks and balances on each other, the Mexican president has nominal, but no effective checks and balances on his power except, perhaps, influential PRI advisors and power-brokers.

Under this arrangement a Mexican president rules a country of about 70 million people with absolute authority for six years. The PRI is also directed from the top, and the person who is PRI leader and president can usually count on absolute loyalty from members who want to advance in the party, government, or the bureaucracy. The PRI-dominated Mexican Congress rarely, if ever, disputes a presidential decision.

The presidential system itself is an unpredictable factor in Mexico's economy. ''For one thing, the president's policies can change overnight,'' says Denis. ''Secondly, he can move to being leftist, or populist. If you would like to put it this way, they are all opportunists. Any way the wind blows, they will go with it.''

This opportunism sifts through the society and exists at every level, Denis points out, and even drifts into the business management style. In practice, what emerges is *la mordida*, the bite.

''And it can be an asset,'' says Denis. ''If, for example, you were in the U.S. or Canada, and you have a court trial coming up, it will take four, five, six months to solve this problem. In Mexico you could solve it within twenty-four hours with money. You save time. Time is money."

It all seems a rationalization, though. In February and March of 1984, while Mexico's austerity program tightened the vise on poor and middle-class Mexicans, a daily hue and cry developed in the editorial and letters pages of the *Mexico City News* over allegations of corruption in the Echeverría Alvarez and López Portillo administrations. These two former presidents of Mexico were alleged to have vast land, industrial, and financial holdings worth billions in Mexico and overseas that they hadn't owned when they entered office. Then there was the outcry over the $1 billion that the oil workers' union executive had allegedly skimmed from the contracts Petroleos Mexicanos (PEMEX), the state oil company, had been forced by law to give them during the heyday of oil exploration.

The greatest growth of the Mexican middle class began after the rule of President Lázaro Cárdenas (1934–40). During Cárdenas's rule land was redistributed, education opened to the masses, illiteracy reduced, and industrial and power projects initiated and/or nationalized.

The Cárdenas legacy was to the middle and upper classes. A new generation was educated and was added to the aspiring middle class. Cárdenas's successors built on this foundation; the wealthy became wealthier and the middle class swelled. The poor had more children and, consequently, stayed poor.

Throughout the forties, fifties, and sixties, Mexico had a steadily growing economy. A further explosion in educational opportunities expanded the size of the middle class and its economic and social horizons. This middle class became the administrative and entrepreneurial class of the developing nation. Meanwhile, the country's economy grew at a modest 4 to 6 percent per year, inflation was moderate, and the middle class continued growing and believing in future growth.

When vast reserves of inland and offshore oil were discovered in the mid-70s, pandemonium broke loose in the Mexican economy. This was Mexico's chance to cash in on high and seemingly ever-increasing oil prices. Revenues from oil could be used to expand Mexican industry and services, physical and social, necessary for national development.

The oilfields, however, had to be developed first, so money was borrowed. The capital came from international banks eager to lend out OPEC petro-dollars. Basically, Mexico financed a massive development program by mortgaging her projected oil cash flow.

The Mexican economic boom was on, and inflation immediately rose by 1977 to 28 percent. The figure dropped to 19 percent in 1979 but hit 28 percent again in 1981. Mexico was in trouble, but no one who read the signs bothered to do anything because the money kept pouring in. Besides, everyone knew oil prices were going to keep rising forever.

In early 1982 the oil market began softening as oil-producing countries, new and old, increased their production levels. By mid-1982, with $90 billion in foreign debt and the loss of $10 billion and clients from some very stupid actions by the Mexican government in late 1981 and 1982, Mexico watched the bottom fall out of the international oil market. While oil export prices plummeted, inflation jumped over 30 percent; the next year, 1983, Mexican inflation shot up to more than 100 percent.

During the growth and boom years the living was easy for the Mexican middle class, and every cent they earned, and all they could borrow, was spent, usually on durables. When they could afford to, the middle class bought homes and cars. They were caught in a psychology of acquisitiveness and immediate gratification at all costs, a psychology that descended from the presidential level.

The economy had expanded so rapidly it appeared to explode; monetary expansion was equally explosive. Oil prices had increased to $20, then $30; by early 1982 they were approaching $35 a barrel. By all projections—official, of course—prices would continue rising to $60, maybe $90 by the late 1990s. Monetary officials expanded the monetary base in relationship to the money *projected* to come in. The populace followed suit.

"Look, the price of oil was going up 12 to 15 percent annually," says Denis, "so that was factored into the national budget. The Mexican fiscal authorities were not expert in commodity markets. Had any stock or commodity broker in Chicago been called in as an advisor, he or she would have said, 'What goes up comes down, and sooner or later there is going to be a crash in this market.'"

But the realities of the marketplace weren't taken into account, and Mexico went its merry way, spending, borrowing, and expanding its monetary base. According to one official from the Bank of Mexico, fully half of its $90 billion foreign debt was accumulated in 1981 alone.

The only influential person who really knew what was going on was the head of PEMEX. Being an oil trader, he understood what to expect and prepared for it. When 1982 was shaping up as the beginning of the world oil glut, he lowered the price of Mexican export oil, hoping to make up the price cuts through greater sales volumes in new markets. When the PEMEX price cuts were announced, then-President López Portillo fired the PEMEX head and abrogated the new oil-pricing contracts.

"Firing him on the spot for acting on his own initiative was one thing," says Denis. "To renege on the contracts, that was the dumbest thing they could do."

Why was that such a blunder? In 1973 the first oil shock was caused by OPEC, led by its Arab members, reneging on existing contracts and raising prices, and it didn't cost them contracts. But in 1973 the OPEC nations had no competition, nor was there a world oil glut. It was a seller's market, and OPEC, essentially a cartel, controlled prices. By 1982, however, it was a buyer's market with an over-supply of oil and hungry non-OPEC oil producers eager to sell their oil. When the Mexicans proved unreliable, their clients turned to other, more amenable, suppliers, and for some months Mexican oil revenues were nowhere near projections.

"Then you have the normal presidential cycle, which occurs every six years," says Denis. "It implies additional spending, monetary expansion, and uncertainty; mostly uncertainty and a retraction of business. People don't invest. They want to see who the next person will be."

When loose government fiscal and monetary policies combined with the shambles in the oil industry and the cyclic impact of the presidency, the result was a tremendously overvalued peso. Six months after the inflationary consequences of the troubles showed up, the government finally acted, and the peso was devalued about 20 percent. Then, in reaction to outcries from labor—it was, after all, an election year—the government decreed a general wage increase of 30 percent. But Mexico is an under-developed nation, and her industries are labor intensive. In those export markets in which Mexico participates, her competitive edge is provided by cheap labor. The 30 percent wage increase, therefore, not only wiped out whatever competitive position Mexico had regained by devaluation, but also rendered her even less competitive than before devaluation.

At this point the peso was again overvalued, and the Mexican populace knew it. Those with the wherewithal rushed out to buy U.S. dollars and hid them at home or, using the preferred method of holding cash assets, got them out of the country.

The capital flight was on. To protect Mexico's precarious economy the government had to end the exodus of money. The second round of devaluation came 1 September 1982 when all banks in Mexico were nationalized, exchange controls were imposed, and banks were closed until 6 September. During those five days all foreign-currency accounts—mostly deposits by foreigners, usually tax-evaded money—were converted to peso equivalents. Then the peso was devalued a further 50 percent.

"Mexican banks had been paying 12 percent interest on those dollar accounts, and it was tax-free interest," says Denis. "The rest of the world, primarily the United States, was paying 10 percent, minus tax. Suddenly, the people (foreigners) who had known how easy it was to get money in and out of the country, and about the interest rates, took a 50 percent loss in dollar terms, and couldn't get what was left out of the country because of the new currency controls."

At the same time, to prevent a run on banks by depositors now getting a negative return on savings after inflation, the government decreed that interest rates on savings were to be increased fourfold to about 50 percent per annum. But the increased interest rates were meaningless if the foreign depositors could see no hope of getting their money out of the country. Foreign depositors who lost money weren't speculators; they had put their money into what appeared to be secure, high-interest, tax-free accounts. Besides, the increases in interest rates meant nothing in real terms because, despite offering 50 percent return, the peso was put on a devaluation slide of 17 centavos per day against the U.S. dollar, and there was no chance they would recover what they had lost.

"If you had $100,000, you now had $50,000," says Denis. "The speculative ones, a tiny minority, went into the Mexican stock market and made 200 percent on their money the first year. The rest, they came here and bought jewelry or exchanged their money wherever they could for whatever they could and got it out."

The Mexican stock market went into a false boom as people rushed into it hoping to make up their losses, forcing prices to rise across the board. Also, the Mexican stock market is a very exclusive club, with a very small investor base made up mostly of insiders who can manipulate stock values. When fresh blood and money entered the market, the major players cleaned up, and the new players made small fortunes at the expense of late comers who perceived the market as a safe haven.

Overall, economic conditions worsened for Mexicans. They had to live with the double punch of inflation and devaluation. Merchants had seen their inventory values eroded by 100 percent, so they raised their prices 100 percent. In the meantime the Mexican consumer's devalued peso had half of its original purchasing power. So, while peso *earning* power held steady, or was even increased to recapture some income erosion, the average Mexican's *purchasing* power was cut by 400 percent.

Follow:

Item X in U.S. dollars =	$100
In pre-devaluation pesos 12.5 × 100 =	1,250 pesos
Item X raised 100 percent in U.S. dollars to	$200
Price in 50 percent devalued pesos 25 × 200 =	5,000 pesos
Purchasing power percentage cut	

$$\frac{5,000 \times 100}{1,250} = \qquad 400 \text{ percent}$$

Says one observer of the Mexican economic scene: "The Mexican middle class was caught holding cash. They had always liked to keep a large part of their wealth in cash, because tax evasion here is an institutionalized behavior pattern. Cash transactions avoid the problem of records. Overnight, their money was worth one quarter what it was before devaluation, and a person with a pre-devaluation income of $30,000 U.S., was making $10,000 U.S."

Karla, in her late thirties, is the mother of three children aged fourteen, seven, and three. She and her husband, both working professionals, barely get by on two salaries that total about the equivalent of $20,000 U.S.

"Each week I go to the store for groceries and the basics," she shrugs. "The prices go up little by little, two pesos, three, ten. It never stops. And increases in salary do not cover the increases in the prices of things we need to go on."

Three years ago Karla and her husband were riding high on their salaries, traveling to the U.S. for weekends, spending money freely, and managing to save a bit. Now, it's a battle to get to the end of the month.

"Where do I start?" she asks. "The children are growing, they need meat, milk, eggs regularly. So I buy carefully, substitute the brand names for the *marca libre*, the no-name, products. I go to the Friday outdoor markets. Still it is expensive."

Rising food prices and, for that matter, price rises on everything, are part of the cost Mexico has to pay to bring inflation under control and deal with her staggering foreign debt. The first step the administration had to take was to control government expenditures. Food subsidies, designed to keep farm earnings profitable and consumer prices bearable, represent a large portion of domestic spending. They were cut. This reduced the amount of income left in the consumer's hands as discretionary disposable income, and Mexicans stopped buying consumer durables, many of which were imports. The cap on consumer demand reduced imports, eased pressure on Mexico's balance of payments, and cut the outflow of foreign reserves.

"Now, in Mexico City," Karla sighs, "it is not as safe as it used to be. We have bank robberies and kidnapings." She shakes her head in amazement. "And extortion. A woman will go to the grocery store, and a man will take her child and threaten to kill the child if the mother does not pay ransom by buying groceries for the man. And the streets...they are not as safe as they were. And the subway...."

The result of the changes in Mexico, generally a socially and politically stable country, is uncertainty. "And fear," says Karla. "We just live for now. We do not think about the future. We do not think about buying a house. It is too expensive and to borrow is impossible. We keep our car longer. We spend less. We work harder and earn less."

The banker who expressed his concern about the middle class and the new urban poor wasn't worried about their welfare. His concern was that the discontentment and resentment of the middle class against a government that governed badly could explode into widespread violence.

"All it would take is someone who could mobilize them, really get them organized, to cause real trouble in Mexico," he said.

That may or may not be conjecture, but there has been an increase in crime in Mexico over the past two years that has repercussions quite visible on the streets of Mexico City. Pass a bank, or a cluster of banks, and look around. Somewhere in the block you'll see a policeman who, in addition to a large calibre pistol, is carrying a rifle.

An American journalist who covers Mexico for an international wire service expressed a different view of middle-class attitudes: "Everyone was quite cynical here about the overvalued peso and the boom," he says. "They were aware of what was going on and rode that boom for all it was worth; now they're paying for it. The poor here are always poor, and the middle class aren't coddled. They grab off what they can, when they can, and the distribution of wealth is as inequitable as anywhere in the world."

The real fear in Mexico came about during the transition between the López Portillo and de la Madrid administrations. People were worried no one was really in control. The nationalization of the banks occurred because economics in Mexico went haywire. Banks were offering U.S. dollars at whatever rate they could squeeze from anxious buyers, and a quick operator who could sprint well could profit on the spread of exchange rates for American dollars, which fluctuated wildly *from bank to bank*.

"And don't believe what they say about Mexico being poor, or any other developing nation crying poverty," he laughs knowingly. "This is a rich country, with a lot of poor people. It's rich in oil, raw materials, and natural resources, even agriculture."

The oil boom simply spread the money around a little farther, though somewhat thinly. It was not uncommon for Mexicans to fly to U.S. border cities for holidays, weekend shopping sprees, or to buy fixed assets. When the boom went bust in August 1982, California Governor Edmund G. Brown asked U.S. President Ronald Reagan for economic disaster aid for San Diego and Imperial counties. These border areas were suffering from the sudden drop in Mexican cross-border consumer trade resulting from the first peso devaluation.

Shortly afterward, when the September 1982 devaluation and currency controls were introduced, southern Texas, especially Laredo, also suffered a severe recession. And real estate agents in border areas had to come up with creative ways for Mexicans barred from taking money out of Mexico to meet mortgage payments on property they had bought as investments.

"I know Mexicans who are wearing Mexican-made clothes for the first time in ten years," says the American journalist. "They used to go across the border and come back with cars loaded with clothes and electronic equipment. And these were working-class as well as middle-class Mexicans. It was just so much cheaper to buy in the States with the overvalued peso than to buy here."

Now, however, the new economic regime in Mexico has taken its toll.

A walk from Alameda Park to Plaza de la Constitución will lead you past a huge outdoor shopping mall on a series of streets that are cobbled and closed off for pedestrian traffic. Everywhere you look, clothing, jewelry, leather, luggage, and shoe shops offer a bewildering array of consumer goods.

Enter a jewelry shop and ask the price of a silver bracelet.

"Two thousand pesos, Señor."

"Fifteen hundred."

"Eighteen hundred."

"Sixteen fifty."

"Seventeen hundred, Señor. The lowest I can go."

"No tax?"

"No tax."

"Deal."

The tax in question is a 15 percent value-added tax on everything. If you bargain on the price and don't ask for a receipt, you save on the bargaining plus the 15 percent tax. Rest assured that a good portion of the money taken in by the shopkeepers is diverted somewhere the tax department can't get it.

It's easy for a shopkeeper to plead poverty because Mexicans aren't buying these days, and there just aren't enough tourists to keep every merchant afloat. So how do they keep going?

One manager of a foreign bank operation in Mexico tapped his chest. "I keep them going. And my colleagues in other banks. They're so far into us, we have to keep them going." He pointed to a foot-thick stack of documents on his coffee table.

"One day's financial restructuring for Mexican business, big and small," he said. "I spend most of my time reading these things."

What about industry? He shrugged. "It's hanging on, waiting for the rest of the world to experience economic recovery, to sell to them."

Will it work? "Not a chance. They don't know, or maybe they don't want to learn how to do business out there. They produce for the domestic market and want the rest of the world to buy their surpluses."

Essentially, the problem is that Mexico has operated under the illusion of self-sufficiency for too long. With a population of 70 million, Mexican industry has been able to produce and sell on economies of scale that make purely domestic operations profitable. So they have not had to compete on the world market.

"Except in the oil industry," says the American journalist. "The requirements of exploration forced part of Mexico's industry to work well. PEMEX wasn't buying rigs or drilling equipment just because they were made in Mexico. So dealing and competing on an open world market causes de facto quality control. There are companies here that hold patents on world-class equipment developed specifically for the oil industry."

Those patents and products represent a prominent exception to the rule of Mexican industrial output, which fails to meet world-class trading standards because the Mexican consumer isn't as demanding of consistent high quality as consumers in other markets. When Mexican industry is forced to compete on world-class standards, it produces.

"Correct," says Denis. "The real problem, and the reason the great Mexican export drive is a myth is that, barring important exceptions, Mexicans don't understand international marketing and don't seem to want to learn."

As an example, he pointed to domestically produced pre-sugared instant coffee. Immensely popular in Mexico, the product has a captive market. The manufacturers decided to try selling their surpluses overseas, and went worldwide to sell to the world market. That was their version of market research. The manufacturers were perplexed to find no one wanted the product.

"If it had been the Japanese," observes Denis, "they would have asked around, 'What do people want? Pink coffee?' They would hide their surprise and ask 'How much? For delivery when?' and go back, orders in hand, to make pink coffee."

There are many facets to the picture Mexicans and observers drew about Mexico. The country is in what is probably the deepest recession it has suffered this century, and it won't climb out of it easily or quickly.

Despite the depth of the recession, there are success stories in the Mexican industrial scene. One is Elmet, an industrial abrasives manufacturer. Jointly owned by an American firm and the Mexican government, Elmet was actually going broke before the recession. The government subsidized the money-losing operation to protect jobs. Under the direction of President Miguel Pedrajo and Administrative Director Eduardo Vanegas, both brought in to save the company, Elmet was turned around and is showing a profit during the recession. How?

"It is a very simple principle," says Vanegas. "You work from cash flow. If your business produces cash, it is a business. If it is not producing some kind of cash, you are in trouble."

He pulled out a cash flow statement and jabbed at it as he spoke. "For us, the cash flow becomes the first and most important financial statement of the company. But this is a different kind of cash flow."

He leaned over and pointed to the figures in the top left-hand corner of the statement. "This is cash I have." He pointed to a set of figures at the bottom right-hand corner of the statement. "This is the dividend I need to return to the shareholders and cash to work with." He ran his fingers along various rows of figures, pointing out known future expenses and increases, and predicted expenses and increases, all allowing for an inflation rate slightly above government forecasts.

"They are my costs. And this..." He pointed to another row of figures. "This is the income I need to get from cash on hand to dividends. So I tell my people, 'this is how much you must sell, so I can pay the bills and stay in business.'" And should his sales staff sell more, so much the better, because Vanegas has to monitor his cash flow each month to ensure Elmet is on target, not only for sales, but also for the assumption of inflationary erosion of revenues, so he can adjust the coming month's plans accordingly.

"This way I will know if I am making money or losing money. No matter what my profit and loss statement says, if I don't have the money for paying salaries this weekend, I don't have a business."

It also takes hard work. Vanegas and Pedrajo worked two years to bring Elmet into a profit position. "Because we worked like hell," said Vanegas. "You also survive by thinking as quickly and creatively as you can. And what is creative thinking financially? The quickest that produces the right answers."

But how do you know they're right?

Vanegas smiled triumphantly. "You are keeping your head above water while your competition is sinking."

The key to the turnaround and survival of Elmet is more than good bookkeeping. "It helps," says Miguel Pedrajo, the company's president. "But you have to work hard. That is the only way to survive in business, and in life. But you must start by not spending more than you have. You, a company, government. There is no free lunch in life."

The people who painted this picture were short on details as to how Mexicans survive in the economic troubles, mainly because they're doing it right now and trends haven't become that apparent. The same people, however, were long on advice to carry back to North America.

1. Count on the family. In Mexico, if out of a family of seven only five are working, all seven and their families are supported by the five. If, suddenly, only two are working, all seven can still count on support.
2. Don't take yourself too seriously. Look at the Mexican

middle class and weep. They actually believed the government needed them but, when push came to shove, the middle class suffered first and most.

3. Don't let any political party stay in power too long. A party in power too long thinks it can take the long view and manipulate an economy despite economic realities. Also, a party in power too long builds a civil service that operates according to the party's dictates, not what's good for the country. In Mexico, the Institutional Revolutionary Party has been in power so long the civil service has become an arm of the party. Senior civil servants are often also important members of the party. The party serves its members, and the civil service serves the party's purposes.

4. Beware of rapid and sudden monetary expansion. A major indicator that Mexico was going wrong was the explosion in the money supply.

5. Be ready to run for cover when the currency is over- or undervalued. Another major indicator that Mexico was going wrong was mass purchasing of imported consumer durables that were cheaper than similar domestically produced goods. When it's an open secret that anything is cheaper across the border because the U.S. dollar is cheaper to buy than it should be, Mexicans suggest playing the game or getting out.

6. Don't overspend. This applies to individuals and government. Live within your means, and try to improve your life and security in real terms with secure investments. Secure investments tend to be those that your government can't get its hands on.

Chapter 13

THE HARD PART BEGINS

IN A PLANE ABOVE NORTH AMERICA, about an hour away from home, the cabin staff pass around coffee. It's lukewarm, but it's North American and, even though exotic coffee is wonderful, anything that smacks of home is comforting.

The past fifty-two days have provided a sensory overload of odors, images, sounds, and colors.

Exhaustion has worked its way right into my bones. I've traveled across eleven time zones, the Atlantic Ocean, and the Mediterranean Sea twice. My feet have touched the soil of nine countries on four continents. In total, I have clocked 40,500 kilometers/25,200 miles in air travel, and calculated in nine currencies, with a minimum of two and a maximum of four exchange rates each. I've worked in five languages, one of which, Spanish, had three different versions.

During the trip I've had the good fortune to meet and interview many people from different walks of life. The openness, friendliness, and honesty of most of them helped broaden the scope of my understanding of people and the world in which we live.

Also, during the trip people lied to me, tried to cheat me, con me, break into my hotel room, and pick my pockets, literally and figuratively. And because I walked around looking intently at the world and continually asking questions, every pimp, shill, con artist, prostitute, and black market operator I passed on the street thought I was looking *for* things. I was offered all manner of inducements to part with my money. They, too, helped broaden the scope of my understanding of people and the world in which we live.

Now the material has to be organized, and there's so much to tell Henry.

Dave is back, and we don't have to worry that we can't deliver the manuscript because of delays caused by war, riots, civil disturbances, strikes, lockouts, acts of God, tropical diseases, or whatever else was written into our contract.

"It's completely upside-down, Henry. People think all the time about how to keep the value of their earnings. So they look for a standard of value that's stable, such as American dollars."

What is he talking about, as he paces back and forth, his hands chopping the air to emphasize what he's saying? Now I'm worried. Were our critics right? Are the political, social, and economic histories of the countries he visited really so different from ours that the methods used to cope with hyperinflation will not be valid here except at a very simplistic level?

Will the material and information he brought back help us construct suggestions with a positive approach? Can we tell our story without frightening people with doom and gloom? On the other hand, can we make people see that propaganda claiming the recession is over and prosperity is just around the corner is only a politician's myth?

Dave disappears, locking himself into his apartment–office. The first chapter shows up. I begin to read. Halfway through Italy I begin to relax. I see the parallels. There is a message for North Americans. Halfway through Israel it becomes clear. We have a winner!

The story unfolds. The parallels are beyond our wildest dreams; no, better yet, nightmares. I'm impatient for Spain, Argentina, Mexico. Finally, it's all there—the parallels, the contrasts, the all-pervasive specter of excess government spending and its impact on our lives. A sense of urgency grips me. Phrases such as "we are living in the eye of the hurricane" and "the lull before the storm" keep going through my mind. It's not too late. We in North America still have a chance.

Dave and I sit down to summarize. And the blueprint for you, for us, begins to take shape.

———◊◊◊———

Part 3

BLUEPRINT FOR SURVIVAL

Chapter 14

GENERAL PRINCIPLES

WHILE WE BELIEVE HYPERINFLATION is inevitable in Canada, it's virtually impossible to predict when it will occur. The uncertainty of expectation is no less frightening than the uncertainty of circumstances that rule when hyperinflation has set in.

We would all be better off if hyperinflation never happens. The way to prevent it is clearly marked, and some alternatives are outlined at the end of this book. We believe, however, that any suggestions for change will not get reasonable consideration at the hands of our political leaders.

To prevent hyperinflation:

- We would have to demand action, not rhetoric, from our leaders.
- Politicians would have to own up to the mistakes they have made in the past and change political direction.
- Citizens would have to act responsibly and co-operatively within the limits of strict economic measures.
- All of the economic measures would have to be applied equally to all segments of society.

We believe that no government, unfortunately, will behave responsibly. To do so would mean failure to get re-elected, and the business of political parties is re-election.

All we can recommend, therefore, is that you get your own economic life in order and ready yourself for a rough ride. While we can't predict when hyperinflation will occur, we can point to the signposts that generally accompany the decline into hyper-inflation. We can also provide some strategies for surviving the inevitable.

The key indication is government spending. When government budgets run in deficits for a number of years in succession, monetary expansion to pay the bills usually follows. This debases the currency and becomes a major inflationary force.

Another major indicator is that the party in power has been in power too long. A party accustomed to almost automatic re-election begins to think that regular voter approval means they have the right answers. When too-successful politicians make mistakes, they're reluctant to admit their fallibility and to look for other policies that will work.

A third factor grows out of the first two. Watch the perform-ance of the national currency on world exchange markets. For example, the world currency traders might be trading the Canadian dollar at 77 cents U.S. because they believe that is all it's worth. Meanwhile, the government might be bolstering the dollar to 78 cents U.S., which is what it wants the currency to be worth.

At this point the currency is overvalued. An overvalued currency is identified by trading trends. Watch for:
- regular downward pressure on the currency in international currency exchanges;
- reluctance of other countries to accept the currency in interna-tional business transactions; and
- regular attempts by government economic authorities to shore up currency values through overseas borrowing.

It is extremely unlikely that anyone reading this book will ever starve. Government give-away programs will always pro-vide at least a bare subsistence. But, is that what life is all about?

To protect ourselves, we must learn to think quickly but not to outsmart ourselves. No one can guarantee us wealth; we can only earn it. With a little planning we can build a strong base for financial security, though wealth is very much a factor of luck—guessing correctly what will happen before it does. *Maximize your chances: Diversify your holdings because no single investment or investment plan is guaranteed.* There are too many variables. This was summarized beautifully by the foreign-currency administrator of an Israeli bank quoted on page 129 as saying, "Investment performance, no matter what, is irrational. We have no control over how anything behaves."

Even American dollar investments may not be the answer. Certainly it has been for the last few years, but at the time of this writing there are worldwide rumblings that the U.S. dollar is over-valued relative to other currencies. So, it is up to you, in the final analysis, to inform yourself and make your own decisions.

Whatever you do, go slowly. If you win, don't re-double the stakes next time out. Put away part of your winnings and diversify along the lines of the "gambler's process" on page 62. Remember that the key to surviving and profiting from inflation or hyperinflation is to be able, first, to profit in relatively normal non-inflationary economic times. Hanging on to what you make is the real test for success, but eventually all profitable aspects of inflation lose against the erosion of the value of money or become illegal; many inflationary schemes are destroyed by recession.

Let's destroy one of the greatest myths about inflation. Many people think that, if severe inflation is anticipated, the name of the game is to borrow more and more money in the hope of eventually paying off all debts with cheaper dollars. The problem is that when you buy property in inflationary times, you pay inflated prices. When the value of the property drops during a recession, your debt load could wipe you out. *Borrowing heavily only makes sense if you can correctly predict the start of the inflationary cycle and you get in early.*

A couple of examples will make this clear. Assume that today in North America the real estate market has bottomed out and will soon begin to rise. You acquire a rental property for $100,000 and you hypothetically obtain 100 percent financing.

Sure enough, inflation runs rampant through the economy and you sell that property for $1 million in three years' time. Clearly, you have made a profit.

Now consider the buyer. Assume the buyer pays $1 million and obtains it all through financing. Then the government recalls the currency and issues new bills at the rate of one new dollar for each ten old dollars surrendered. At this point the second buyer at best owns a property worth 100,000 new dollars against which he owes an equivalent amount of new money.

But notice we said "at best." If the change in currency is accompanied by a recession, the value of the property itself could drop on the open market by as much as 50 percent. Under those conditions it could prove difficult to find a buyer able, or ready, to offer more than 50,000 new dollars for the property. The owner would be completely wiped out.

This isn't to say don't borrow. As long as you are comfortable with your debt load, borrow all you want, but assess your position clearly. You may be making a good living now, but examine how recession-proof your job or business is. You can't pay back debt if you are unemployed. All governments are eventually forced to tackle their deficits, and the first items to go are government subsidies and contracts. If your job or business is largely dependent on government, be very very careful in borrowing. You may be more vulnerable than most.

Let's consider some financial-planning specifics. In Chapter Two we discussed the consumer price index and what it means. At this very early stage we concluded that the cornerstone to economic security is to enter retirement with interest-sensitive investments, such as a house and one or two late-model cars fully paid off. The middle section of this book reinforces this very basic planning. In many countries it is impossible for young people to afford to buy homes and their only hope is to inherit a family dwelling or win a very large lottery.

In fact, just to show how your thinking should always be open to change, consider the question of whether or not a second home or vacation property is a good investment. In Henry B. Zimmer's recent book *How to Profit from the Next Canadian*

Real Estate Boom a very strong argument was made that a summer cottage is a terrible investment for Canadians. This is because, in Canada, mortgage interest on money borrowed to acquire such a property is non-deductible and, if the property is ever sold, the capital gain will be taxed. But are the tax consequences really the be all and end all? Certainly, as the book points out, there are ramifications in making investment decisions beyond the tax implications or, in fact, pure dollars and cents. Owning a country house is very much a lifestyle decision: If a family can afford two homes and really has the use for a vacation property, by all means go out and buy.

Yet, with the implications of future hyperinflation taken into account, we have a new perspective. When heavy inflation hits North America, our children will not be able to afford to buy homes of their own. If you have two children and are interested in subsidizing their welfare, there is an advantage to owning two properties. When you die, you can leave your city house to one child and the country house to the other. The child who inherits the country house could sell it for whatever value the property commands at that time and immediately use those dollars to acquire a functional principal residence. This is all part of good conservative financial planning and the actual value of the dollar at that time doesn't matter.

Assume you acquire a country property for $100,000 today. Sure enough, with heavy inflation, the price at the time of sale is $1 million. Your child can take that $1 million and buy a more suitable property as a permanent residence. On the other hand, assume that all our suppositions are wrong, or that the inflation which we describe is followed by a severe depression. At the time of inheritance the country house can only be sold for $50,000. If that is the case, it can reasonably be assumed that the value of city houses has fallen as well. Even if your child is unemployed or is struggling to make ends meet, the proceeds from the sale of the country property can be used to finance or pay for a principal residence.

When it comes to the family car, the message has to be directed towards those people who are a few years away from retirement. You must target to buy a brand new fuel-efficient car at the time you retire. If in the next year or two car prices start to jump substantially, buy that much sooner. In fact, if you're really concerned, you might consider buying a new car today, putting it up on blocks and having it available when you need it five or even ten years into the future. The vehicle will be out of style, but it will provide reliable transportation. After all, if people drive cars today that were built in the 1960s, why shouldn't you be able to drive a 1985 model ten years down the line?

Next consider durables: furniture, appliances, televisions, stereos, video equipment. Remember, the Canadian economy is far more precarious than that of the United States. We are much more dependent on imports. The Canadian dollar has fallen dramatically in the last three years and, if our assessment is correct, the slide has just begun. Take stock of what you have and what you need and, if your income is relatively secure, what you want (which may differ from what you actually need). Incurring some short-term debt for durables is fine, as long as you don't over-burden yourself and become a slave to consumerism. Don't become so dependent on your tangible assets for self image that, by losing any, you become depressed or despondent. Refer to the sixteen basic rules to surviving hyperinflation at the end of Chapter Four about Italy. Rule number one is number one for a reason. "Take nothing so seriously or hold it so dear that losing it will destroy you, financially or emotionally. Whatever you do, don't take yourself too seriously. This business of surviving the money game is a game. Be flexible, and be able to take a tumble and still land on your feet."

Buy durable clothing so, when a recession hits or prices climb too quickly, you can get by wearing the same apparel for several years if need be. Should you be stockpiling certain kinds of foodstuffs or at least training yourself to do your grocery shopping more efficiently? Should you be developing an expertise in nutrition? The specific answers to those questions are up to you but, overall, we suggest that you invest in yourself and your family first. To the extent possible ensure your comfort;

231

it's more important than wealth.

One of the most important lessons learned in researching this book was, to some extent, severe inflation and economic depression have similar results: They create havoc with the average family's earning power and ability to stay ahead. Also, while we see that hyperinflation is inevitable, we caution that it won't last forever. So, while preparing for inflation, you must make your life as depression-proof as possible.

From what we've been able to determine, the people in the world who manage to stay ahead of inflation are generally either efficient entrepreneurs or hard workers willing to hold down two jobs. We are both firm believers in entrepreneurship, although there are several lessons you must learn first. Many people dream of owning a profitable business, but it's hard work. There are no guarantees of profit, and for most it's a twenty-four-hour-a-day proposition.

While this is not a book on how to start or run your own small business successfully, there are some points you should consider. First, the ideal small business is neither capital intensive nor labor intensive. You should not be forced into a position where you mortgage your soul to a bank for financing or to a union for labor. If the business can be run by members of your immediate family, well and good.

Next, the products or services your business provides should be as recession-proof as possible. Ideally, your business will provide goods or services needed on a recurring basis, so you can deal with the same customer many times over. Your products or services should also be affordable whether times are good or bad. On the one hand, we can caution you to stay away from dealing in expensive luxury items although, on the other hand, we can see leisure industries as dominant businesses of the future.

You've undoubtedly learned in reading this book that high unemployment is as much a fact of life in the countries visited as it is here in North America. Despite government propaganda, we believe high unemployment is likely to continue, especially in light of the technological revolution.

The jury is still out on the question of whether computerization will create more jobs than it replaces or the other way around. Certainly in the next ten or fifteen years, even if computerization creates jobs, they will be in areas totally foreign to traditional skills. Ultimately, people in their forties, fifties, and even sixties will be victims of their inability to be retrained.

As explained earlier, though, the government will not allow anyone to starve. To prevent bloody revolutions, subsidies will be paid, and the only problem for the unemployed will be how to use their time effectively and profitably. There is usually no profitable solution, so the next best thing is using one's time so that the hours and the days pass as painlessly as possible. Anyone who caters to these people by providing relatively cheap entertainment will profit, at least until a particular business becomes saturated by competition. A good example of an inexpensive leisure industry today is the business of providing video tapes to an expanding home video market. This business may already be saturated in your area, so you'll have to come up with a better mousetrap.

For many people, the key to maintaining a reasonable lifestyle will be the ability to create and hold down a second job. The ideal situation is to turn a hobby into a profit-making venture. For example, if your hobby is carpentry, you may be able to work two nights a week or on the occasional weekend helping friends and neighbors renovate their homes. Obviously any money you receive should be reported for income tax purposes to the authorities. If you fail to do so there are severe penalties, and we cannot and do not condone tax evasion. What you do, however, is largely a function of your own conscience and, of course, your own assessment of whether or not you will get caught!

The topic of tax evasion is a very sensitive area and one which, unfortunately, permeates this book. To ignore its existence in hyperinflated countries would be dishonest and yet we certainly cannot promote it. If nothing else, our commentary on tax evasion should serve as a warning to government. Raising taxes to the point where they are perceived to be prohibitive will only produce wholesale evasion. If people feel their backs against the economic wall, many will decide that there's no choice but to opt out of the system. If it ever comes down to a choice between buying groceries and paying taxes, the tax people will lose every time! The lesson to government is that it cannot indefinitely cover its overspending by continuing to bleed the populace.

From an article in the *Financial Post* magazine issue of 1 May 1984 entitled "What You Don't See Can Hurt You" by Andrew Allentuck, we extract the following quote: "Today, in this country, taxes in total take 51% of our incomes, more than the cost of food, shelter and clothing combined, according to a study by Vancouver's Fraser Institute, a think-tank with a free-market philosophy. The average Canadian family with an income of $33,325 will pay $17,335 to various governments in various taxes in 1984. Of that $17,335 only $5,763, or 33 percent, is income tax; the remaining $11,572, or 67 percent, of the tax is composed of commodity taxes hidden in the prices of goods. Sales taxes, for example, total $1,976. Add $1,703 for excise duties and/or taxes on liquor, tobacco, and entertainment, to name a few; $560 for customs duties; and $567 for automobile, fuel, and license taxes. In all, says the institute's assistant director, Sally Pipes, it would be necessary to work six months and eight days just to pay fifty-three different taxes."

Let's summarize the viability of various investments in an inflationary environment. First, let's deal with gold, which gave us our biggest surprise. From a North American perspective gold has been anything but a spectacularly well-performing investment in the last couple of years. But, since the gold price is measured in American dollars, we felt, at least before this project began to unfold, that gold would be considered by residents of the countries visited as a prime hedge against inflation. As the value of local currency drops compared to the U.S. dollar, automatically the value of gold increases.

Surprisingly, gold does not appear to be a high priority in these countries, not as long as the U.S. dollar holds value and American inflation rates are low. To some extent it is respected, but ownership is also feared. Gold is heavy, and in large quantities it's difficult to transport. In some cases, ownership of gold by private citizens is illegal, and in many cases there is the fear that at the whim of government private possession could become illegal. Of course, gold can always be stockpiled in a secure location, perhaps Switzerland or the Channel Islands. And yet, if the domestic situation becomes intolerable or, at best, difficult, how do you get to your gold?

Certainly gold is seen by many as a partial hedge, but the adage don't put all your eggs in one basket holds true. Gold jewelry is perceived by many people in Europe, South America, and other parts of the world not only as a hedge against inflation but also as insurance for survival. You can always barter your life, if need be, for some of this glittering metal.

Gold has other drawbacks as well. It is not easily divisible into very small quantities. For example, if you had a quarter-ounce gold Kruggerand and wanted to use part of it to buy ten loaves of bread worth one-tenth of an ounce Kruggerand, it would be difficult for the seller of the bread to make change. Another problem is that gold in and of itself has little intrinsic value. No country bases the value of its own currency on the amount of gold it owns. It is certainly conceivable at some point that politicians will decide or decree that gold should have no value at all.

Also, gold price fluctuations are difficult to predict. If Russia harvests an inferior wheat crop one year, it may be forced to dump large amounts of gold to buy wheat. Much of the gold hoarding in this world is done by Middle Eastern countries. The Arabs could suddenly dump their gold if they need revenues over and above oil income. It's a very uncertain situation. This is not to say that middle-income and upper-income North Americans shouldn't have some gold in their portfolios. Remember what we said on page 160: "[Gold] doesn't always perform as expected if you are looking for quick profit. It is, however, a different situation if you are looking for long-term security. Then a rousing chorus of voices says to buy gold, and not to let anyone know you have it until you're ready to sell."

One of the reasons gold is not as popular as we would have

thought is that investors in other countries have an alternative—
strong paper currencies. A thriving market, both white and
black, exists in currencies, the most popular being the U.S.
dollar. Paper money is much more compact than gold, easier to
carry, easier to store, can be bought and sold in smaller denominations, and can be readily exchanged from day to day.

From a Canadian perspective, it appears that the U.S. econ-
omy is significantly healthier than the domestic one. So, for
Canadians looking for a hedge against a falling domestic dollar,
U.S. currency may be the answer. In the long run, however, the
U.S. dollar will fall too. The United States with its near $200
billion annual deficit cannot easily avoid its destiny, making the
U.S. dollar a safe haven for investment for only a short period of
time.

Another major lesson learned is that we all owe it to ourselves
to become expert on world affairs, world currencies, and relative currency values. We can't predict what will happen to the
Swiss franc, the Japanese yen, or the German mark, except that
these are the kinds of currencies—backed by strong economies,
frugal governments, or both—you want to understand and hold.
So, if you value your economic prosperity in the turbulent years
ahead, you must be willing to learn.

Now consider real estate, other than the home or the vacation
property. Traditionally, more affluent investors in all the countries visited have become involved in real estate ownership.
Certainly there are problems. Real estate is registered with
government, liable to taxes, and is not fluid. On the one hand,
real estate can be subject to rent controls and, on the other, there
is no control over interest rates. So, certainly, there is substantial
downside risk.

In North America, at present, there is also tremendous upside
potential. First, it is possible at the time this is being written to
acquire both commercial and residential rental property with
five-year fixed-rate financing. There is the penalty of paying a
few percentage points more than if you arranged shorter-term
financing, but our advice is to consider it an insurance policy,
rather than increased interest. If you own property at the time

the inflationary spiral starts, you are bound to profit in the medium term. Your toughest decision will then be when, or if, to sell.

For example, as explained in the chapter on Argentina, there is a tradition among the more affluent residents of Buenos Aires to own a large family apartment as well as other rental properties. When hyperinflation takes its toll of middle- and upper-class people, you could move into one of your own apartments and rent your prime properties to others at high rents. Alternatively, if you own an apartment building and are concerned about the welfare of your immediate family, friends, or other relatives, you could subsidize their living expenses, if you wish to do so.

If you buy real estate, don't pay an inflated price on the assumption rents will automatically escalate and there will always be 100 percent occupancy. The trick is to pay a realistic price based on today's rents and then sell to someone greedier than yourself who is willing to buy when the boom hits its peak.

If you are looking at real estate as a long-term investment and decide on a commercial property, make sure your rents are large enough to pay off the debt within a reasonable time. You can be destroyed if you provide commercial tenants with long-term leases and you're forced to refinance your holdings at significantly higher interest costs. By paying off your property quickly, you'll find that you'll have an ongoing cash flow to work with to enable you to diversify into other activities.

What about the stock market? To a large extent, this international tour reinforced a good deal of what we already suspected about the stock market. Specifically, the market does not behave predictably. In most of the countries visited, the local stock market has gone through a series of booms and busts— no different conceptually from results in North America. In times of heavy inflation, it can be reasonably anticipated that there will be at least a short-term boom in the market.

Eventually, as interest rates escalate, investors draw funds out of the market and put them back into interest-bearing certificates. Moreover, inflation leads to recession and many businesses have a good deal of trouble trying to stay afloat when they cannot control the cost of supplies, labor, or their own sales. In other words, the stock market is not an infallible long-term investment. The booms are created by short-term greed as investors flock to get in. Then, after a short peak, each boom is usually followed by a collapse.

This is not to say that a balanced market portfolio isn't worthwhile. Invest in stocks that behave in a stable fashion in both good times and bad. Also recognize that, to play the market effectively, you must look at international investments. If it is within your psychological make-up to do so, and you're willing to expend the time, effort, and the money (by hiring a professional counsellor), then look towards the international scene. For example, North American markets at a given point might be stagnant or in decline, while there's a booming market in Bombay. If you perceive that, for argument's sake, the German mark will be a very strong currency for the next two or three years, you might consider investing in the German market. Alternatively, if the German mark appears soft, consider Japan. This is certainly much easier to say than to do. Most people are not comfortable placing their assets thousands of miles away. For the small investor this isn't practical, but for the large investor, it is almost mandatory. If you can't develop the expertise yourself, find reputable professionals who can help you.

One of the biggest surprises is that, despite weakening economies, investors in many of the countries visited continue to place their trust and money in domestic government bonds. Certain factors must be considered if you hold government bonds. First, only buy government bonds when the yield is real. This means either the interest rate exceeds the inflation rate by a substantial amount and/or there are tax concessions that make bond ownership attractive. To some extent you might expect that there's little risk to buying government bonds. After all, any government can print money to meet its obligations. In the long run, however, you must be extremely careful: If currency is devalued by 50 percent, you lose half your investment.

In some countries the attraction of bonds is (as explained on page 156) as a method of holding black market money. The government provides term notes with an interest rate that is positive after an inflation adjustment and, most importantly, the bond is also an untitled bearer instrument, which means it can be traded back and forth without any controls on ownership or taxes.

At the time this is being written, a government bond or, for that matter, any chartered bank or trust company term deposit is not an unreasonable investment for Canadians within a registered retirement savings plan or a pension plan program. As long as the yield is tax sheltered, it is still possible to get a rate of return which compounds faster than inflation.

Realize, though, if our dollar is suddenly devalued and/or heavy inflation starts up again, the investor will lose money. Much of this loss can be prevented by moving into the stock market just before this inflation returns—if you can predict correctly when, in fact, this will take place. Even if you can't predict accurately, you will probably be able to recoup a good deal of your loss by reacting quickly and moving into the market immediately after the first devaluation occurs.

What happens when the stock market eventually peaks and interest-bearing investments still appear unattractive? At that point if you have funds registered for tax purposes, you may have to opt for one of several choices such as a qualified investment through a Canadian institution where the investment is denominated in a currency other than the Canadian dollar. This is assuming such investments are available and would qualify within a tax sheltered plan. Alternatively, it may become more expedient to collapse your plan, pull the money out, pay your taxes, and enjoy complete flexibility in your investments with what is left. Another plan of action is to pull your money out, evade your taxes, and run! Fortunately, these are not decisions that have to be made today.

Finally, another surprise emerged from our voyage through many lands. This is the high value placed by many knowledgeable people on coins and stamps. As explained earlier on page

128, there is much more support for these collectibles than any of the other exotic investments including jewelry, antiques, and art. The explanation received in the various countries was the same—these items have a true, easily defined value to collectors worldwide, and they do tend to appreciate. Coins and stamps are extremely portable, stamps more so than coins, and most of the time authorities such as customs inspectors don't have any idea of their value. They can easily be transported across international boundaries and converted from a weak to a strong currency. Also, information as to transactions in coins and stamps is not readily available to the tax department.

Our perspective on coins and stamps has changed considerably as a result of this research. Previously, we viewed collecting as a hobby in which you would have to be interested before buying and selling should even be considered. In other words, why own stamps if you have absolutely no interest in their aesthetics?

Today, our perspective is somewhat different. You may want to own ten to perhaps one hundred stamps. They may not be part of any specific collection; they may not even be related to each other. They don't have to be stamps issued by the same country or government. All that is required is that, among true collectors, these stamps have perceived value that will increase at least to the same extent as worldwide average inflation figures.

Of course, if you develop an expertise and find you enjoy collecting, so much the better. The more knowledge you have, the easier it will be to buy intelligently, and the more difficult it will be for someone to cheat you.

No matter how you decide to invest, you must become adept at using a simple hand-held calculator that adds, subtracts, multiplies, and divides. Remember that at 50 percent annual inflation you will have to think ten times faster than you are thinking today. At 500 percent inflation you must think a hundred times as fast in order to survive—let alone prosper.

———— ∾∾∾ ————

Chapter 15

SPECIFIC STRATEGIES

IN THE PAST, Henry Zimmer has used the "earnings profile" approach to illustrate specific strategic planning for individuals in different income brackets. Specifically, in a 1982 book co-authored with V. Jeanne Kaufman entitled *Reshaping Your Investment Strategies for the 1980s*, a chapter was devoted to an examination of the positions of five different individuals in various income categories. These included: the executive, the employee or novice investor, the professional, the owner-manager of a business, and the single career woman. The authors suggested various investment and tax-planning strategies that they felt appropriate for these individuals and their personal situations. There were also other models for individuals not in the above categories, for example, the childless professional couple who rent their home.

In this book we thought it would be useful to adopt the same approach using the same profiles. We will highlight our current thinking and compare it with some of the key points from the original analyses. We must stress that no single plan is suitable for all executives or professionals. As we have pointed out, a good deal depends on the living requirements of the individual and/or family and the degree of investment risk with which each is comfortable. Many of our suggestions, however, are quite adaptable to people in various income brackets, even though goals and objectives may differ. With the aid of this material, you will be in a better position to comprehend the implications of hyperinflation and the different tactics you could adopt to fit your personal investment strategy.

The Executive

Profile: Extremely conservative

Age: 49

Marital status: Married; spouse with no income; two dependent children, one in college and a second in high school

Salary: Earns $125,000 a year as president of a chocolate bar manufacturing company

Disposable income over and above living requirements: $1,500 per month

Annual contributions to his employer's pension plan: $3,500

Assets:

    Home: fair market value $300,000; cost $180,000

    Term deposits: $180,000 at 10 percent

    Stocks in employer's company: fair market value $20,000; cost $5,000

Liabilities: Mortgage: $75,000 at 13 percent due in three years

Strategy This man is a typical executive with few investments other than his home and perhaps a small stock position in the company for which he works. Though his income is substantial, he has not aggressively pursued a diversified portfolio. Also, his wife has no income, and one of the children is now of college age.

In the original analysis, methods of minimizing taxes were emphasized. These include income-splitting techniques, which take advantage of the Canadian tax structure. The idea is to try to generate investment income in the hands of a spouse who is not otherwise taxable, to ensure a greater after-tax retention. You should note that this type of planning is only effective in Canada and not in the United States, because, under American tax law, it is generally advantageous for a husband and wife to pool their incomes, so it really doesn't matter who earns what.

The original recommendations were to use a good portion of the term deposits to pay off the mortgage. From an income tax standpoint this idea still makes sense since, in Canada, mortgage interest on a personal residence is non-deductible. Because the mortgage is small compared to the fair market value of the home, we now question whether or not paying off the mortgage makes sense. It is not as if the executive has an inflated debt against an inflated purchase price. He may find within a few short years that he can pay off his debt out of one or two month's income. In fact, if the executive is willing to adopt a slightly more aggressive attitude, perhaps now would be a good time to re-mortgage the home for a greater amount and use the excess financing to acquire some kind of real estate investment such as a summer home or vacation property. Alternatively, perhaps a small apartment building, a duplex, or even a small commercial structure would be a suitable investment.

The executive in this case study should take stock of his position with his company. Is the company itself on solid ground? Is the marketability of the company's products likely to remain stable in inflationary times and in the severe recession which usually follows? If the executive's position is secure, he appears to have too much invested in term deposits. Now might be a good time to spend some money. Perhaps some of the household furniture should be replaced while prices are still relatively cheap. Now may be a good time to buy that new stereo or a VCR.

Keeping all those eggs in that term deposit basket is not prudent. He should diversify: $20,000 in gold or in a strong foreign currency; another $20,000 in blue chip stocks; $10,000 or $15,000 in stamps or coins. In the last two years our executive has already lost almost $20,000 in buying power when comparing his Canadian term deposits against the U.S. dollar.

Next, it would be worthwhile for the executive to carefully review the terms of his employer's pension plan. If it is an inflation-indexed program, he is covered, but not completely. The next question becomes: Can the company afford to pay an indexed pension? Fortunately, the executive is probably only five or six years away from having no dependents other than his spouse, so his cost of living should drop. Even if his pension proves to be deficient, he is not likely to be badly hurt by economic turmoil.

The executive should examine his existing stock portfolio, which consists mostly of shares of his employer corporation, acquired at a very low cost and with considerably higher present value. It is not always good planning to be "married" to the shares of an employer's corporation. Not only should the past performance of the investment be taken into account but future potential should also be considered. If little growth is anticipated or the business stands to suffer drastically from increases in the cost of imported raw materials, perhaps the shares should be sold. Tax will have to be paid on the capital gain, and the balance may then be used to make other investments.

As company president, he probably has some expert knowledge of the manufacturing process. If he knows the sugar and/or cocoa bean markets, he might consider selling his stock and investing the proceeds in the commodities market. Commodities investments are very risky, but he can afford a speculative investment—as long as he is comfortable with the risk.

The Employee

Profile: A novice investor; uninformed, too willing to take risks, has no specific goals or objectives except getting rich quickly
Age: 32
Marital status: Married; wife has recently begun working and earns $12,000 per year; two children, both in grade school
Salary: $30,000 per year
Combined disposable income over and above living requirements: $500 per month
Assets:
   Home: fair market value $100,000; cost $80,000
   Term deposits: $4,000 at 10 percent
   Stocks: fair market value $3,000; cost $5,000
   RRSP: $5,000 in Canada Savings Bonds
Liabilities:

Mortgage: $60,000 at 14 percent

Charge accounts: $2,000 at 19 percent, payments of $150 per month

Bank loan for stock: $4,000 at 14 percent

Automobile payments: $180 per month

Strategy Here we have a young family trying to get on its financial feet. The major family objectives discussed in the original profile, namely, establishing equity in the home, remains the same. The employee must realize that he isn't likely to become rich quickly. Slow but sure is the way to go. The stocks should be sold and the loss realized. The charge account balances, bank loan, and car payments should be eliminated as quickly as possible.

Fortunately, the employee's spouse has recently begun to work. There is probably the temptation to spend, perhaps to take a costly holiday. Don't! Every extra penny not required to maintain a reasonable standard of living and to purchase required durables should go into establishing equity in the home. It is too early for this family to consider an aggressive investment policy. At this point, the only outside investment that makes sense is the registered retirement savings plan. The employee is in approximately a 50 percent tax bracket, so it only costs about 50 cents on the dollar to continue such an investment program, and the RRSP does provide needed liquidity in the event of an emergency. When inflation heats up, it may then become advisable to switch the RRSP funds out of Canada Savings Bonds into growth-oriented investments in the stock market, but these would have to be watched very carefully.

Perhaps most important, the employee should cultivate a hobby or skill which can be turned into a profitable small business venture. Alternatively, preparing for or taking a second job would make good economic sense.

The Professional

Profile: A high flyer trying to recover from the decline in the value of his investments caused by the current recession

Age: 45

Marital status: Married; wife is active in his practice with an income of $15,000; two children, both in high school

Net income from his practice: $80,000

Disposable income over and above living requirements: $1,000 per month

Assets:

    Home: fair market value $225,000; cost $150,000

    Stocks: fair market value $25,000; cost $45,000

    Commodity contracts: fair market value $20,000; cost $35,000

    Automobile: cost $45,000

    Term deposit: $2,000 at 10 percent

Liabilities:

    First mortgage: $130,000 at 13 percent

    Second mortgage: $45,000 at 15 percent

    Car loan: $40,000

Strategy This man is like many successful self-employed professionals earning significant incomes but unable to manage their money well. This professional has expensive tastes and enjoys taking risks. He understands that he is still young and can recoup any losses he may suffer on his investments.

As discussed in the original profile, this man needs to do much more than review his investment portfolio. He must examine his method of investing. He is a classic example of the many high-income earners who invest rashly or without discipline and lose significant amounts of money. This person has lost a fair amount of money, at least on paper, in the stock market and on commodity contracts. He may be better off getting out of these markets for the time being and seeking a more solid financial base. The $45,000 automobile matched against a $40,000 loan is not good conservative planning. Of course, a car is an important asset, but it isn't really necessary to own a luxury car that is so heavily financed. Our professional would be a lot better off with two smaller, perhaps more fuel efficient, vehicles. A good mix would be a $15,000 sedan for formal and business occasions and a small runabout for everyday use.

The professional is certainly in a position to make some

investments. If he sells his stocks, commodity contracts, and expensive automobile, pays off his car loan and uses some of his cash to buy two less expensive cars, he would still have about $30,000 left over. Perhaps he and his family would enjoy a home in the country; this could be considered an investment. The cost of the investment should be modest though. His debt load between first and second mortgages is, at present, approximately twice his annual income, and it's unlikely that he would be comfortable with substantial additional debt. If a second home does not appear to be desirable, perhaps other investments should be considered such as gold, strong currencies, stamps, or coins. A key point to consider is that the professional doesn't usually have the time to monitor his portfolio closely; therefore, he should probably stay away from the type of investment choices that require day-to-day follow-up.

The Owner–Manager

Profile: Conservative; devotes all his energy to his own small business

Age: 55

Marital status: Married, wife active in business with an income of $20,000 per year; three children, two married, one in college (self-supporting)

Corporation pays the small business tax rate and earns a net income of $100,000 per year after salaries are paid

Excess cash generated (not required for business expansion): $25,000 a year or about 25 percent of net income

Corporation debt: $20,000 to shareholders on a non-interest-bearing demand basis; relatively low debt load

Personal income: The owner–manager receives a salary of $75,000 annually

Assets:

    Home: fair market value $200,000; cost $75,000

    Term deposits: $50,000; $25,000 in the name of each spouse

    RRSPs: husband $35,000; wife $30,000

    Art collection: fair market value $30,000

    Canada Savings Bonds: $40,000 in wife's name at 10 percent

Liabilities: Mortgage on home: $20,000 at 8.75 percent due
  1997

Strategy This profile is a portrait of a successful but conservative husband and wife who spent their lives building up a business, but without developing an appreciable investment portfolio. Their risk tolerance appears minimal.

The first planning step would be to take a very close look at the business and see if it is ready to cope with hyperinflation. Are the fixed assets, capital equipment, machinery, furniture, etc., up to date and serviceable enough that they won't have to be replaced when prices jump? Are labor costs controllable? Can the company ensure an adequate supply of raw material or product for manufacture or resale? Is the company's pricing structure flexible enough to pass costs along to customers, without losing them, when this becomes necessary? Will there be a high demand for the company's products in time of heavy inflation? Is the owner–manager concerned about competition both from within and outside the country?

Above all, the business must be protected. If that objective can be met, the owner–manager and his spouse should have no problems surviving the next few years.

The owner–manager in this profile is just a few years older than the executive profiled earlier. He too might take a close look at his home surroundings to see if any furniture needs replacement, or if there are durable goods he wants to buy. He might then examine the position of his children, who may be self-supporting now but might not face a secure future. If the owner–manager wants to protect them, he can. Perhaps by using his term deposits and Canada Savings Bonds as the downpayment, he could invest in a small apartment building. If one of the children should lose his or her job, the owner–manager can always provide an apartment free or at reduced rent.

The owner–manager is not likely to be in a position where he wants to play the stock market if he hasn't done so up to now, but expanding the art collection with surplus earnings may be a reasonable alternative. If real estate doesn't appeal to the owner–manager, perhaps some funds should be shifted into foreign currency or into gold. It may be advantageous to diversify some of the assets outside North America.

There are important tax considerations as well. In Canada, since the corporation gets the small business tax rate, it is only taxed at between 15 percent and 25 percent of its profits depending on the province in which the corporation carries on its activities. Thus, the company itself is capable of investing from 75 cents to 85 cents on the dollar. To some extent, as mentioned previously, the company should maintain a cash reserve for emergencies or ensure at this point that its plant and equipment are adequate for its needs and do not have to be replaced at the much higher prices we expect will prevail over the next couple of years.

It should also be kept in mind, though, that the corporation could make investments in gold, art, real estate, or even foreign currency, in the same way as a Canadian individual. A private corporation is simply an extension of its owners and can have a broad-based investment portfolio. The company can invest 75 cents to 85 cents on the dollar after taxes whereas the owner–manager only has 50 cents on the dollar after personal taxes.

But remember that a corporation must provide not only an annual income statement but a balance sheet as well, so the authorities know exactly what a corporation's assets are and where they are. A big question which therefore faces the owner–manager is whether the tax advantages of using additional dollars today within his corporation are worth the potential grief of having the government knowing exactly what assets he has.

Some thought should also be given to ensuring continuity of the business. Perhaps certain key employees should be made shareholders, so the business can continue effectively even if the owner–manager and spouse are unable to participate. An alternative is to wait until the inflationary spiral is upon us and sell the business outright, at which point the owner–managers could retire or perhaps stay on as employees.

In putting together this sample profile we have not considered the value of the business as a family asset because each case is different. Although the business is extremely profitable, it may be that its goodwill is related to the owners themselves and the business by itself may not be particularly saleable. This is certainly a major factor in the overall planning picture.

The Career Woman

Profile: Conservative; so far has taken no interest in learning about investment alternatives

Age: 38

Marital status: Single

Salary: $40,000 per annum

Disposable income over and above living requirements: $800 per month

Annual contributions to her employer's pension plan: $2,400

Assets:

    Term deposits: $24,000 at 10 percent

    Jewelry: $14,000 original cost

    Antiques and art: $40,000 original cost

Liabilities: None

Strategy This woman is typical of a high-income single person with extra disposable income and no dependents. She lives in a luxury apartment and has conservatively put aside more than a half-year's income, which is invested in term deposits. She has, over the years, allowed herself the indulgences of some jewelry, antiques, and collectibles.

A great deal of the career woman's personal welfare depends on job security. After reading this book, she should try to determine how strong her position is and what her chances are of having an increasing income over the next twenty or twenty-five years that would keep pace with inflation. If her job is secure, then the most important decision she has to make is whether to invest in a home or a condominium.

The purchase of a bungalow or cottage probably wouldn't be attractive because of the maintenance involved. She should then look to a condominium apartment or townhouse. To ensure a small debt load and establish equity, a large downpayment is suggested. This means cashing virtually all the term deposits and eliminating a good deal of the liquid security that our career woman possesses. A great deal therefore depends on her health, job stability, and the potential of being transferred by her employer. Perhaps buying a home now, when prices are low and long-term fixed interest rate financing is obtainable, can be the biggest decision she will make. And yet, it's a tremendous commitment.

As in most of the other profiles, the career woman should take stock of her furniture and other durables. If she wants some new living room furniture, a better stereo, or a microwave oven, now is probably the best time to buy. You should note that the profile makes the assumption that she does not own a car. By living in an urban environment, she has probably arranged her lifestyle so an automobile is not necessary; as long as it continues to be unnecessary, her cost of living will be substantially less than if she had a car. For some people it will always be cheaper to use the public transit system or taxicab in lieu of owning a vehicle.

While the career woman's jewelry cost her $14,000 it should be recognized that this is not really considered by many people to be an investment so much as a durable that holds value. Jewelry is attractive, it may have sentimental value, and it may become extremely important if ever our society degenerates to the point where property such as jewelry could be the price of food or one's life. If the career woman wants to take part of her excess disposable income to purchase gold or other precious metals or stones from time to time, there are better ways of purchasing these items than as finished jewelry.

On balance, the career woman in this profile is in a relatively strong position. Her income is approximately equal to that of the employee and his spouse profiled earlier in this chapter. The big difference, though, is that the career woman is responsible for herself alone. To some extent that makes her position, in light of the coming hyperinflation, quite attractive.

Other Models

An examination of the position of a young professional couple renting a city apartment would probably result in a profile similar to that of the career woman. When it comes to suggesting inflation strategies, a good deal depends on whether or not they intend to have children. If they do, their profile would then more resemble a cross between the employee or novice investor and the professional.

A fifty-eight-year-old married employee still a number of years away from retirement, who is perhaps concerned about making serious mistakes in his investments, would likely be best advised to take the most conservative approaches suggested in our profiles. This individual is close enough to retirement that he might not have time for a second chance, so he must be careful to adopt a conservative and profitable investment approach, and limiting his investments to savings bonds or term deposits is not the answer.

The same considerations would apply if we were to examine an older husband and wife who do not own a business, are not in professional practice, but have some $30,000 to $50,000 to invest. Also, the widow or divorcée with somewhere between $50,000 and $100,000 should find that several of the options presented in this chapter suit both her needs and temperament.

You should be able to identify with at least one or two of the specific examples. Many of the suggestions are equally applicable to people in differing situations and income brackets. Our approach emphasizes the need to take action without incurring extraordinary risk. We recommend that you stabilize and balance your financial portfolio through diversification while there is still time. Remember flexibility and timing. If you make a mistake, don't hesitate to sell out, cut your losses, and go on to something else. Surviving and profiting from the coming hyperinflation is a challenge we all must face and meet as best we can.

Chapter 16

SPEAKING THE UNSPEAKABLE

O UR COUNTRY is in an economic crisis.
Politicians in power are unwilling to admit that we are on the brink of disaster, because they, with our co-operation, created the crisis. They did so in the name of social justice, to ensure that everyone shared in the wealth.

The government of Canada was constituted to provide "peace, order and good government." It was to guarantee an environment of peace and order so Canadians could get on with life and business without interference. Good government implies that interference will also not come from government.

Good government must lead to ensure that society works; however, politicians forgot that good government must also follow the precept that business, operating within guidelines that ensure social peace, is the only means to prosperity.

As one of the many people interviewed for this book observed, government should work like air conditioning—operating unnoticed until something goes wrong, then repaired immediately. Our government, unfortunately, is in the way, demanding too much of our attention and economic resources, diverting us from the business of getting on with productive lives and businesses. Our government needs fixing.

But a government is only a reflection of the people who elect it. As such, we must recognize that we can't lay all blame for our country's ills at the feet of politicians. We, the citizens, must take part of the blame, and change our ways if we're to avoid runaway inflation and eventual hyperinflation.

The problem is that government spends too much money on social programs, and crown corporations—business and industrial ventures that are costly wastes of human and financial resources.

Government spends because we, the citizens of this country, have grown to expect, and demand, that it take care of us and provide us with jobs. It's unproductive to argue which came first, the programs or demands for the programs. All that matters is the recognition that government has us dependent, like addicts, on social programs that remove the incentive to take care of ourselves and each other.

We must also recognize that government is a major player in the marketplace, not to produce efficiently, but to protect jobs by supporting inefficient industries. Rather than creating an environment which fosters development of new efficient industries that create more new jobs, government is putting money into industrial activity with no future.

There was a time when government entered the business world as the legislative arbiter regulating relations between employers and employees, business and business, country and country. Government fulfilled its role.

Unfortunately, once in as arbiter, government wormed its way into other areas of business. Now government not only *regulates* business but also acts as though it can *conduct* business better than business can. Government, however, is not motivated by competition for profits, and business conducted or backed by government often forgets profits altogether.

When it comes to governing, we can't, and shouldn't, expect government to make a profit. If anything, profitable government takes too much money out of the economy and is as much of a disservice to society as when it takes money to cover deficit spending. We have every right, however, to demand that government balance its books.

As it stands now, our government is in a frightful state of economic insolvency and is plowing more deeply into debt every minute. Total government debt is well in excess of $180 billion, a figure most of us find incomprehensible. A graphic representation of our national debt would better be: $180,000,000,000.

What every one of us must understand is that this debt is ours. The figure represents $7,200 of debt for each of 25 million Canadians, debt we did not individually incur. The figure of $7,200 per Canadian may not mean much, but think of it in terms of a family of five—$36,000. Consider that every baby born in this country is born owing $7,200.

We can't possibly each go to Canada's creditors and lay $7,200 on the line and wash our hands of responsibility. But we have to understand that the need is critical to stop this erosion of Canada's equity immediately.

The consequences of not doing so are very simple: Eventually we will not be able to meet our foreign debt obligations, perhaps because our natural resources are depleted or we are no longer able to sell them as cheaply as Third World countries. The world will no longer extend us credit. The Canadian dollar will devalue drastically. Because we are net importers of manufactured goods, our cost of living—inflation—will skyrocket, and economically we will be in the same mess as Argentina and Mexico.

What must be done to change this situation is neither simple nor painless. Government must stop over-spending! Failure to do so means everyone (except those who have prepared for economic chaos) will suffer.

What follows is a set of suggestions we have framed to deal with these problems. They are not hard and fast solutions but, rather, are ideas to be debated from which solutions may develop. We feel that we cannot justifiably criticize without offering alternatives to the existing situation. Canada is at an historic turning point. We can direct our destiny, or strike a Royal Commission of Inquiry and slowly fade into oblivion as a country that failed to meet its potential.

1. Government must encourage industrial self-sufficiency, productivity, and efficiency. Government must also get out of private business.

For too long it was believed that our natural resources were an inexhaustible source of wealth. During the late 1940s and 1950s we lived on the income from our resources. In the 1960s and the 1970s we borrowed against them. In the 1980s we have to sell them in ever-increasing quantities to pay our debts.

Unfortunately, unless we make fundamental changes in our economic structures, we'll never get even because, though we export more resources than we import finished goods, the day will come when the lumber, minerals, oil, and natural gas won't bring in enough revenue to pay for what we buy.

This will happen for two reasons. First, developing countries with large debts are selling off their resources for whatever they can get just to get their hands on hard currency. Our resources will one day become non-competitive, unless our dollar keeps dropping in value relative to the U.S. dollar.

Second, the prices of imported goods will keep rising while our resource revenues remain stable, or shrink, and we'll eventually end up spending more on imports than we receive on exports.

As it is, we give away our rapidly depleting natural resources, rather than use them to maximum profit in efficient domestic industries. If Canada is to prevent the slide into hyperinflation, it must opt for industrial development and a policy geared to the opportunities the future offers rather than the easy outs offered by bolstering non-productive industries.

This means private investment in Canada, domestic and foreign, must be promoted and offered an environment in which it can thrive and profit. Productive industries must be encouraged and the non-productive allowed to wither. Supporting non-productive industries with no prospect of turnaround simply contributes to deficits and inflation.

This does not mean all requests should be rejected out of hand. We can look at the turnaround in the Chrysler corporation, accomplished with government-guaranteed loans. Then again, look at the example of Maislin Trucking which, despite government loan guarantees and cash infusions, folded.

However the judgments are made, they must be made by individuals motivated by profits, not politics or civil-service perceptions of safe bets.

The true judge of a company's ability to right itself is the marketplace, so perhaps an independent national industrial council of financial, industrial, and labor representatives could be established on a rotating five-year basis. The council's mandate would be to examine applications and allocate aid to needy potential winners at a reasonable rate of return on aid. All industries which receive government aid, or grants, like the oil and gas industry, should be required to provide, and fulfill, performance guarantees.

To ensure that the private-sector inflationary factor of an expanding economy does not spiral out of control, business and labor would have to co-operate to ensure that productivity, rather than cost of living, dictates wage, salary, and price levels (see comment 2 below). Government's role at the bargaining table would be to ensure productivity is the key to settlements. Any settlements not linked to productivity should result in tax penalties, with the revenues put into a fund to be administered by the national industrial council.

To ensure that the public-sector inflationary factor is minimal, government must sell off crown corporations that could be operated profitably by the private sector. The present freeze on civil-service hiring must continue, and civil-service salary scales should be linked to private-sector salary levels so they follow, rather than set, standards for the workplace. In addition, the tax system must be overhauled (see comment 4 below).

The aim of these policies must be to promote an attitude which seeks high efficiency in industry and business on the Japanese model. Japan, with no resources except her population, imports all of her raw materials but manages to re-export the inflation factor of volatile costs such as those of oil. This is done by linking all work-related rewards—cash bonuses, company-sponsored travel, public recognition—to productivity.

Canada has all the natural resources she needs to be an industry-based economy except, it seems, the will to produce.

2. Wage and salary increases must be linked to productivity.

Domestic inflation must be limited as much as possible to that which results from economic growth and expansion. To this end the inflationary practice of salary and wage settlements based on cost of living at all levels of industry, business, and government must be stopped. Instead, government could offer the civil service efficiency bonuses. Between business and labor a system of profit-sharing programs, bonuses, even equity positions could be created. Providing all participants in business and industry a stake in improving productivity will lead to increased efficiency.

Whatever is done, automatic cost-of-living increases must end. They are a form of indexation which partially, and temporarily, protect income from inflationary erosion but in no way address the problem at its source.

3. Tax incentives must be established to promote movement of population to industrial areas. Alternatively, tax incentives must be established, within the framework of a cohesive industrial policy, for industry to locate in undeveloped, but populated, areas.

Canada suffers from the industrial handicap of having a small, badly distributed population of 25 million. This creates economic and political problems that work against industrial development.

For one thing, economies of scale are difficult to achieve unless industries are price-competitive on the export market.

Second, Canada's population distribution works against rational government and industrial development of this country. Population concentrated in certain areas spurs pockets of industrialization. They provide labor pools and proximity to markets and communications networks. They create their own dynamic and create service jobs to back up the industrial population.

Most importantly, besides jobs, large population centers offer amenities that make urban life enjoyable.

Industrialized areas house concentrations of voters, power blocks manipulated by political parties which then make concessions to those regions at the expense of others. What results is pockets of prosperity surrounded by pockets of economic depression.

These depressed areas become financial drains on the productive centers. They force government to divert revenue into unemployment and welfare payments. Government also puts money into very visible make-work projects that only create interim, but no long-term, jobs.

Two alternatives present themselves: People can be encouraged to move to the large industrial centers, or industry can be encouraged to establish in depressed areas.

Either solution would provide the opportunity for the unemployed to become productive. Coercion, however, is not the way to get people to move.

Tax credits could be used to promote movement of population out of depressed areas into industrial areas.

Mass migrations, however, contribute to urban sprawl, which creates social problems. Also, people can't be counted on to leave a favored region, or home, simply because jobs appear to exist elsewhere. So, alternatively, industry must be given an incentive to locate in non-industrialized regions of the country.

The incentives might not necessarily have to be tax incentives, though they could be a starting point. What is necessary, though, is an industrial policy which recognizes that industry cannot locate in an area that does not provide the necessary services, i.e., good, cheap transportation networks, energy, and raw material sources. Money would have to be invested in broadening the industrial infrastructure—modernized railroads, upgraded highways, pipelines. Building the infrastructure would create construction jobs and, after completion, lasting jobs in the service and maintenance sectors.

4. The tax structure must be revamped to establish a

minimum corporate tax based on accounting profits and a minimum personal tax on income greater than $50,000.

This measure, besides being a revenue earner, is also a confidence builder. It must not be used as a showpiece: It must be implemented and enforced fairly with no exceptions. One of our greatest problems is that the national tax burden is carried by too few people. This is a prime incentive for tax evasion.

The tax system is seen as unfair, confiscatory, and confrontational. Despite any pronouncement from government that it enjoys the confidence of the public, taxpayers suspect where their money goes, how the government manages to spend all of its tax revenues, plus a hefty deficit. Taxpayers resent tax authorities who are seen as vultures employing questionable, unsavory, and insensitive tactics.

Taxpayers also resent the fact that too many people and corporations get away without paying a fair share of taxes.

In dealing with a similar situation two decades ago, when it was found that many high-income earners were paying no taxes, the United States government enacted minimum tax regulations regarding accelerated depreciation of capital goods, stock options, capital gains, and large itemized deductions such as mortgage interest. In essence, any of these deductions could have been used to reduce tax exposure to zero. Tax authorities closed the door to ensure that everyone pays a minimum of taxes.

The only way this country is going to get out of the present economic mess is if each individual and every corporate entity shares the weight, each according to ability. While tax incentives must be maintained to encourage investment by business and individuals, there must be a minimum tax each pays for the services government provides.

Government policies must also be revamped to allow for the two following suggestions.

5. The universality of all social programs must end.
No one must be allowed to suffer the indignities of poverty or

starvation. To this end all social programs must be administered according to need. This includes old age pensions, family allowances, unemployment insurance, and health care.

According to Michael Walker of Vancouver's Fraser Institute, writing in the *Financial Post* in April 1984, a saving of $8 billion per year would be realized if universality of social programs were abandoned for families earning $17,400 or more. If the cut-off point were family earnings of $23,200, the savings would be $6 billion. Both of these figures would make appreciable dents in the annual budget deficit.

Ironically, this would also make for a more equitable administration of social programs. Basically, we are all in this together. If government continues debasing the currency through overspending, we will all eventually suffer. By taking the strain off government finances, we can ensure that all receive their share of the common wealth according to need.

The argument that means tests are degrading is an intellectual diversion from the gritty facts of life. The social, emotional, and spiritual costs of being thrown on unemployment, or forced to resort to welfare are more degrading than any mandatory means test could ever be.

For example, in no way would any Canadian who has paid into the Canada Pension Plan be prevented from claiming what is rightfully his or hers. All pensioners, however, are not living on or below the poverty line; some had the financial vision and ability to build a future on a more secure basis than public pension plans. Therefore, if a pensioner can afford 100 percent of the cost of health care, he or she should pay the full cost. If, however, a pensioner needs a subsidized health plan, it should be subsidized to the degree the pensioner needs.

Another example is the baby bonus, which persons at all levels of income receive. The program should be altered so it provides parents with a choice. When a child is born, parents could apply for baby bonus payments, or they could choose to take an increased child tax credit for as long as the parents support the child at home until the child is eighteen. Undoubtedly, those who need the baby bonus payments to subsidize feeding and clothing the child will opt for the cash; others will opt for the tax credit.

Turning to medical care programs, we can take another approach to extra billing. Let any doctor who wishes to extra bill do so. Let the marketplace decide if that doctor remains in practice.

The same sort of judgment should be applied to every existing government social program. Any program that operates through direct payment should be altered to offer the choice of direct payments or tax credits. Not only does this provide a workable alternative, but the alternative provides a saving in the costs of administering direct-payment programs.

6. Re-establishment of the extended family should be encouraged through formal tax credits.

Government social programs such as welfare are stand-ins for the sort of community and family self-sufficiency and interdependence that was lost as society became industrialized, urbanized, and mobile. Mobility broke down the extended family.

We have to get back to being responsible for ourselves and each other, and get government out of our everyday lives. The place to start is the family. Individuals who support other family members related by blood, marriage, or adoption should be allowed a tax deduction or credit which is reasonable relative to the amount spent to maintain the family member. For example, if you support your widowed mother and she is able to forego her old-age pension, the tax system should compensate you in some manner.

Watch the family unit start pulling together again.

Failing implementation of these schemes, another alternative exists. Under present conditions in which the Canadian economy is a hybrid of resource seller, with a small industrial base, and finished goods buyer, the dollar is over-valued. It hovers in the 75 to 78 cent U.S. range because the government can't afford to let it float to its own level. To keep the dollar in that range, the government borrows heavily overseas, which is self-defeating.

The pressure on the Canadian dollar is a result of the erosion of confidence in Canada's ability to order her economic affairs and achieve a state of financial solvency. Every time the dollar drops, inflation creeps up. Every time the government borrows overseas, the deficit climbs, our debt picture worsens, and inflation creeps up even further.

To stop this, the Canadian government must impose strict currency and exchange controls on our dollar. The government should then stop shoring up the Canadian dollar on world currency markets and let it float to its real trading value relative to the U.S. dollar.

We recognize that the short-term consequences are going to be inflationary. Import prices will soar, and people won't be able to afford to buy imported goods. But once buying stops, imports will stop flooding into the country. This will improve our balance of payments problem and bring in short-term surpluses, as our now-cheap natural resource sales will jump.

Then, interest tax credits should be allowed for loans for industrial development to implement an import-substitution program. The new industrial output from Canada would not only meet domestic demand but would also be price-competitive on the world market because of the favorable exchange rates on the Canadian dollar.

Industrial prosperity would result.

The only problem with this proposal is that so much of the Canadian economy is owned by foreign interests. These interests might not appreciate the massive write-downs in assets they would suffer as a result of devaluation of the Canadian dollar. If the program is successful, though, the loss will only be temporary.

Undoubtedly, there are many policies that could be implemented and many new directions Canada's economy could take to right the present situation. We have no claim to any particular wisdom that can solve Canada's economic problems.

We do know, however, that present conditions cannot be allowed to continue. The platitudes and promises of political candidates are not the solution either. Action to save Canada, our home, is what is necessary.

Unfortunately, we see too many politicians who, in the blind pursuit of power, refuse to take the courageous step of facing the Canadian public and telling us the economic realities. Perhaps they are all too aware of the fall of the Clark government in 1979 when the finance minister proposed raising gasoline prices 18 cents a gallon to raise the revenues necessary to pay off the national debt.

The Clark government fell on the basis of facing the truth. We'll never know if that government might have succeeded in cutting the federal deficit. What we do know, though, is that the re-elected Trudeau government raised gasoline taxes more than 18 cents a gallon, and yet our federal deficit has mushroomed in the ensuing five years.

We are in the midst of a crisis no politician will admit exists. Economic survival of this country will only come about if we declare war on deficit spending. If the national economy survives, we will all survive. If the national economy collapses, everyone, without exception, will suffer.

The options are to leave the country, save the country, or arrange your finances for survival. Whatever happens, arrange your finances for the unexpected. After all, you never know what some shark of a government will do that affects your economic well-being.

———⁓⁓⁓———